CARRA

MY AUTOBIOGRAPHY

www.**rbooks**.co.uk

CARRA

MY AUTOBIOGRAPHY

BANTAM PRESS

LONDON • TORONTO • SYDNEY • AUCKLAND • JOHANNESBURG

TRANSWORLD PUBLISHERS
61–63 Uxbridge Road, London W5 5SA
A Random House Group Company
www.rbooks.co.uk

First published in Great Britain
in 2008 by Bantam Press
an imprint of Transworld Publishers

A CIP catalogue record for this book
is available from the British Library.

ISBN 9780593061022 (cased)
ISBN 9780593061039 (tpb)

All photographs personally provided by Jamie Carragher, with thanks to Liverpool FC, the *Liverpool Daily Post*
and *Echo*, Trinity Mirror, and the photographers who have followed his life and career over the years.
Every effort has been made to obtain the necessary permissions with reference to illustrative copyright material.
We apologize for any omissions in this respect and will be pleased to make the appropriate
acknowledgements in any future edition.

Addresses for Random House Group Ltd companies outside the UK
can be found at: www.randomhouse.co.uk
The Random House Group Ltd Reg. No. 954009

The Random House Group Limited supports The Forest Stewardship
Council (FSC), the leading international forest-certification organization. All our
titles that are printed on Greenpeace-approved FSC-certified paper carry the FSC logo.
Our paper procurement policy can be found at www.rbooks.co.uk/environment

Typeset in 11/16 pt Sabon by Falcon Oast Graphic Art Ltd.
Printed and bound in Great Britain by
Clays Ltd, St Ives plc

8 10 9 7

To everyone who's helped me on my journey from Marsh Lane to Anfield and the most illustrious stadiums of Europe: my best friend and wife Nicola, my beautiful children James and Mia, my mum and dad for making me the person and player I am, my brothers John and Paul, and everyone in Bootle I consider part of the Team of Carraghers.

Contents

Acknowledgements

I was determined to ensure when the time came for me to tell my story it reflected how I play: completely honest. That's why I imagined I'd wait until I'd played my last game before putting pen to paper. In normal circumstances it's difficult for players to express how they really feel until they've retired. But as I approached my thirtieth birthday I suppose I hit that age where I had so much to get off my chest I couldn't keep it in any more. My wife, Nicola, thinks I've got grumpy old man syndrome forty years too early, so with so much to be said about my life, career and Liverpool FC there was no way I could have waited another four or five years to do this book. Besides, no one might be so interested after I pack it in!

As an avid reader of sporting autobiographies, I couldn't wait to get started. On the Liverpool coach heading to an away game, on a flight to Europe or just lounging around a hotel awaiting kick-off, I'm usually hiding behind the latest football book to hit the shelves, so I knew it was only a matter of time before I took the plunge. I've often felt I had more of interest to say than those I was reading about; and in some cases I was so impressed by the story I felt inspired to follow suit.

I had a fair idea in my mind what makes a good read. Without wishing to sound big-headed at all, I often find myself inundated by interview requests during the course of a season. It made sense for me to present my story and my views in my own way rather than see myself plastered across different newspapers from one week to the next, with little or no control over how I come across. That's why I instructed my agent of the past ten years, Struan Marshall, to accept an offer from the publishers Transworld, and work on *Carra* began.

As well as my family and close friends, to whom I've dedicated this book, I'd like to thank Struan, his assistant Kathryn Taylor and Andy Sterling for all their help with this autobiography and throughout my career. Thanks also to the Transworld team, including Giles Elliott and copy-editor Daniel Balado, and finally thanks to writer Chris Bascombe for piecing together my story and putting up with my attention to detail and constant changes. *Jamie Carragher, July 2008*

In the summer of 2007, Jamie and I met in the reception of the Grand Hyatt Hotel in Hong Kong to begin work on this book.

Pre-season is a time when the line between optimism and delusion is unavoidably blurred. Liverpool's Far East summer tour was enhancing the same expectations we'd both grown accustomed to across the previous decade – Jamie as a player and me as a Kop season ticket holder and LFC newspaper correspondent. As Jamie handed me his notes, mapping the journey he'd take through his memories, he left suitable gaps for the successes in the months to come.

A year in the writing, *Carra* was intended to conclude triumphantly in May 2008 with Liverpool's elusive nineteenth

League title or sixth Champions League win. But just ten minutes after our first meeting I conducted my second interview of the day, this time on behalf of my former employers at the *Liverpool Echo*, and assistant manager Pako Ayesteran succeeded in bursting the bubbles I'd been inflating moments earlier, painting the picture of a football club in turmoil behind the scenes which was still far from ready to capture its 'holy grail'.

'This club is not ready to win the title,' Ayesteran stated.

His words were scarily prophetic, but I doubt even he foresaw the extent of the imminent disturbance. Within three months Ayesteran had left Liverpool, Rafa Benitez's position was under threat, and the recent American takeover was creating one dramatic headline after another. As Carra reviewed plans for the book, there was a growing realization the finale would not be one of triumph but of painful reflection on a traumatic season.

Jamie always intended this to be far more than a traditional, clichéd footballer's autobiography, and the background against which it has been written underlines why. It's a record of a turbulent yet triumphant time in the club's history, as the modern Liverpool Football Club has fought a continuous battle with the ghosts of its past. The paradox is, while Liverpool has been gripped by uncertainty and instability, Jamie has been a permanent symbol of what it used to be, what through players like him it quite often still is, and what it eternally aspires to be. Without him, Anfield would have been a far grimmer place over the last ten years. It's his efforts as much as any which have ensured regular honours for Liverpool, and safeguarded a place among the European elite.

Liverpool has been blessed with great servants over the course of its illustrious history, but none has managed to represent the aspirations of the club and its city more than Jamie Carragher. Helping him to tell his story has been my writing equivalent of winning the Champions League, a cup treble and the Premier League, all within the space of twelve months.

I'd like to thank the Bascombes, the Wooseys, the Connollys and the Boileaus for their constant support; Paul Joyce of the *Daily Express*, whose assistance and advice was, as always, invaluable; LFC statistician Ged Rea; and Roddy Frame for providing the eternally inspirational soundtrack to all my writing efforts.

Most of all, I'd like to thank my wife, Paula, for her proof-reading expertise, and Jamie for keeping his long-term promise to resist the temptation to allow one of the Sunday supplement crew to muscle in and grab the ghost-writing gig.

Chris Bascombe, July 2008

Foreword by Kenny Dalglish

I was still Liverpool manager when I first saw Sharpy. That was my nickname for the eleven-year-old Jamie Carragher, who provided an early demonstration of his Scouse cheek by turning up for five-a-sides at Liverpool's School of Excellence wearing the Everton kit of his childhood hero, Graeme Sharp.

Carra was a striker in those days. I'd head to the Vernon Sangster Leisure Centre, just adjacent to Anfield, and join in the games with my son Paul. I couldn't fail to notice the impressive forward in blue. He made sure I always took my place in the opposing side, so I doubt he ever won a game!

The fact he brazenly strolled in wearing his Everton strip said a lot about the young Carra's character. He showed no inhibitions, regardless of the surroundings. It's a positive attribute he's taken into his adult career. Whether he was playing a five-a-side aged eleven or excelling in the San Siro or Nou Camp in the Champions League, he's never changed. I love seeing that sense of dedication, professionalism and pride in the people of Liverpool, which is why the city became my adopted home after I moved from Scotland. Nobody epitomizes these qualities more than Carra.

I'll bet while Carra was scoring goals, picturing himself celebrating in front of the Gladwys Street end, somewhere at Everton's training ground there were young lads in Liverpool kits pretending to be Ian Rush.

It wasn't just Carra's provocative choice of kit that made him stand out. He was a prolific goalscorer in his age group, and my youth scouts were telling me they had high hopes he'd progress through our ranks. As I've seen his career develop since, winning so many honours at Anfield and breaking modern appearance records, it's given me immense pride to see that the work of people like me and my staff at youth level at the time – Steve Heighway, Hugh McAuley and Frank Skelly – helped such world-class players emerge.

I always said if you can't find top-class footballers in a city as passionate about the game as Liverpool, you must be doing something wrong, and we didn't do a bad job during my time in the form of Carra, Steve McManaman and Robbie Fowler. We recognized the importance of bringing through youngsters who have an affinity with the people they play for. You can get that with those from other areas – I hope I'm proof of that – but it's always extra special for lads on The Kop to see someone they can relate to. If I have any regrets since leaving Liverpool, missing out on the chance to manage Carra, Robbie and Stevie Mac is one of them. Every manager in the world would have loved to have such players in their side.

It's amazing someone who was such an Evertonian has now come to represent everything positive about Liverpool, but it's a tribute to him he's handled this transition so well on and off the park. Being a local boy and playing for Liverpool or Everton brings its own pressure. In many ways, it's much harder. There are distractions to contend with growing up in full view of the

Merseyside public and there's a responsibility not only to represent the people on the pitch, but to conduct yourself in the right way off it. Far more is expected of you, but Carra has coped with it admirably.

Liverpool has a long list of legendary defenders, but Carra's name will sit comfortably alongside those of Ron Yeats, Tommy Smith, Emlyn Hughes, Phil Thompson, Alan Hansen and Mark Lawrenson. The difference is, after ten years of distinguished service in so many different positions he's still going strong and has plenty still to achieve in the game. We're not talking about a player in the past tense here, but someone who'll have many more chapters to add to his life in football. He's a credit to himself, his club, his city and his family, whose competitive streak I can absolutely vouch for.

In fact, all that remains is to urge everyone to remember the following. When you're reading about my amusing brush with Carra's dad during a notorious fixture between Bootle and Crosby Schoolboys, recalled during the course of the book, keep this in mind.

It was never a penalty.

1
Marsh Lane

I was lying on my bed crying.

A pair of football boots was scattered across the floor, and I was still in my soaking schoolboy strip, trying to figure out how within thirty minutes I'd gone from avoiding bruises on the pitch, in a game which ought to have underlined my growing potential, to receiving a good hiding from my dad. I'd been handed a lesson in football and in life I'd never forget. At the age of seven, my destiny was being shaped.

When players talk about defining moments they usually focus on their highlights. I could begin my story writing about European triumphs or FA Cup wins. I could recall my professional debut, or the first time I signed a contract. I could relive a watershed game when I came off the pitch and knew I'd achieve my dreams, or at the very least felt they were within my grasp.

But a career isn't so simple. Only as you get older can you reassess your experiences. Then you appreciate the impact of events you never recognized as life-changing at the time, but which made you the person you are. When my dad hurled that pair of soaking football boots at me, he probably thought he was merely handing me the punishment I deserved. It was more than that. This was the start of my becoming a footballer.

The cause of my dad's rage was a shameful performance for Merton Villa, my first team. I was already showing promise, playing in the Under-11s alongside lads three years older, but on this particular afternoon there was a reason I didn't want to play.

It was raining.

Actually, it was hail-stoning. I'd never faced torrential conditions before, and couldn't summon the desire, energy or courage to drag my drenched body around a sodden pitch. For the first and only time, I faked injury. As the first challenge came in I hit the turf, rolled around and threw in some tears to seal the deal.

'They'll have to substitute me,' my cunning seven-year-old brain conspired. 'I can go home, put my feet up and get warm.'

No substitution was needed. Philly Carragher, my dad, was on the pitch with his own hook before any decision was necessary. He grabbed my shirt, dragged me from the field, pushed me head-first into the car and drove home, leaving me in no doubt about what would follow.

Once in my bedroom, it hailed football boots. My drowned jersey felt heavier by the second as it absorbed my tears. My dad told me I'd let him down as much as myself. No Carragher was going to be seen as such a coward, especially not in public. I needed to understand the value of pride, and to learn to deal with tough circumstances. I knew the next time I played, no matter how demanding the situation, I wouldn't hide.

I hated my dad at that moment, but I've been thanking him for the punishment ever since. Since turning professional, I've played with and against players who've shown the same gutless attitude I did when I was seven. At least my age was an excuse.

Ability can only take you so far. You need character to

accompany it. I was compelled to appreciate and make the most of my skills. There's a saying, 'you are what you're brought up to be', and it applies to me. The best players are a product of their environment. The attitude my mum, dad and the wider community drove into me at an early age became the foundation for how I carry myself on and off the pitch. I've been able to build my reputation on it, to export the distinctive principles of Marsh Lane, where I grew up, to the football stadiums of England and Europe.

People see where I'm from, Bootle on Merseyside, and consider it deprived. Economically it is, but there was nothing underprivileged about my childhood. I feel blessed to have been born there. I'm proud of my city and even prouder of the district where I still belong. Wearing my Liverpool shirt gives me a responsibility not only never to let myself down, but to make my family, friends, city and district proud of me. Without this outlook I would never have become a successful footballer. My heart and soul were born and bred in Bootle.

Maybe it was easier for me to develop a fighting instinct earlier than most. It was a necessity. I was lucky to be born. Everything that has followed has been a bonus.

My book of revelations begins with the most dramatic: if my mum hadn't been a Roman Catholic, I might have been aborted.

Paula Carragher was given the option of a termination due to complications halfway through her pregnancy. She was told I had spina bifida – a birth defect that affects the spinal cord. She was too religious to consider abortion, no matter how disabled I'd be. 'Our Lord told me to have the baby,' she still claims. She's very holy, my mum – at one time in her life she considered becoming a nun – and had already suffered two miscarriages before I came along. She's since had three sons – her holy trinity, if you like. That's a reward for extraordinary resilience and faith. She made all of us attend Mass every Sunday when we were youngsters, and she's still sure someone above has been watching over me from the moment I was conceived.

Unlike my extrovert dad, who pops up so much in this story you could be mistaken for thinking the title *Carra* refers to him, my mum has always chosen to remain in the background, asserting a quiet influence. But she's the rock on which my family was built. I owe everything to that agonizing decision she took thirty years ago.

Her prayers were answered, because when she had her final scan the condition was different to the doctors' diagnosis. As I hope I've proved in the years since, there's no problem with my spine. The trouble was in my stomach rather than on my back. I had a condition called gastroschisis: I was born with my bowels outside my stomach. If you ever see me changing shirts with an opponent after a match, you'll get a good view of a scar and notice the absence of a belly-button. Thirty years ago it was serious, and I spent the first six weeks of my life in Alder Hey Children's Hospital holding on for survival like Liverpool did in extra-time against AC Milan in Istanbul. Just like my cramp-ridden body in the final stages of that 2005 Champions League Final in the Ataturk Stadium, I must have looked a right state, but I managed to pull through, and it's never been a problem to me since.

So it was amid trauma that I, James Lee Duncan Carragher, was delivered into the world on 28 January 1978. James was a tribute to my granddad. I'd like to inform you I was also named after two genuine greats of the game, Duncan Edwards and Jimmy Greaves; sadly, as my dad was a fervent Evertonian throughout the dismal 1970s, Gordon Lee and Duncan

McKenzie were on his mind when I arrived. McKenzie was dropped by Lee for an away defeat at Middlesbrough in the FA Cup on the day I was born, so my name shows Dad's sense of humour more than his former love of the Blues. The guardian angel my mum talks about was obviously a Kopite, dropping the first hint my destiny lay in the opposite direction to Goodison Park.

I was baptized in honour of Merseyside football, and the initiation ceremonies have continued ever since. My first memory of my dad is of him on the Wembley pitch kissing Graeme Sharp after the full-time whistle against Watford in 1984. I was six, watching *FA Cup Final Grandstand,* when he jumped on to the screen dancing like a madman. This wasn't his first time on the pitch. He confronted Everton manager Gordon Lee during the FA Cup semi-final replay with West Ham in 1980, shortly after Frank Lampard senior scored the winner. Whatever he thought of Lee, it didn't stop him naming me after him.

Football was my dad's life, and he passed it straight into me.

He managed two nearby football teams, The Brunswick, also based on Marsh Lane, and his Sunday League team Merton Villa. As soon as I could walk, I'd be standing on the touchline watching him impersonating a top-class football manager. He wore a long duffel coat, like all those charismatic bosses in the 1970s, and treated every game like it was the most important event of the week. He'd even employ the football psychology managers such as Bill Shankly were famous for. 'You're the best striker in this league, much better than everyone else,' I once heard him say to one of his forwards. 'You could score a hat-trick today.' Five minutes into the game, he'd turn away from the pitch in disgust, look at the spectators and say of the same player, 'He's a fucking shithouse!'

My football training began like this, absorbing the lively sights and sounds of the Merseyside amateur leagues, and travelling to their most notorious venues, such as Brook Vale in Litherland, Buckley Hill in Sefton, Stuart Road in Bootle, and Windy Harbour, which, appropriately, is now the site of the Liverpool FC Academy in Kirkby. As a besotted spectator, the closest I got to playing on a full-size pitch in those days was sprinting towards the goalmouth at half-time, taking advantage of the nets for a fifteen-minute game of headers and volleys.

I was mesmerized, not only by the football but by the whole culture that accompanied it: the togetherness, the banter, the aggression, the celebrations in victory, the despair and conflict in defeat. I was eased into this world, then locked into it.

Everyone loved their football, no matter what their level. In the Sunday League, anyone who turns up can get a game. If a goalkeeper enjoys eight or nine pints too many on Saturday night and fails to turn up on Sunday morning, there'll always be someone at the bar ready to step in. Mysterious hangover bugs often sweep across squads on Sunday mornings. On one occasion the manager of The Chaucer, the pub which was the focal point of my community, had no option but to turn to the untried goalkeeping talents of one of his locals.

Jimmy Smith's long-awaited opportunity had arrived.

Those who know Jimmy will tell you he's a great lad but he's also not the full shilling. Strictly speaking, he wasn't registered to play, so it was explained to Jimmy that for the duration of ninety minutes he had to pretend he was called 'Kenty' – the name of the absent keeper. Things progressed well until Jimmy conceded a penalty for an atrocious tackle, and the referee decided it was worth a booking. 'Unlucky, Kenty!' everyone on the pitch and touchline shouted loudly, reminding Jimmy of his secret identity, though not completely convinced their new recruit could maintain his act.

'What's your name, son?' asked the ref.

You could see Jimmy struggling with this tough question, trying to ensure he didn't let his team-mates down.

'Kent,' replied Jimmy proudly, the sweat pouring off him as he focused on his special task.

'And your first name?'

There was a pause as Jimmy's confused mind considered the possibilities. Then his face lit up, he stiffened his back, and he confidently offered his response.

'Clark,' he said.

The referee simply wrote the name in his book and carried on none the wiser.

This incident obviously provoked laughter, but generally these games were taken as seriously as Champions League qualifiers. There's a famous quote attributed to the legendary American football coach Vince Lombardi: 'Winning is not everything, it's the only thing.' It's the opposite of the fluffy romantic notion that says 'it's not the winning but the taking part'. Lombardi later tried to distance himself from the sentiments behind his famous line, concerned things would be taken to a dangerous extreme by more cynical, ruthless coaches. Perhaps he'd heard about my dad's antics. Whenever I hear the saying now, I think of my dad's career as a manager.

He adopted the philosophy with a religious fanaticism. Several escapades earned him a season ticket at county FA disciplinary hearings. I'm not sure if hitting a referee with a corner flag, as my dad once did when upset with a decision, will ever be recognized by UEFA as a fine example of sportsmanship. The victim, George Kane, went on to referee in the Football League.

Fortunately, he never got the chance to wreak his revenge on me. Another time my dad was so convinced his team weren't capable of equalizing he ordered his physio to break one of the crossbars to force an abandonment. The plot was foiled when a replacement was erected, and the game went ahead. My dad later vowed to be more respectful of officials. One day he discovered the referee for an important match several miles away in Kirkby was from Bootle, so he charitably offered him a lift on his team bus. The goodwill lasted ninety minutes. After his team's defeat my dad drove home, deliberately leaving the poor ref stranded. Never mind the FA, even the local radio station was disgusted: the incident was mentioned on Billy Butler's BBC Radio Merseyside show the following day.

The message being sent to me was clear: win by all means possible.

Life off the park was just as colourful. Marsh Lane is the type of area that has contributed to Liverpool's reputation. It's a mad mix of cynical and kind-hearted, funny yet tough personalities. The regulars of The Chaucer possessed the only degree that matters – a BA in how to be streetwise.

For generations, the people here have been bred to be survivors. Bootle was bombed to virtual destruction during the Second World War; it was the most shelled area of the country during the Blitz. Later, poverty set in because the dockyards, once the main source of employment, were abandoned. Entire communities were stricken. A grey landscape was left sandwiched between the wealthier suburb of Crosby, leading towards the middle-class towns of Formby and Southport, and the bustling Liverpool city centre two miles to the south. The residents must have felt they were being squeezed and taunted into submission. It's no wonder many of them turned petty crime into a trade. Even now the police in Bootle are seen as a hindrance rather than a help. There must have seemed no alternative to bending the law, beyond packing your bags and jumping on a boat or train, which many did. Instead of walking around feeling defeated by their circumstances, the people here kept their chins up and fought back to support their families, and they didn't care what it took. You've two choices in a situation like that: sink or swim. Ninety per cent of people here keep their head above water.

Those I grew up with didn't simply strike back with violence or thieving, as the stereotypes suggest. The most destructive weapon I ever saw in The Chaucer was a sharp tongue. Some of the hardest men I've met have been reduced to nervous wrecks by a witty put-down. You need to be shrewd as well as resilient where I'm from.

The unconditional belief that friends and family come first, no matter what it takes, has been passed on to sons, daughters and grandchildren. It's the Lombardi philosophy applied to real life. That's why this is the place I love, warts and all.

Many football autobiographies slip into the cliché of rags-to-riches tales, every chapter sprinkled with sentimental accounts of how a multi-million-pound player once couldn't even afford his own bootlaces when he was younger. You might be thinking my description of life in Marsh Lane in the eighties is following the trend. But mine is no story of a poor Scouser. Whatever preconceptions you may have of my childhood are wrong.

We lived in one of the biggest houses on Knowsley Road in Bootle. My mum is still there. She and my dad are grafters. They worked hard to make sure we had the best of everything, and if there was anything more to be done to make the life of their children better, so be it. I was never short of the best kits and football boots. I felt well off compared to some of the other lads in the area. One called my dad Arthur Daley, because on top of his building job he always seemed to have some scam on the go that meant we could go on our summer holidays to Spain.

His own dad, James, was a character too. 'Mr Drysdale' the drinkers in The Chaucer used to call him, after the bank manager from *The Beverly Hillbillies* who was considered tight with his cash, because he never got a round in. 'I drink in my own time,' he'd tell them. Regrettably, his wife, my Nanny Carra, was drinking in her own time too. She suffered from alcoholism. It reached such a bad stage she once mistook her poor dog for the living-room rug. 'That rug is in a right state,' she said as she was falling asleep in front of the fire. She'd picked it up and thrown it into the kitchen before she realized it had four legs.

We weren't a family of scallies though. There were a few nutters, maybe, but not scallies. My uncle, Pat Carragher, was a well-respected policeman. I thought he was a millionaire. He lived in a huge house on Victoria Road in Formby, where some Liverpool and Everton players live now. We'd turn up with our swimming costumes and towels to head straight for his sauna and jacuzzi. It was as if we were on one of our trips to Butlin's. Forget Mr Drysdale, we were like the Clampetts whenever we visited him.

The rest of the time we were more like the Royle family. When I heard one of Peter Kay's stand-up routines I could have sworn he'd visited both my nans' houses when I was little. Me and my younger brothers Paul and John spent alternate Sunday afternoons there, and later at my dad's sister Auntie Ann's. It was the same warmly familiar routine each week. We'd be outside playing football before being shouted inside to gather around the table for Sunday roast. When that was eaten, we'd fight for our speck in front of the television, munching away at the biscuits piled on a plate on the coffee table as we watched *Bullseye*. Family get-togethers saw my mum and dad's Dr Hook and Drifters back catalogue getting played to death, while I'd moan at Mum for dressing me and Paul in identical clothes, as she always did.

Paul, who is a couple of years younger, seemed to like this habit more than I did. He looked up to me when he was really young, so much so that when I started primary school and was kitted out in my St James uniform, Paul insisted on my mum buying him the same outfit. He ended up going to nursery in a school uniform he didn't need to wear for another two years. He soon stopped this fixation.

He has a shorter fuse than me, which I discovered to my cost when we were a little older. I tried to let him beat me at pool during one visit to The Chaucer, leaving the black over the pocket for a simple tap-in. Paul did a Ronnie Rosenthal and missed the sitter. His response to my laughing was to belt me with his snooker cue. I'm always on my guard when we're playing pool now, just to be safe.

My dad's family might have been home to some eccentrics, but Mum's side, the Vasallos, who were originally from Malta, were just as lively. Her dad, Paul, worked on the boats, and often returned with all manner of different goodies from his journeys abroad. The family even had a pet monkey at one point. My mum's mum, Ellen, is my only surviving grandparent, and I know how much pride she takes in all her children, and her twenty-one grandkids, and her six great-grandchildren.

My mum and dad split up when I was ten, and there were fears I'd go off the rails and manipulate some sort of 'victim' status, being from a broken home. I was caught robbing sweets at school, which prompted the parish priest to come and talk to me about the perils of a life of crime. He had nothing to worry about. This was when Mum's strength came to the fore. She juggled her work behind the bar with bringing up three sons. She works in Southport as a nurse now, determined as ever to consider others before herself. Of all the people in my life, she's the one I respect most. Paul, John and I never wanted for anything as kids. Everything was done for us. Whether it was cleaning, cooking or any other housework, she waited on us twenty-four hours a day. The way we've been brought up is to her eternal credit, so when she feels proud of any of our achievements, I feel doubly pleased because it's she who made it possible.

Despite the separation, she knew I already had stability in my life, not only because of her, but because of football. My second home was the Brunswick Youth Club – the Brunny – where we'd spend every school holiday having a kick-about in the gym in the afternoon and playing pool in the evening.

My dad may have moved out of the house, but he remained as influential as ever. As I got older he'd take me to The Chaucer, or to the pub he owned, The Salisbury, otherwise known as The Solly, where in an hour I'd learn more words of wisdom and tricks than I did in a year at school. After I broke into the Liverpool first team, a bemused stranger saw me at the bar of The Chaucer and felt obliged to approach me with a word of advice.

'Do you really think you should be in here?' he said. 'This pub is terrible for drugs.'

'No it isn't,' came a voice from the other side of the room. 'You can get anything you want in here.'

You didn't strive to keep your feet on the ground, they were stuck there as soon as you walked through the doors of a Marsh

Lane boozer. If anyone was perceived to be letting his head drift towards the clouds, he'd soon be dragged back. I once saw Tranmere Rovers midfielder Kenny Irons being brought to earth with a thud when he was overheard criticizing a fellow player, with the words, 'Who the fuck do you think you are, Marco Tardelli?'

I'd be captivated by the personalities surrounding me, although when fame arrived it sometimes felt I was being held responsible for every indiscretion of my friends. I later introduced one of my Liverpool team-mates, a certain Michael Owen, to Chaucer regular Tom Foley, and it seemed like an innocent enough meeting. Tom liked to rub his hands together – a gesture Michael later copied after scoring a famous hat-trick at St James's Park against Newcastle – and was known to 'have his fingers in one or two pies', so Michael and I ended up on the front of the *News of the World* due to our 'association' with someone with a criminal record. The reporters must think we have a duty to check the background of everyone we meet.

I don't take a moral view on any of the lads I grew up with. I take people as I find them. I served my apprenticeship as a permanent touchline mascot to my dad's teams, but I earned my stripes by earning the respect of the people of Marsh Lane. I wasn't going to be allowed, nor did I want, to forget my roots because I'd made it at Liverpool. Football has never been a way of escaping my working-class background, but a means of celebrating it. These fine people still remember the young lad who stood on the touchline with his dad every Sunday. I'd never turn my back on those who made me who I am.

Of course watching football was never going to be enough for me. I craved a piece of the action. I was supposed to wait until I was eight before I could play for the Merton Villa junior team, but I lied when I was seven to persuade the manager, Peter

Halsall, to pick me. This was the beginning, I hoped, of a glorious career as one of Everton's greatest ever strikers.

That was a distant fantasy. You've no idea how good you are, or might become, at that age. Throughout my years at St James Primary, I had no notion of the level of my talent. How could I know? You're judging yourself against lads who live in the next house or street, not the rest of the country. I was content enough starring for the school team, trying to impress the headteacher, John Rourke, whose pride in being an Everton season ticket holder meant he could immediately count on my respect.

My secondary school was Savio High, where the most famous former pupils were Peter Hooton, the lead singer of The Farm, and former Liverpool defender Mark Seagraves. His cousin Gary, or 'Siggy', was my best mate in class. I treated my school trials in the same way as my first training sessions under a new manager, determined to show what I was capable of. And the more I played, the more I sensed how highly I was rated. I'd be in training sessions with lads my own age and the Savio High teachers would shift me to join the older boys in more organized competitive matches. Mike Dickinson, one of those teachers, was also the physio for England Schoolboys (he's now working for Everton), so I guessed he could compare me to players from across the country.

I was still playing for fun rather than seriously considering turning professional. The first real hint I had of my ability arrived courtesy of Dad having a pint too many as I played pool in The Solly.

'Is your lad any good?' he was asked.

I was lining up another pot, pretending not to pay attention, but his response made me tremble with anticipation.

'He'll play in the top division in England,' said my dad, who didn't realize that I was listening in.

I wanted to believe him, but part of me still imagined it was the drink talking.

Even when I was first invited to train with Liverpool the implications didn't sink in. When I was nine, I finished top scorer for the Bootle Boys side, which represented all the schools in the area. Again, I was playing in an age group above mine. (Ian Chapman was the manager of Bootle Boys. When he told me he was a Manchester United fan I jokingly said I was certain I'd learn nothing from him, but he proved me wrong and led us well.) Anfield scout Harry Hodges spotted me in the Bootle Boys team and asked five of us to train at the club, introducing me to the School of Excellence coaches Hugh McAuley and Dave Shannon, who'd have such a major influence in later years. I made sure they remembered me by turning up to train in an Everton kit and taking the nickname 'Sharpy', after my Goodison hero Graeme Sharp.

It wasn't long before Kenny Dalglish, the Liverpool manager at the time, knew who I was too, although this had nothing to do with my performances on the pitch. Once more I had my dad to thank. The meeting of Bootle and Crosby Boys led to Carragher clashing with Dalglish on and off the park.

Kenny's son Paul was playing for Crosby, and he was on the touchline with one of his top scouts, Tom Saunders, to show his support. It was 1–0 to Crosby when, late in the game, we were gifted a dubious penalty to equalize. Kenny wasn't impressed by the decision and had a pop at the referee. This was the signal for my dad to show his colours.

'Keep your fuckin' mouth shut, Dalglish,' he said. 'You should know all about dodgy penalties after the amount you get at Anfield every season.'

Before I knew it, Kenny and my dad were virtually coming to blows. Saunders had to step in to keep them apart.

My position at Liverpool could have been precarious if Kenny's ego had been insulted, but the opposite happened. Ever since, he and my dad have laughed about it. Kenny probably thought if I was anything like my dad, no one and nothing was going to intimidate me. Reputations count for nothing in football, after all.

Unlike any Liverpool manager since, Kenny had a hands-on approach at the club's School of Excellence, which later became The Academy. I hear Alex Ferguson does the same at Manchester United. Kenny would watch training sessions, know the names of every nine-year-old, and want to meet their families. His dedication undoubtedly brought good long-term results, ensuring Liverpool were a step ahead in signing the best young players, even passionate Evertonians like me, Robbie Fowler and Steve McManaman. Who says no if Kenny Dalglish or Steve Heighway knock on your front door? If a bright young prospect is undecided whether to move to Anfield or Goodison nowadays, I'm certain a quick visit from the current manager would seal the deal.

By now I was becoming increasingly aware of being a level above most of my team-mates at school and in the Bootle Boys side, but this began to cause problems. Football was no longer about fun, but critical to my mood for the rest of the week.

It was not pretty watching ten-year-old James Carragher in action. If anyone tracked down former colleagues who played alongside me as a schoolboy, I'm sure they'd hear a selection of horror stories regarding my attitude. They hated being in my team. I had no concept or appreciation of other players' limitations. Perhaps I was still lacking an understanding of my own ability, believing anyone could reproduce my form if they put their mind to it. More likely, I was intolerant of less talented footballers to a point where I could be accused of being a bully.

I wanted to win too much. This isn't a bad quality, but at such a tender age it must have seemed a bit strange. Most ten-year-olds will play the match, go home, watch telly eating a bag of crisps and forget about it the next day. I'd think about a defeat for days. Instead of enjoying my football, I was too intense. The 'winning is the only thing' philosophy was poisoning me. There were times I was substituted for being too aggressive towards my team-mates. The influence of watching all those adult amateur league battles had sunk in too deep.

By the start of my second year at Bootle Boys, the age rules meant I was playing alongside lads in my own year. It became even clearer to me how much better I was, and it wasn't a responsibility I carried well.

We played Wirral first game of the new season, a team that included David Thompson, my future Liverpool team-mate. I'd decided I wanted to play centre midfield so I could dictate the play much more. It was 0–0 at half-time, so the manager ordered me back upfront and I scored a hat-trick in a 3–0 win. My central midfield career was over, temporarily at least, after forty-five minutes. I was a striker for the rest of the season.

I was talking a great game on the pitch, and usually playing one too, but I was stinking places out with my behaviour. On my Anfield debut playing for Bootle Boys, I scored at The Kop end, but Heighway pulled me after the game and slated me for not being a team player. 'You need to start appreciating your team-mates,' he said. It was the second key warning of my novice career, and it hit me as much as my dad's flying boots.

The opposition felt the heat of my anger too. As Bootle's best player, I'd often be targeted by opponents, and if I ever felt I was being provoked, I rarely bit my tongue or controlled my temper. Yet again, the conduct I'd witnessed standing on the sidelines had been embedded into my repertoire. The Sunday League was always a scally zone.

At the start of my Merton Villa career we'd regularly lose 7–0, but we improved every season. Medals began to arrive, and personal recognition came with them. Soon we were the best team in the Bootle and Litherland District. We also won a national tournament held in Southport and moved into the stronger Walton and Kirkdale League, playing the best sides in Liverpool.

Our rivals were a team called Pacific, who had a player everyone recognized as a top prospect, Jamie Cassidy. Jamie would have been a certain Liverpool regular if he hadn't suffered so much with injuries. He damaged his cruciate and broke his leg just after breaking into the reserves, and never fully recovered. Their striker, John Murphy, also went on to score lots of goals for Blackpool. They were a formidable side, and they beat us to the league title, but then we met each other in the Sunday League Cup Final.

That game, held at the Long Lane playing fields in Fazakerley, meant as much to me when I was twelve as the moment Andriy Shevchenko fluffed his penalty in the 2005 Champions League Final. We won 5–4, and I scored twice. As Everton midfielder Stuart McCall presented the trophy, I revelled in a collective sense of achievement. Good as I was, it had needed a monumental team effort to win that cup. I was proud of the whole side's efforts, not only my own. Another box in the 'things to do to become a top footballer' had been ticked.

After McCall handed me my medal, I just muttered 'Thanks' and walked back to my seat. If he'd wanted to chat longer, I could have listed all his playing statistics, how many goals he'd scored, and maybe even offered a bit of advice on what more he could be doing to live up to the standards of the great midfielder he'd replaced, Paul Bracewell – a player who inspired my gelled haircut at one time. This is because when I wasn't playing football, I wanted to be reading or talking about it.

Every youngster in Liverpool likes to keep a stack of magazines under the bed for some quiet late-night entertainment. *Shoot* was my choice. Its arrival every Saturday morning was pencilled into my mind's diary. I'd collect my order from the newsagent and read every sentence. I wasn't interested in pinning posters on the wall, but in finding out any detail about every top player. I'd keep each edition for years, so I'd always have a private library for later reference. Today, I'd test my memory for games and goalscorers against anyone in the country. I studied results, fixtures and players in such depth I'm now able to answer many football trivia questions instantly. If I wasn't a footballer, I'd have gone on *Mastermind*, my specialist subject 'Shoot magazine during the 1980s'.

One edition from spring 1988 still traumatizes me. I was convinced Everton had signed Ian Rush from Juventus because he was on the cover of *Shoot* wearing the blue kit. I ran home shouting to everyone, 'We've signed Ian Rush!', only to read the article and discover it was an April Fool joke. I wasn't laughing, and graduated to the more mature *90 Minutes* shortly after.

If I ever met one of the professional players featured in the pages of *Shoot*, I wasn't as surprised as some youngsters would have been because I was lucky enough to become accustomed to it. I was training twice a week at Liverpool, at the Vernon

Sangster Leisure Centre – which is due to be demolished to make way for the new stadium on Stanley Park – and was used to seeing the likes of Dalglish and Everton's manager Howard Kendall on the line during schoolboy games, watching their own sons. Kendall's presence would always prompt me to try to find an extra yard. Liverpool had spotted me, but privately it was Everton I still hoped to join.

At the age of eleven, I was given my chance.

Ray Hall, who ran Everton's School of Excellence, had actually been pursuing me for some time, and eventually I allowed my heart to rule my head and accepted his offer. We only signed annual contracts at Anfield, so at the end of my second season I informed Steve Heighway my Liverpool career was over and my spiritual home awaited.

Hall was excited by his new signing. A day before my first training session he called my mum to ask her the name of my favourite player.

She didn't know. 'I think it's Tony Cottee,' she said.

The following morning I arrived to be met by a smiling Hall.

'I know who your favourite player is,' he said.

'Graeme Sharp?' I replied.

Hall's face turned white. He'd brought me Cottee's shorts as a welcome gift. I wasn't exactly gutted, but I wasn't performing cartwheels either.

My dad warned me leaving Liverpool was a mistake. He had no intention of stopping me joining Everton; all he said was there was no reason to leave Anfield. Within a few months I realized he was right. I loved Everton, but there was no comparison in terms of the coaching, organization and standard of players, and the glory days of the mid to late eighties were over. At Liverpool, everything was focused on passing and moving. When a player tried to pick up the ball, Heighway would shout at them like they'd committed a cardinal sin. 'Are you a goalkeeper, lad?' he'd yell. 'Put that down!' I missed working with him and wanted to go back.

I asked my dad to approach Heighway and ask if there was a chance of a return. Thankfully, Liverpool agreed. I signed my first longer-term contract when I was fourteen, on schoolboy forms.

Phil Thompson was waiting for me at Anfield when I went there to put pen to paper. 'You'll never be as good as your arl' fella,' Thommo said. He probably still had the bruises from meetings between Kirkby and Bootle twenty years earlier.

The only time I've left Liverpool since that day was to head to Lilleshall, the FA School of Excellence for players between the ages of fourteen and sixteen. Heighway tried to stop that happening. 'I don't want you to go,' he said. 'I know you've got to, but I believe you're the best fourteen-year-old in the country and I want to coach you here. They'd better not ruin you.' But this was my first opportunity to test myself against lads from across the country and in Europe. Besides, winning a place at Lilleshall was a huge accolade.

Any doubts I had about my abilities were quashed as I packed my bags and headed south for the final selections, after making the cut at the North-West trials, held in Preston. I was in competition with future internationals like Frank Lampard. I made the squad of sixteen, Lampard didn't.

By winning a place, I felt I had everything I needed to realize my ambition.

Lilleshall was the perfect grounding for a young professional. It was like being at boarding school, but I loved every minute. They were two of the best years of my life. I suspect it was harder for my family than for me during this time. Going away from home was exciting. Other than holidays or away matches, I'd not spent any time outside Bootle. But to see me wave goodbye at fourteen, even if it was only for a while, wasn't easy for my mum. Top footballers often get a bad press because the supporters only see our wealthy lifestyle, but there are sacrifices to be made to get to the top. There's no doubt some lads find it tougher than others, and homesickness is a problem, but I didn't see Lilleshall as a hardship. I missed my family too, but never so much I wanted to leave. I saw it as character-building. It helped me grow up quicker because you had to look after yourself rather than rely on your family to do everything for you.

The venue itself was superb. It was like living in luxury. It was a two-mile drive from the gates to the front door. I thought I was arriving at a mansion.

As far as I was concerned, I was joining a specialist school for footballers. We had to attend lessons and do all the usual school stuff, but we also trained with the best coaches every day and were all given our first taste of international football while we were there, so there was always something to look forward to.

After it was shut down, critics argued it was too elitist, focusing too much on a select group to the cost of others. This doesn't make sense to me. The fact I could go from a Bootle Sunday League side to Lilleshall proved how fair the scouting system was, while even those who didn't get in didn't necessarily suffer from having to stay with their clubs. What Lilleshall guaranteed was that the most highly rated youngsters in the country were given every chance to progress, and if any of those went on to represent England, as I did, it was a success. Ray Clemence's son Stephen and Gavin McCann were the other players in my year who went on to play at the top level. My Liverpool team-mate and former rival from Pacific Jamie Cassidy was also there. We shared digs. He's responsible for my now being known as Jamie rather than James. To my family and friends, I'm still James, but during my spell at Lilleshall, Steve Heighway would refer to the 'two Jamies' away from home, so at Liverpool it's stuck.

Our eyes were opened to the standard of player elsewhere, but also to the financial differences between the Scousers and others. Me and Jamie were proud of our YTS contracts, while others were telling us about being paid as much as £10,000 in signing-on fees. In every sense, this was a taste of a world beyond Liverpool, which broadened our horizons.

By the end of my first year there I couldn't wait to go back. Steve Heighway had other ideas. Lilleshall played Liverpool towards the end of year one and I didn't play well. 'That's it, I'm bringing him back here,' Heighway told one of the coaches. 'They're ruining his game.' I heard this news later. He was wrong, though. I'd simply had a poor match and there was nothing to worry about. I was progressing at least as well as I would have had I stayed on Merseyside.

I was overlooked for England Schoolboys, but made my international debut representing Lilleshall at Under-16 level, partly because the aptly named no-nonsense Keith Blunt was manager, and he seemed to take a shine to the street fighter from Liverpool.

Yorkshireman Blunt was my type of boss. It was he who convinced Heighway it wasn't necessary to take me out of Lilleshall. He coached Joe Cole later, who told me how when he tried a Cruyff turn in the centre circle he was met with a scream of disapproval. 'Stop!' cried Blunt in his Brian Glover-inspired accent. 'We won't be having any of that nonsense here, lad.'

I was one of the smallest players in our group, but what I

lacked in height I compensated for in spirit. I heard a few years later Wayne Rooney was shown a photograph of me standing beside Marlon Broomes, a six-foot-tall defender who's played for a host of First Division clubs, and asked, 'Which of these do you think became an England international defender?' Marlon dwarfed me, so the point was made: there's an obsession with physique at a young age, but it's no indicator of where a career can go.

Coaches like Blunt saw my attributes, although my language gave him the opportunity to indulge in a form of physical torture. There was a rule that anyone caught swearing had to do a lap of the pitch. Suffice to say, I ended up resembling a marathon runner. The Bootle Tourette's syndrome was no help to me: I cursed every misdirected shot or pass. I might as well have been wearing spikes rather than boots. I couldn't be bothered with the school lessons either. I was only interested in football. Michael Owen attended Lilleshall a couple of years later and told me the headmaster would discipline the players by shouting, 'We're not going to have another James Carragher here!' Michael, or Mo as I'll refer to him, said that by the time he met me he thought I must have been some kind of nutcase. My legend went before me, and it had nothing to do with football. I was even banned from the final graduation ceremony, or the 'caps day' as it was called, after a scuffle with a classmate on my last day of school. My dad ordered me to turn up anyway, daring them not to let me join in. No one said a word and I received my cap, presented by Jimmy Hill, with the rest of the players.

My international bow came when Blunt picked me upfront against Italy in Sardinia, and left a shy striker called Emile Heskey on the bench. I scored in a 2–0 win, the Italian keeper Gianluigi Buffon having no answer to my lethal finishing. Sadly, the return game with the Italians ended with tragic news. A coach from The Chaucer travelled to Walsall packed with my supporters, then returned to discover one of the locals, Stevie Porter, had been killed in Spain the same afternoon. Stevie would have been on the coach but for his holiday; his son Michael was one of those who'd come to see me play. His mum was waiting for him to deliver the news when the bus got back.

Other outings for the Marsh Lane boys were less traumatic. My next game was away in Holland, a 1–1 draw, with David Thompson on the mark for us. This fixture was my dad and his friends' first European expedition to support me. Included in the party was the landlord of The Chaucer, Jimmy Roberts, who'd had his eyes gouged out during an horrific incident some years earlier. Naturally enough, thoughts turned towards a slice of the action in Amsterdam's red light zone.

'I'm not getting involved in any of that, Philly,' Jimmy told my dad.

'Don't worry, Jimmy,' my dad replied. 'We've brought you here as our eyewitness in case any of our birds accuse us of getting up to no good. You can tell them you didn't see us do anything.'

My second year at Lilleshall saw me briefly flirt with going back to Everton. Lilleshall's match with Liverpool ended in a 2–0 win for the representative team, for which I was playing upfront alongside Andrew Ducros. He began his career as a trainee at Coventry but has spent most of his days playing for non-league clubs such as Nuneaton and Burton Albion. He must think back to those days in 1993–94 when Graeme Souness tried to sign him for Liverpool. Ducros was taken by Souness and Sammy Lee into the office at Melwood after the game and told the club had liked his performance so much they'd like him to join. He got on the team bus heading back to Lilleshall understandably chuffed, while I – a Liverpool player – sat there still waiting for my first hello from the Anfield manager.

I was so livid that quitting the club on the spot seemed a valid option. After five years, this was how they treated me? By trying to sign my striking partner? Making me feel like an idiot in front of all the Lilleshall players? I wasn't going to lie down and accept this. I got ready to fight back. Ray Hall had also watched the match, saw how angry I was, and told my dad he'd happily sign me again. 'Let's see how Liverpool feel if I go somewhere else,' I thought.

Unfortunately for Ducros, Souness didn't remain in the job long enough to take him to Anfield, and my revived thoughts about heading back to Goodison lasted no longer than the coach journey home. I made up my mind to put my Everton sympathies to one side and prove to Liverpool they didn't need to be considering any alternative to me.

One of my final games at Lilleshall was against Portugal during the Under-16 European Championship in 1994, on the same day the old Kop closed before it became seated. We won 1–0 against the hosts, and at a celebratory team meeting after the game Blunt said it was appropriate for me to lead a rendition of 'You'll Never Walk Alone'.

As a Liverpool player, it was easy.

As an Evertonian? I was opening a can of worms in my head.

2

Everton

On 26 May 1989, Michael Thomas ran through the heart of Liverpool's defence and scored the most notorious last-minute goal in Anfield history, handing Arsenal the title. In a Bootle pub just a couple of miles away, an eleven-year-old Evertonian, his dad and his mates began celebrating as if their own team had won the League. A group of lads went outside and scrawled graffiti on the wall.

THANK YOU, ARSENAL.

The eleven-year-old laughed his head off, encouraging and applauding the offenders who were chalking the headline he dreamed of reading on the back of every newspaper the following morning.

That boy was me. I thought of myself as the biggest Blue in Bootle. On that depressing night for Liverpool, the club I would eventually come to love, their defeat meant as much as any of my own team's victories. I didn't simply want to bask in the glory of Arsenal's win; I wanted to rub it in under the noses of every Red in the city.

My earliest football experiences had been with an Everton

team that competed for the League and FA Cup every year and which also enjoyed European success. By 1989, the only satisfaction left at the end of the season was this failure of Liverpool's to parade the championship. Nowadays, the Goodison trophy room is a museum of former glories.

This is part of being a football fan, and we should make no apology for it. The ultimate pleasure is a cup or League victory for your own side, but taking comfort in the disappointment of others is strangely satisfying. Anyone who takes a hike up the moral high ground and says they're not happy to celebrate when their rivals lose is a liar. You're always looking for these consolations as a supporter because it sustains your interest when your own ambitions are foiled. Seeing clubs you don't like suffer is all part of the tradition. Every side does it, not just Everton, though circumstances dictate some are condemned to feel this way more than others.

As an Evertonian, I was thrilled whenever Liverpool lost, mainly because it improved our chances of winning the title. As a Liverpool fan, those feelings are now reversed, and other sides have been added to the list of teams whose defeats I celebrate. Seeing Manchester United and Chelsea come a cropper makes me feel the same way I did about Liverpool when I was eleven years old. I'd never go as far as writing graffiti on the side of my house, but I'm sure if United ever lost a cup final in the last minute the drinks would be flowing.

I've thought a lot during the course of writing this book about my feelings towards Everton, and they must be as complex as anyone's in the city. My attitude has changed towards Everton as I've grown older. I used to love them, but there are things about the club I can't stand now.

There are two Evertons in my life: the Everton before

Liverpool, and the Everton after. The club I loved in the 1980s and the team I see now are poles apart in my mind. I refer to the Everton of the eighties as 'us' and the modern Everton as 'them'. I can't stop myself discussing what 'we' did when I think of Howard Kendall's first wonderful side. That's why I'm dedicating a chapter to Everton. They're part of my life as much as Liverpool. It's a blessing and a curse to feel this way. It puts me in a unique position to observe the relationship between the clubs, but it forces me to confront some uncomfortable truths.

I was Everton-mad growing up. I was a regular at all the away games as well as at home. Evertonians talk fondly about the legendary European Cup Winners' Cup semi-final against Bayern Munich in April 1985. Never mind the Goodison second leg; I was in Germany with my dad for the first game too, getting my bobble hat swiped by some Munich fans outside the ground.

I'd be in a bad mood for days when we lost. Worse than that, I'd be inconsolable when our rivals won. Nothing meant as much to me as my Everton top, which I even wore while training at the Liverpool School of Excellence. Liverpool were the target of my poison in those days, even after I'd joined them. I thought the Liverpool fans were cocky and arrogant – a characteristic they'd earned after years of success – so naturally I rejoiced when they were beaten. They reacted the same way if Everton lost, although you still hear the more dishonest claim otherwise.

One of my earliest memories of the Merseyside derby rivalry came courtesy of Everton's defeat to Manchester United in the 1985 FA Cup Final, which I attended as a seven-year-old. As our coaches returned to Bootle shortly after midnight I vividly recall a group of Liverpool fans who'd been waiting for our arrival so they could give us stick. We'd won the League and the European Cup Winners' Cup, and had enjoyed arguably the best season in our history, so we were hardly in mourning. But there they were, desperate to twist the knife, even if that meant celebrating a United win. Any time I hear Liverpool fans say they're more bothered about Manchester United than Everton, I think about that night and those lads who must have been standing outside for hours for no other reason than to have their moment of fun at our expense. They're probably the same people who say Liverpool fans don't care about Everton. Oh really? So you weren't celebrating Norman Whiteside's winner? I wouldn't be surprised if 'Thank you, United' was written on the wall of a few Liverpool pubs that night. In my opinion the derby rivalry is bigger and far more important to the city than the one with United.

Liverpool and Everton fans had to take it as much as dish it out to each other back then, but it wasn't underhand and was always based on what was happening on the pitch. We could share the bragging rights because in the mid-eighties we were undoubtedly the two best teams in Europe. My loyalties were exclusively to my heroes in blue, and I wasn't shy of showing Liverpool fans, players and staff how I felt about my team, even while I was training alongside Anfield legends. In fact, signing for Liverpool made me want to show my true colours even more, even if it sometimes got me into trouble.

I remember returning with the Liverpool reserve squad from a mid-afternoon game early in 1996 while Everton were playing an FA Cup third round replay at Stockport. The radio match commentary was on as the coach made its way back to Melwood, and naturally I was listening to every word and urging Everton to win. Stockport scored, and Ronnie Moran and Sammy Lee, who were in charge of the reserves at the time, couldn't hide their delight.

'One–nil!' shouted Ronnie, the sense of joy inescapable.

Sitting at the back of the coach, I simmered away inside, praying we'd get back into the game.

Then my moment came. Everton equalized. I couldn't resist.

'Get in!' I screamed.

'Who the fuck was that?' shouted Ronnie, who as the first-team coach was still in the dark about my youthful loyalties.

I wouldn't say it was the cue for a witch hunt, but Ronnie might as well have been holding a pitchfork as he swooped to find the culprit.

The next day I was hauled before our youth coaches Hugh McAuley and Dave Shannon for one of those 'quiet chats' footballers have to get used to during the course of a career.

'Listen, Jamie, you've got to sort this out,' Hughie said to me. 'The senior staff have high hopes you'll play for the first team. It's time for you to start behaving like a Liverpool player.'

I walked out of that meeting having heard the warning, but it was going to take more than a gentle pep talk to stop me loving Everton.

The first time I was named sub for the senior team was an away fixture in Middlesbrough in 1996, and even then my mixed loyalties couldn't be hidden. At half-time I was warming up with the other subs as the latest scores from elsewhere were being read out over the tannoy. Everton were winning 2–0 at home to Newcastle. It was the day Alan Shearer was making his debut for the Geordies, so I was pretty impressed by the Blues' efforts.

As I was going through my routine, I spotted my dad, who'd come to the front of the stand. He was eating a meat pie as the half-times were announced and I made the mistake of giving him the thumbs-up to show my approval of the Everton score. Had they been paying any attention, a few thousand Liverpool fans in the away end might have seen how happy I was too. It wasn't the most diplomatic way for an up-and-coming player to curry favour with his own supporters. I could see from the way my dad's face turned a rather unattractive shade of beetroot he was livid. 'I could be ducking football boots again when I get home,' I thought as I headed back to the changing room.

He was far less diplomatic in his use of language than Dave and Hughie when he caught up with me, but even then the message was only partially accepted. Every true football fan will tell you how hard it is to shake off those feelings you have for your team. Most of us never have to do it, and even for those of us who succeed, it certainly can't be achieved overnight. I had to go through a prolonged spell of enforced indifference before I deserted Everton. My first taste of Liverpool first-team involvement at Boro was a tentative step in the red direction.

That didn't mean I stopped treasuring childhood memories of following the Blues. Giving them up was not part of my Liverpool 'transfer'. There are Goodison legends from the golden period I still admire and copy today, many of whom I've since had the good fortune and pleasure to meet on a regular basis. They made those early football experiences magical.

The first League game I ever watched at Goodison was at the start of the inspiring 1984–85 season, at home to Tottenham. I was six years old. We were comprehensively beaten, 4–1, and I don't remember anything about the game other than seeing Harry Cross, a famous character from the now-departed Scouse soap opera *Brookside*, leaving the ground early. Judging by the faces of everyone around him, it was the only decent cross anyone saw at Goodison that day. He'd seen enough, but even though we lost, I was yearning for much more.

My dad started taking me to away games that season. On the train to Ipswich – which must be the ground furthest away from Bootle in the country – he introduced me to all the most famous Evertonians, like Eddie Cavanagh. Eddie ran on to the Wembley pitch when Everton won the cup in 1966 and had earned himself iconic status ever since. Meeting him was like a coming-of-age ceremony. The nod of approval from Eddie was an acknowledgement you were now a true Blue. I wasn't just a home-game regular but part of an away-day elite.

Being seen on the pitch, particularly if you were caught by the television cameras, was like a medal of honour. One of the most recognized Blues in the city was Eric Crainey, who jumped on Graeme Sharp when he scored the famous winner at Anfield that season. Later there was Jimmy Sanders, who ran to Neville Southall when he was involved in his half-time sit-down protest against Leeds in 1990. It takes some courage to run on to that hallowed turf, and a bit of fitness too: you have to be an Olympic hurdler to avoid the rugby tackles of the stewards and policemen when they chase you off. I also heard many examples of my dad getting on the pitch. At one time the players must have thought he was the physio. 'I'll get on there one day,' I'd say to myself, and I wasn't necessarily thinking it would be as a player.

That season was captivating from start to finish. I was lucky, or maybe it was fate, to have such an exceptional Everton team as my introduction to top-class football. They didn't simply beat virtually everyone home and away, they tore them apart, playing high-quality football. I didn't go to games fearful we wouldn't win, I'd be guessing the margin of victory. So confident was I of our success, I'd already be thinking about how our rivals would do before a ball was kicked, and how far ahead we'd be in the table by the end of the afternoon.

Match of the Day became the second most important event of the week, after the game itself. My dad would video the show and I'd watch it repeatedly until I'd memorized every word John Motson and Barry Davies said.

Back then there weren't cameras at every ground. You were only given decent highlights if you were near the top of the table, so Evertonians became used to earning top billing and having the pleasure of seeing the afternoon goals from another angle. If you weren't one of the main games, you had to settle for a clip on the local news. In October 1984 we beat Manchester United 5–0 at Goodison, but *Match of the Day* weren't there to film it. The goals were only shown on the BBC filmed by one of those dodgy long-distance cameras. It was literally sixty seconds – a bit like the graveyard slot the modern side gets after midnight on *Match of the Day* now, only with a cloudier picture. We had the tape and it circulated the whole of Bootle for the rest of the week as if it was a piece of treasure for every Blue to get a glimpse of.

I'd mimic radio and television commentaries from Everton's most famous wins of the time, repeating them when we were recreating goals during our own kick-abouts. 'Gray's there again. Oh, I say!' I'd shout as I re-enacted the striker's diving headers against Sunderland in 1985. 'Everton's hold on the cup has been re-established' was another quote which stayed with me from the FA Cup run that season. Motson and Davies provided the soundtrack to Everton's epic victories.

When I couldn't go to the game, for whatever reason, listening to the radio was torture. You hear the full ninety minutes on local and national radio today, but two decades ago it was second-half commentary only, with a couple of brief reports in the first half between the songs the DJ played. It was terrible trying to guess what was happening without the likes of Teletext, mobile phones or *Soccer Saturday* providing instant updates. From a young age I wanted to see the action every weekend, not be miles away imagining Peter Reid, Kevin Sheedy and Paul Bracewell exchanging passes before Trevor Steven crossed for Graeme Sharp to head us into the lead.

The worst experience that season was tuning into the vital away match at Spurs in April 1985. They were our rivals for the title so I'd developed a pathological hatred for them, checking their fixtures and willing them to concede goals as much as I urged Everton to score. Everton had an old-fashioned system of arranging the final scores on boards around the perimeter of the pitch to keep supporters informed of others' results. You had to match the game with the corresponding letter or number in the programme notes. I never had the patience to hang around and work it out. I'd run out of Goodison after a game, straight into the shop across the road and shout, 'How did Spurs get on?' More often than not that season I was told they had won. I'd go home disappointed, which was ridiculous after having watched my own team deliver another superb performance.

By the time we played Spurs at White Hart Lane we knew if we won, the title race was over.

'Now we're off to Tottenham where we hear there's been a goal,' the radio host said just ten minutes into the game.

For a second, my stomach ached with anxiety.

'It's Andy Gray for Everton!' yelled the commentator, his voice hoarse with excitement.

I felt I was on the pitch, scoring the goal myself. At the very least I wanted to be there joining the celebrations, especially when the game ended 2–1 to the Blues.

I never fully appreciated how good that team was at the time. Watching players of the calibre of Peter Reid gave me a perfect education in how to play football. My dad loved Reid more than any player. I've met him many times, and it's even better when someone you admire is such a great man off the pitch too. Whatever he's doing in football, wherever he's a manager, I always want him to be successful. 'Watch and learn from him,' my dad would tell me. 'Look at the way he never gives the ball away. Look how much the game means to him. Even if he's having a nightmare, he'll never hide.'

We didn't hide in Munich for the first leg of that Cup Winners' Cup semi-final. I was out there with my dad, my Uncle Peter and their mates Tommy Valo and Davey Mull, sampling the delights of the European away-days that would become part of my life.

'Have you come here for a fight?' we were asked by the Germans when we arrived.

'No, we've come to show you how to play football,' we'd say back.

Everton fought as hard as usual for a 0–0 draw, and me and my dad went back to our hotel. Before long we received a call in the room from Tommy and Davey.

'We're at the players' hotel,' they said. 'Get down here.'

I saw all the Everton players, and when the team coach left I chased it down the road. Our left-back John Bailey saw me, made the driver stop the coach, and then gave me a can of Coke. It was a small gesture, but when you've travelled all that way to see your team, that kind of thing stays with you for ever. I suppose it's one of the reasons I've always got time for those who make the effort to follow Liverpool in Europe.

In the second leg, I was given my first taste of true Scouse passion on a European night. I've enjoyed plenty of similar occasions as a Liverpool player, but as an Everton fan, nothing beat that semi with Bayern Munich. The Germans didn't know what hit them, other than a lot of Everton boots and plenty more heart and soul. Only English fans, maybe only Scousers, create an atmosphere like that. And only in the 1980s could players like Andy Gray get away with volleying German defenders up the arse for ninety minutes like he did that night.

Sharpy was my hero, but I loved Kevin Sheedy too. Had Sheedy played in my era, David Beckham would be considered the second greatest deadball expert in Premier League history. At home to Ipswich in that 1984–85 season, Sheedy put one free-kick to the keeper's right only for the referee to disallow it. Not a problem. He placed the retake to the left to put Everton ahead. It finished 2–2. I was awestruck.

I've also Sheedy to thank – or should that be blame? – for providing me with my first lesson in the fickleness of supporters, something I've also become used to as a player. It came during the FA Cup semi-final against Luton in 1985. I was the unofficial chairman of the Sheedy fan club, and he played in that game after being out injured for a few weeks. Kevin Richardson had been deputizing and playing well, but Kendall brought Sheedy straight back.

It was obvious he wasn't 100 per cent fit, and he wasn't having a good afternoon. The fans standing near me were crucifying his performance, no matter what he did. If he lost the ball, they'd shout; if he passed to a team-mate, they'd still criticize him. As his biggest fan, I took all the stick he was taking personally. I prayed for just one chance with a free-kick. When it came, I knew what would happen next. I rehearsed my celebration in my head like a military operation. Sheedy stepped up and kept his part of the bargain with another sweet left-footer, and I put my plan into action. The fans were ecstatic. I turned towards those who'd been slaughtering him as if they were all Luton fans and screamed my approval directly into their eyes. Of course, they were oblivious, celebrating as much as the rest of us, but to me Sheedy's free-kick had delivered a message loud and clear to his critics: keep your thoughts to yourself next time.

Sheedy's equalizer kept Everton in the competition, and Derek Mountfield's winner allowed me to fulfil my first important football mission. As the jubilant supporters celebrated, seven-year-old James Carragher found himself on the pitch, jumping on the backs of the Everton players. 'I'll be on the television tonight!' I sensed triumphantly as I returned to my standing position.

Eddie Cavanagh had a youthful new member of his exclusive club.

As I got older, it didn't matter where or when Everton played, I'd be there. Usually in body, always in mind, and mostly in both. Never mind the second-half radio commentaries, we'd always make sure we got in somehow, even if we didn't have a ticket.

Wembley trips seemed a normal annual event then. We could plan our year around May for a cup final, or August for the Charity Shield, or March for the, er, Zenith Data Systems Cup. Remember that one? I suspect many have tried to forget it.

The 4–1 defeat to Crystal Palace in 1991 was memorable for at least thirty Bootle kids who headed for Wembley with my dad. He led them all to the stadium and told the stewards it was all arranged for the youngsters to go in for nothing. 'They're all from care homes in Liverpool,' he explained. 'I've heard they're all allowed in for nothing on a Sunday. It's a free gate on Sunday, isn't it?' The stewards looked bemused and found a room for the youngsters to stay while they found some officials. My dad then explained he had his own ticket and would be going to his seat in five minutes, so if the thirty lads weren't allowed in the stewards would need to stay and look after them. Unsurprisingly, thirty seats were found, taking the attendance that day to a whopping 41,030.

Some London performances were more remarkable than others, and not solely because of the result. I was hysterical in 1985, but that had nothing to do with Norman Whiteside's winning goal.

An hour before kick-off I was with my dad and Paul when we saw a cockney tout, a spiv straight out of a classic *Only Fools and Horses* script, offering tickets down Wembley Way. He took out a bundle of about twenty to sell, so my dad grabbed them to dish out to the genuine fans who didn't fancy paying a fortune. Unfortunately, he turned straight into a policeman who arrested him and the tout on the spot. I was seven and Paul was even younger, but we had to watch as my dad was pounced on and pushed into the back of a police van.

We were taken on board the vacated Everton team coach to calm our tears, then my dad's mates took us in to the match, but all we were thinking about was what had happened to our dad. Would he be stuck in London overnight? Then, twenty minutes before the end of the game, I felt a pat on the shoulder. God knows how my dad found us, because it was still terracing then. I was so relieved to see him, and finally I could enjoy the match. Then Whiteside scored and made the day even worse.

'What's just happened?' I distinctly recall a fan standing next to me asking as the United players and fans celebrated.

Everyone looked at him, and someone said, 'What do you think just happened? They've scored, you stupid bastard.'

I felt like punching him, but my seven-year-old right hook still needed work.

Strange as it sounds, I don't remember being too upset about losing the cup final that season. We had the League and the European Cup Winners' Cup under our belt; the FA Cup, which we'd already won a year earlier, would have been a bonus. The end-of-season party in The Chaucer went on until three a.m. as we'd fulfilled the ultimate ambition of beating Liverpool to the League title for the first time in fifteen years.

As we danced on the pool table in the early hours, I could never have imagined Everton would win only one more title in the next three decades. At that time the competition between the Merseyside rivals was enjoying a golden period. Annually we engaged in a struggle for local and national supremacy. The Everton team in 1986 wasn't as good as in 1985, but in my opinion it was still superior to the Liverpool side that won the double. Oddly, I believe the Liverpool team that threw away a nine-point lead in 1987 was a better side than the Everton team that took the championship. Liverpool collapsed at the end of that season when it looked all over.

If Evertonians want to talk about crucial events in the mid-eighties that changed the course of football history, there's one that stands out for me: Neville Southall getting injured while playing for Wales, just before the title and cup run-in in 1986. I'm still convinced that if Southall had stayed fit until the end of the season, Everton would have won the double.

Southall's the greatest keeper Britain has ever had. One

performance I saw him give, away to Coventry in 1988, remains the finest I've seen by any keeper; and the saves he made in the 1–0 cup replay win against Liverpool in February 1991 – the game that followed the famous 4–4 draw immediately before Kenny Dalglish resigned – are still talked about today. He was a goalkeeper who regularly won games, and I'm certain he'd have made the difference in 1986.

I've watched the 1986 FA Cup Final on DVD plenty of times over the last few years, and I still can't believe how much in control Everton were. Liverpool weren't only on the ropes midway through the second half, they were getting a standing count. One mistake by Gary Stevens, giving away the ball outside his own box, changed everything. After being a punchbag for over an hour, Ian Rush came back with the knockout blows. I was devastated when I left Wembley that day, feeling as low as I can ever recall as an Evertonian.

I looked at my dad, expecting to see the same expression I carried, but he never got as down as I did. 'I'm sure I care more about Everton than he does,' I'd say to myself. That wasn't the case. He was just more experienced and wiser about such matters. He was certainly more used to seeing Everton lose than I was. He'd suffered the Gordon Lee era.

Everton's sole goalscorer that day, Gary Lineker, left that summer for Barcelona. He was a great striker, and no one can argue with his goals record when he was at Goodison, but the team did better without him in 1985 and 1987. I didn't take to Lineker when he was an Everton player, and he seemed perfectly happy to get out of the club when the Spaniards made a bid. In my mind, and in that of many Evertonians, Lineker came first in his world and Everton second. I've spoken to some of his ex-team-mates since, and their views confirmed my suspicions.

When, the following summer, Howard Kendall left the club (to be replaced by his assistant Colin Harvey), with Everton sitting proudly as champions, things started to go wrong. Only the appointment of David Moyes fifteen years later threatened a revival. The players who arrived in subsequent seasons, such as Tony Cottee, Pat Nevin and Peter Beagrie, weren't in the same class as we'd seen before. World-class players were replaced by average ones, and in some cases that's being generous. Sharp, Reid, Bracewell, Sheedy, Steven and the rest would grace any all-time greatest team list. How I'd love the two wide men I watched in 1985 in my Liverpool team. And what did we have now? As Alan Ball told my dad after he sold Beagrie (a player famous at the time for celebrating goals with a somersault) from Stoke to Everton, 'I've just sold Everton a fucking circus act.' Goodison legend Alan didn't know whether to laugh or cry when he negotiated that deal.

The 1989 FA Cup Final against Liverpool was the last major occasion for most of that great Howard Kendall side, and the best chance for Harvey to win a trophy, but for obvious reasons that was a fixture unlike any before.

As in 1986, I travelled to the semi-final and to Wembley as a Blue, although my feelings after both matches were vastly different. We'd been at Villa Park on the afternoon of 15 April, aware of events unfolding in Sheffield during Liverpool's semi-final with Nottingham Forest, but only hearing the full horrific details when we arrived home. We knew the match at Hillsborough had been abandoned, and as we travelled back to Bootle there was none of the celebrations you might expect having reached the FA Cup Final. We sensed all wasn't well.

Once the depressing news of the ninety-six deaths of those innocent Liverpool fans had sunk in, winning the FA Cup meant nothing to us. The final was an irrelevance compared to what the Liverpool fans had suffered, and there was a real feeling of solidarity inside Wembley that afternoon. It was an exciting game, which Liverpool won 3–2, but none of it compared to 1986. The defeat never hurt. As an Evertonian, quite correctly I felt like a guest at Wembley that day. It would be the last time I'd travel to see the Blues for a major final under the Twin Towers.

After all those Wembley and European jaunts, relegation scraps now became our main priority.

I was at Lilleshall in May 1994 when we played Wimbledon in the game that could have led to relegation. I came home to my mum's for the weekend, but neither me nor my dad had a ticket for the game. Wimbledon went 2–0 up, prompting an urgent phone call.

'Come on, lad, we're going up there,' my dad said. 'We won't get in, but I just want to be at Goodison now, whatever happens.'

We weren't alone feeling this way. It seemed every Evertonian we knew who couldn't get into the game was standing outside the ground. People talk about the religion of football, and at a moment like that it's true. It was a spiritual matter. Everton were about to be relegated. It would feel like a bereavement. And what do you do at funerals? Meet your friends and console one another.

We got to a turnstile and banged on the door. A steward opened it, my dad somehow blagged us through, and we got in for the last thirty minutes. Everton were still trailing, 2–1, and we were expecting to witness the death of our proud record as the longest-serving member of the top division.

We saw all the drama unfold as Barry Horne and Graham

Stuart turned it around and Everton survived with a 3–2 win. I was euphoric and headed straight for my first full-on night out. 'You can forget Lilleshall tomorrow,' I thought as I headed for a debut on Liverpool's nightclubbing scene. My coaches weren't happy when I failed to turn up the next day, but I'd do the same again. I wasn't going to miss those celebrations for one coaching session. It was one of the most enjoyable hangovers I've ever had.

My professional commitment to Liverpool started to take over shortly after this and, naturally, my perspective altered as my emotional attachment to Anfield grew. My eyes were opened to the more unattractive side of the rivalry between the clubs, and I increasingly began to notice the cruelty and spitefulness in many of the jibes thrown at Liverpool and its players by Evertonians.

Merseyside's local paper, the *Liverpool Echo*, repeats the same article every time Liverpool and Everton meet, asking readers, 'Whatever happened to the friendly Merseyside derby?' They put on rose-tinted glasses and walk down a picturesque memory lane at Wembley in 1984, 1986 and 1989, crowded with Reds and Blues skipping jovially arm in arm as the chant of 'Merseyside' echoes in an upbeat Scouse twang across London. I was there, and it's a comical exaggerated perception of how it really was, but it's right to say there was more unity on show then than now. The fans are segregated these days and seem to have developed a maliciously blinkered view of their history, where everything positive is exclusively a consequence of their own valiant efforts, and all things negative are the responsibility of conspiracies, refereeing decisions or, in Everton's case, Liverpool. The atmosphere is much meaner than I remember as a fan. Local journalists sense this and always have to be balanced and make sure they don't upset one side more than the other when discussing the topic. They usually end up upsetting both by getting into a tangle of contradictions, saying neither one thing nor the other.

As someone who's been a Blue and a Red, I feel more qualified than most to offer my opinion on where it all went wrong. I can't avoid the conclusion that the bulk of the responsibility lies in the reaction of many of Everton's fans to the barren spell the blue half of our city has gone through, and their treatment of Liverpool players who are my friends. It's added a sinister element to the rivalry which wasn't always apparent, and it has forced me to undergo a complete transformation in loyalties.

I'd never go so far as to say I hate Everton in the same way some Liverpudlians claim – that's much too strong a word. But I hate losing to them more than to any side in the world, in the same way my Blue mates hate losing to Liverpool. That's partly because I hate what Evertonians sing about Steven Gerrard and his family at every derby. It's personal, it's vindictive, and it's disgusting. It goes beyond the kind of banter that is acceptable in any form of life, not only football. One of my best mates, Robbie Fowler, had to put up with similar abuse for years. He wrote in his book how the scandalous drug taunts, invented for no other reason than to try to put him off his game, hurt him and his family. No one should have to suffer that. We know as footballers we're going to get ill treated by opposition fans, but when people start telling lies and then turn them into despicable chants, I'm appalled.

Liverpool fans are hardly blameless in this respect. They have targeted rival players from Everton and Manchester United during our fixtures with some vile taunts. I'm no fan of Gary

Neville, but he suffers when we play United in the same way Stevie does, and Robbie did. So did David Beckham when he was still at Old Trafford. John Terry has also heard foul insults at Anfield. You can't make a judgement about one set of fans without looking at your own.

Nothing can justify this sort of behaviour, but there is a difference with this abuse, inexcusable as it is: it is kept within the stadium. You don't get thousands of Scousers spreading malicious rumours about Neville on the streets of Manchester. And you don't hear Liverpool fans singing about Everton, United or Chelsea players if we're not playing them. Evertonians consistently chant about our lads whether they're facing Liverpool, Reading or Portsmouth. It's not confined to derby day. I even hear it on television when they're playing in Europe.

Maybe the part of me that knows deep down that, Red or Blue, we're exactly the same gives me a different perspective. I find it so depressing to hear Scousers target their own. On Merseyside, you can sense it's become a lot worse over the last twenty years, and I fear the trend will become tougher to reverse unless common sense prevails soon. I loathe hearing Evertonians calling Liverpool fans 'murderers' in reference to the Heysel disaster of 1985, when fighting with Italian fans before the European Cup Final led to the deaths of thirty-nine Juventus fans. Players and fans get abused like this around town now too. I can't understand why this has started in recent years, and it's a big reason why my relationship with Everton has turned sour.

Forget Manchester United or Chelsea. Everton are the team I want to beat more than any every season.

I feel more strongly about it because I followed them for so long. I was one of them. I know what it means to be a die-hard

Blue so I'm speaking as someone who's been there and worn the Everton T-shirt. When you get hurt by those you feel closest to – or perhaps more particularly, when you see your best mates unjustly under attack – there's no way back.

Since Everton lost their way you hear less and less arguing about which club has the better players; there's now more of a preoccupation with wagging an accusing finger at Liverpool at every opportunity. If there's less to celebrate on the pitch, there's more to complain about off it. Liverpudlians have still been able to keep a focus on trophy collection, but Everton's decline has led to a flourishing industry of historical reinvention. The same excuse is regularly put forward: all Goodison's woes began after Heysel, which led to all English clubs being suspended from UEFA competitions. The European ban hurt Everton, that's unquestionable. I watched a fantastic team capable of competing at that level, and there was no one more devastated than me when the club was unable to play in the European Cup. But over a quarter of a century, some Evertonians have somehow managed to manoeuvre the club into the role of victim in the sordid affair.

I was too young to remember what happened that night in Brussels, but I do know the hostility shown to Liverpool fans in the years that immediately followed was nothing compared to now. The clubs were closely matched at the time; there was no reason to presume one side would be affected any more than the other. I certainly didn't chant 'murderers' at Liverpudlians at derby games, and I can't recall becoming involved in arguments claiming the actions of the fans in Brussels had ruined Everton's chances of being successful in the future, short or long term. In fact, if anyone had suggested the tragedy would lead to Everton's decline as an annual title challenger, I'd have mocked them and told them it was no more than the Kopites' wishful thinking. Anyway, Everton won the title two years after Heysel, so the argument about them going into freefall because of it doesn't stack up.

Everton began to lose their way at the top of English football when Howard Kendall followed the money to Spain in 1987. Colin Harvey took over and bought three or four expensive players who weren't up to the job. The claim Kendall wouldn't have taken the cash and left had Everton still been in Europe is one only he can answer, but it certainly doesn't explain the two decades of poor decision-making at every level of the club since. Just like Liverpool after Kenny Dalglish quit in 1991, it was bad judgement in the transfer market which caused the decline in standards. When you buy the wrong players every summer, there's no escape from mediocrity, and no excuse.

Harvey also didn't command the same level of respect from the senior professionals who'd brought the club so much success. His record wasn't bad compared to those who followed him, but at that time Everton expected to be title challengers every season. Unfortunately, the board kept making calamitous decisions. Some of the managers they've appointed since, and the speed with which they've sacked others, has left them behind the Premiership 'elite'. That's what cost them their place as title contenders as part of the traditional 'big five'. There's a massive gap between Everton and Liverpool now in terms of trophies won, and I don't see them getting anywhere near where it was all those years ago when the sides were neck and neck in the silverware count.

As I said, the European ban isn't the reason for this. I know plenty of Evertonians who, deep down, agree the club has only itself to blame. Liverpool suffered because of the ban too, as did Arsenal, but both clubs were run better in the years that followed.

If you really want me to show sympathy for clubs that suffered during that time, I'll save it for the likes of Norwich and Wimbledon, who also missed out on European football. They were unfashionable teams without the kind of history and backing Everton enjoys. Everton didn't need the money as much at the end of the 1980s as they do now, and if you look at the kind of fees they were spending even in 1989, when Cottee's signing broke the British transfer record, it shows why they paid the price later. Poor Norwich are now struggling in the Championship, and Wimbledon no longer even exist. If Liverpool visited Carrow Road or Milton Keynes, I wouldn't expect to hear their fans screaming 'murderers' at us. Those Evertonians who adopt this chant as a sinister club anthem on derby day ought to ask themselves why. That side to the rivalry increasingly disturbs me, though you've got to make a distinction between this and other elements that can be put down to a good old-fashioned traditional love of one team over the other.

I've gone from being someone in the Liverpool side whom Evertonians privately thought was still one of their own, to a player they now feel epitomizes the enemy. At the same time, I've been cut more slack than my team-mates, probably because of my openly Blue past. There are Toffees who still believe I wear an Everton tattoo on my arm. I eventually discovered where this rumour began. 'Which Liverpool player always wears long sleeves to hide an Everton tattoo?' was a question doing the rounds in city pub quizzes. Answer: Jamie Carragher. Has anyone ever seen this tattoo? Can the artist who put it on my arm step forward so I can meet him? My brothers have even become involved in arguments at work with fellas who insist, despite all the evidence to the contrary, I've got the Everton crest on my arm. This has been going on for so long I hope I can knock it on the head once and for all. It doesn't exist. Maybe this myth explains why I've never been treated as badly as Robbie and Stevie.

The reason I wear long sleeves, incidentally, is because I think I've got skinny arms.

I've played in many derbies now, and I can honestly say I've always tried to be as careful as possible with my pre- and post-match comments. There have been times when I've made a point of biting my lip, trying to be respectful. We took a 3–0 beating at Goodison a couple of seasons ago and the DVD of the game was in the shops a week later. It should have been in the horror movie section. I had a nightmare and was nowhere near 100 per cent, but at the time I was asked about our performance straight after the game I said we were beaten fair and square.

Too often I've felt the same courtesy isn't shown to Liverpool by Everton. On their side, you had someone like Alan Stubbs, whom I consider as Blue as they get. I know Alan's from Kirkby so his own fans probably didn't think he was really a Scouser, so maybe that's why he liked to play to the gallery a bit. The Liverpool dressing room was always having a giggle at Alan's expense, because when derby day came along we knew he'd be having a good cry at us over something, especially if we won. But there are times I feel they have zero respect for us. While we tiptoe around making sure we don't cause a furore, many of their former (and current) players have felt they have the freedom to slag us off. It's a small but annoying sub-plot of every derby. The rest of the country might be bemused Liverpool should even care what Evertonians say about us, but within our city it's huge.

And it's not just the Everton players who seem to have developed what I'd call the Goodison persecution complex. I didn't really blame Stubbs for defending his team, even if I disagreed with his comments, but I'd expect their hierarchy to be more considered and careful with their remarks. There are plenty at Goodison who've done the club no favours when talking about Liverpool.

The person I've respected most at Everton during my time as a player is David Moyes. Without doubt he's Everton's best manager in twenty years. And the quip he made on the day he joined about Everton being the People's Club on Merseyside was genius. It immediately got the Evertonians on his side and wound up the Liverpudlians, so fair play to him. Brilliant stuff, I say. That's what it's all about in this city. Make your own fans proud of you, and if it gets your rivals' backs up it's a classic double-whammy. There's no harm in that at all. In 2007, Rafa Benitez tried to hit back when he talked after a game about Everton being a small club that came to Anfield to play for a draw. How did they react? They put a statement on the official Everton website having a go at Rafa. How small-time can you get? It was embarrassing, but it proved my point about the different reactions to upsetting comments.

Let's be blunt about this. If I really wanted to be cocky about Liverpool's achievements, I've got plenty of ammunition. We could really milk our European successes and domestic trophy haul if we wanted, but I firmly believe we've kept a lid on it to make sure we don't unnecessarily upset our neighbours.

I could understand Evertonians being wound up by Rafa's comments in exactly the same way Liverpudlians still get angry about the People's Club statement, but surely the hierarchy has a duty to rise above that? We all have a responsibility as players and fans to be careful what we say and not to inflame tensions even more, but in the heat of battle, or in the immediate aftermath of a game, it's forgivable if mistakes are made. At boardroom level it's a different matter. You should show some dignity and rise above the banter. Everton don't need to justify how big a club they are in England, and certainly not on Merseyside. Rafa only recognized how big Everton are when he arrived in this country. When he was in Spain he had no reason to see Everton as he does now.

What made their reaction even more surprising is it came at a time when the debate about the two Merseyside clubs sharing a stadium was being revived. There was a time when some argued this made sense logically and financially, but tradition ensured there was no prospect of the fans accepting it, especially as the nature of their rivalry changed. I've never wanted it and would never have supported it. Everton sympathizers, however, seemed keen on the idea being discussed and there were regular stories in the *Echo* and *Liverpool Daily Post* talking up the possibility. Once again, there was an inescapable undercurrent of Everton's jealousy of Liverpool tainting my view of their motives.

For years, Everton championed their project to build a stadium on the King's Dock on Liverpool's famous waterfront. Liverpool FC weren't invited to the party. I can't remember a single interview with Everton owner Bill Kenwright in which he said it made sense for Liverpool to head to the King's Dock with his club. Now there's a wonderful arena at the venue, but there's no football club playing in it. Everton's perilous financial situation meant their dreams were dashed.

By then, Liverpool were pressing ahead with the new stadium on Stanley Park. Soon after the King's Dock plan was scrapped, the agenda of some of the Everton fans switched from being boastful about their own stadium to critical of the decision to allow Liverpool to build theirs. Evertonians said they'd been refused permission to build a new Goodison on the park in the 1990s. But even if they had, as with King's Dock, they wouldn't have been able to afford it.

This sense of injustice turned into what can only be described as an unofficial campaign to get Liverpool City Council to agree Liverpool's plans on the condition they spoke to Everton about a shared stadium. They were too late.

By this time my switch to Liverpool was virtually complete. The club had taken over my life, rearranging my head as well as stealing my heart. I was seeing red rather than feeling blue. You can attempt to follow both teams with the same intensity, but in the end it's a straight choice. Try to sit on the fence and you're quickly exposed as a fraud, hiding your true feelings but fooling no one.

I often wonder what kind of person I'd be if I'd never played for Liverpool and was still travelling home and away following Everton. I'd be an elder statesman of the away-day crowd. Maybe young lads would be getting introduced to me and my dad, hearing stories of how we were on the pitch celebrating some of Everton's most glorious victories. Would I have gone swimming with the tide on derby day and joined in the abusing of Stevie and Robbie? I wouldn't have known them if I wasn't a player. But I wouldn't have gone down that path. I know it. If I picture myself alongside fans singing 'murderers', it makes me feel sick. I'm ashamed of it. I know I'd be the one telling those around me to stop, like my dad did to the idiots at Goodison who sang Munich songs at United fans in the mid-eighties.

To me, it's a younger generation that's most guilty of taking the derby rivalry to an extreme, fans who weren't even born in 1985 but who want to believe what they're told, or just want to 'fit in' to impress their friends. It's the same at Anfield. When snotty-nosed teenagers sing about the Munich air disaster – something which disappeared for years but crept back into the game not so long ago – I want to go into the stand myself and rattle some cages. I suspect some of those who behave in this way don't think of the implications of what they're doing. It's self-abuse, really, bringing shame upon themselves and their city as much as hurting the targets of their venom. But no matter how unacceptable they're told it is, they still do it.

Growing up where I did in Marsh Lane, the choice of red or blue was made for me. As I got older, my ability to play at the highest level took me in a different direction and gave me an opportunity few Scousers get: I got to pick sides. I was also fortunate to be given an insight into how both clubs operated at close quarters, and I reached the conclusion Liverpool is a bigger and better-run club.

Originally I only wanted to play for Everton, but when I left Liverpool as a schoolboy to do so, I knew I'd made a mistake. At first I still liked Everton and wanted them to be performing well, but increasingly I became less tolerant. The transformation from loving them to openly wanting them to lose took years to complete, as I said, but when I saw some of my best friends suffering as a result of revolting abuse, naturally, my love for Everton receded. Anfield called me. It was my professional commitment and personal friendships that finally took my heart from Goodison and positioned it slap bang in the centre of The Kop.

Regular first-team football for Liverpool made me increasingly unconcerned about hearing Everton's results, but if you want the date, time and venue of my full conversion from Blue to Red, I can provide the details. It came on 24 January 1999, the day of the FA Cup fourth round tie between Manchester United and

Liverpool – Old Trafford, followed by a ceremonial visit to The Chaucer.

United won the treble that season, but we were two minutes from knocking them out of the cup with the kind of gritty performance we produced regularly during the more successful period of Gérard Houllier's reign. We'd been 1–0 up for the entire match thanks to Michael Owen. Defensively we were outstanding. At the time it was probably my finest game for Liverpool.

We lost two goals in the last two minutes, the winner arriving in injury time. Coming home on the coach was, to that point in my career, the worst feeling I'd known in football. I headed straight to The Chaucer to drown my sorrows, hoping I'd see a few sympathetic mates. I knew I was going to take some punishment, but I thought most people would feel sorry for me.

Perhaps I should have known better. As I walked through the door, there was laughter. Friends, people I'd grown up and travelled around Europe with following Everton, didn't think twice about treating me like any other 'dirty' Kopite. I stood there for a brief second unsure what to do. I could have brushed it off, sat down, ordered a pint and taken my medicine with the help of the much-needed lager I'd craved all the way down the M62. That's what I'd do now, but not then. Mentally and physically drained and demoralized, I turned around and went straight home.

That moment exposed how much my allegiances had changed and how I was now perceived by my own friends. It had taken me ten years to walk those few symbolic miles across Stanley Park from Goodison to Anfield, but without even realizing it at the time, that was the moment the journey finished.

There was a time I would have been sitting with my Blue friends initiating the laughter at the Liverpudlians' expense, just as I did when I saw the Arsenal graffiti in 1989. Now I wasn't a fan, but someone who'd been toiling for his team only to see the biggest win of his career stolen in the worst way possible. When I walked into The Chaucer that evening I was heading for a collision with my own past, and a glimpse of what would have been my future if I hadn't been lucky enough to be a Liverpool footballer. I didn't like what I saw.

As I made my way from the pub and into the Marsh Lane drizzle, I wasn't walking away from my mates at the bar, who were perfectly entitled to have their fun. I was turning my back on that bitter Blue eleven-year-old who'd celebrated Michael Thomas's winner. I was turning my back on Everton.

3

A Liver Bird Upon My Chest

There's nothing like your first time.

The adrenalin rush; the anxiety beforehand, as you want to do yourself justice; the yells of approval as you approach the climax; and the feeling you're sharing something special. That's what winning your first significant trophy does to you.

Holding aloft the 1996 FA Youth Cup with my Liverpool team-mates was as pleasurable an experience as any I've had in the game. It wasn't the greatest performance I've been a part of. In many respects we fumbled through much of the competition, and it was more memorable for its originality and symbolism than its place in the history of the club. But to those of us who played a role in it and went on to represent the first team, the first kick in that tournament signalled the beginning of the end of our apprenticeship.

We began that Youth Cup campaign of 1995–96 as kids, unknowns with everything to prove. We ended it on the threshold of a senior debut, with plenty of ammunition to suggest we'd be around for many years to come. I was eighteen, jogging confidently around a packed Anfield alongside players of the calibre of Michael Owen and David Thompson, clasping medal number one as a Liverpool player, and there wasn't a grain of doubt in my mind this wouldn't be my last. Amid the celebrations, I vividly recall sensing this triumph was the platform for much more. We all knew unthinkingly this wasn't the peak of our success at Anfield, but another important step on our journey. There would be more illustrious finals heading our way in a red shirt. This was like a final exam before graduation, and we'd passed with first-class honours.

If you win a cup as an adult, you want to savour the moment and appreciate it for what it is there and then. As a youngster, there's a different sensation. No sooner are you holding one cup than your mind is racing ahead and you're dreaming of where it will lead. In my case, I felt I'd shown I was ready to be promoted to first-team duties. I'd only have to wait a few weeks for this ambition to be realized.

In 2006 and 2007, those memories came rushing back as I watched Steve Heighway win the FA Youth Cup for the first time in ten years, and then defend it with another crop of fresh-faced youngsters. I sat in the stands alongside Steven Gerrard to offer my support and could visualize myself running about with the cup and how excited I'd been about the years to come. But as I applauded the next generation, I was partly proud and partly saddened by the scenes of jubilation I was witnessing. There must have been a sense of apprehension, hollowness even, as those emerging youngsters hailed their win. None of those players must have felt confident this would be anything but the highlight of their careers in red.

So much had changed at youth level between 1996 and 2006, and players following in my tradition are suffering the most. I've become one of a dying breed – a Liverpool lad playing for

Liverpool. The timing of my arrival as a Liverpool player was as impeccable as one of my most important last-ditch tackles. And given what's happened since, it had to be. Although I believe myself good enough to have played for the club in any era, I'm not convinced I'd have been handed the same opportunities had I broken through a few years later.

The trip from Liverpool's youth side to the first team used to be straightforward. Nowadays it's an obstacle course, the route blocked by a combination of foreign recruits and political infighting between the club's opposing factions at youth and senior level. It's as if we've erected our own barriers between the youth and first team.

Being part of a successful Liverpool youth squad once meant you were tantalizingly close to a full debut. Nowadays, the previously short trip from the Anfield Academy to becoming a household name is a voyage of a million miles. Playing for Liverpool wasn't a distant fantasy for me. Walking through the gates of Melwood as a nine-year-old, I believed it was a genuine possibility I would play for the club. The tragedy for someone at the same age today is that that hope is remote.

The reasons for this have been a constant source of conflict at Anfield, and there have been times I've wanted to get involved in the debate. My playing commitments have meant – up until now at least – I've never allowed my strong opinions to intrude on what is essentially an issue for the club to resolve. All I know for certain is this: the days when Premier League managers were prepared to gamble on or show patience with their up-and-coming talents are over. It depresses me how local lads are rapidly becoming as much an endangered species in the Liverpool first team as players who wear black boots.

Of course it's not just Liverpool suffering in their desire to bring through their 'own'. There's a nationwide epidemic, with an increasing shortage of quality players coming from the academies. Or perhaps I should put it another way: the players coming through the ranks are suffering from a shortage of chances to show they have enough quality.

The stakes in the game are too high to permit a long-term vision with youth development. Managers are under insufferable pressure to get instant results, so they won't take risks with players who, like me, may have needed six months or a year of first-team experience to establish themselves. Some clubs could have gone through three managers by then.

I wouldn't say all the Academy boys who've followed me and Steven Gerrard were necessarily in the same class, but several have been moved on at a stage when they were being judged on their 'potential'. But the longer you spend alongside top-class players and the more you're selected, the better you become. Potential has to be given the chance to grow, and those seeds are only planted on football pitches during games. If you're starved of the minutes, you learn nothing new, progress no further, and slide into obscurity.

The best any reserve on the fringe of the Liverpool senior squad today can hope for is a Carling Cup appearance and a few pre-season friendlies, unless you're a world-beater at seventeen or eighteen. Forget coming into your own at twenty or twenty-one, as so many did in the past. Those who've come through The Academy but aren't playing regularly by then might as well decide where they fancy going on loan.

As I said, you can't blame the managers for their bloody-mindedness, given the enormous demands upon them. They've got to look for the quick fix, and would rather buy an established player they know from abroad than blood an unproven teenager. Fans are also more intolerant than they like to think, and won't stand for experimenting with youth unless it's instantly successful. Supporters will always embrace the idea of their side being packed with local talent, even suggest it's a fundamental ambition of the club, but the passports of the players are consistently shown to be irrelevant when it comes to judging results. The fans are no less forgiving if a Liverpool team full of Academy recruits gets beat. Recent history proves this.

One of the most controversial managerial decisions of the last twenty-five years at Anfield was taken by Rafa Benitez in the FA Cup third round defeat against Burnley in 2005. He was slated for selecting a team packed with youngsters from our Academy, even though a virtually identical side was lauded for beating a full-strength Tottenham team in the Carling Cup a month earlier. Whatever the rights and wrongs of Benitez's choice that particular day, as a result he'd have had to question his own sanity before taking the same decision again.

The next world-class Merseyside teenager to make his Liverpool debut will feel the breath of forty thousand sighs of relief as fears of the extinction of local talent are eased. The hunt for the next Gerrard, Owen or, dare I say, Carragher has become as obsessive as the club's pursuit of the Premier League title, and has led to some high-profile casualties.

Liverpool were spoiled for a sustained period in terms of the idea of Scousers emerging through the ranks and becoming the mainstay of the senior side. In the 1960s and 1970s the club could rely on a steady rather than spectacular stream of local talent. Ian Callaghan, Tommy Smith, Chris Lawler, Phil Thompson, Jimmy Case and David Fairclough successfully jumped from the boys' pen on The Kop on to the pitch, but it was never the case that two or three a year made the breakthrough. For much of the 1980s Liverpool struggled to find anyone good enough from the area. The likes of Sammy Lee and Gary Ablett were exceptions. The double-winning side of 1986 had one Merseysider in the squad, Steve McMahon, and he was signed from Aston Villa. In the great side of 1988, John Aldridge had been brought in from Oxford after spending most of his career outside the city in the lower divisions.

Before Kenny Dalglish appointed legendary ex-winger Steve Heighway to look after youth development, hardly any players had moved from the reserves into the first team for a decade. The School of Excellence, as it was, included many who'd been enticed to the club by Dalglish and Heighway. We continued to represent our Sunday League sides, but we'd head to Melwood once a week, staring at the shiny cars and smart clothes of the professionals in between training sessions. Knowing I'd be sharing the same pitch and dressing rooms with some of the world's greatest players was inspirational.

Heighway's appointment coincided with some spectacular discoveries. A flurry of us arrived around the same time in the 1990s, enhancing the club's reputation for nurturing local talent. Steve McManaman, Michael Owen, Robbie Fowler, Steven Gerrard and I saved the club millions in transfer fees; others like Stephen Wright, Dominic Matteo, David Thompson and Stephen Warnock made millions more through their sales.

Sadly, in recent years this conveyor belt, which was so prolific, has ground to a halt.

If ever a coach paid for achieving too much too soon, it's Heighway. The proficiency with which local boys made the step up heaped pressure on him to unearth more of us on a season-by-season basis. Over £10 million was spent on the new Academy, with extra millions committed annually, but the

School of Excellence days were the club's most rewarding. Heighway eventually left Liverpool in 2007, despite winning two successive FA Youth Cups, partially because he was sick of the criticism. The split between The Academy and Melwood was unhealthy for the club and I felt the youth director was unfairly treated.

There were times I felt unless a youngster was as good as Stevie or Michael, our managers would be too quick to dismiss them, favouring some of their own foreign imports who weren't any better than the Academy lads. And anyway, homegrown players of Gerrard's class come around once every thirty years at any one club. From the moment they make their debuts, they look like world-beaters. Mo was the best player in the side on the day he broke into the first team. Stevie walked into the same category. Their examples should have been enough to convince the senior management that if the quality was there, Heighway would find it and nurture it. Houllier and then Benitez were constantly at loggerheads with Heighway, and frustrated that players of first-team quality weren't arriving from the youth set-up every year. Both had experience of their own as youth coaches in France and Spain, so they resented having no influence in this sphere at Liverpool.

While I understand their sense of dissatisfaction, the club was right to trust Heighway. Managers come and go, but you've got to maintain continuity across as many levels of the club as possible. What was essentially a clash of personalities became something much bigger, and it was detrimental to Liverpool. Changing the youth set-up every few years when a manager leaves makes no sense. The key is for the youth director and manager to work together, but that became increasingly impossible as the conflict cast its shadow across the club. Given the lack of cooperation, it's no real surprise Steven Gerrard remains the last Academy success story, from as far back as 1999.

Houllier and Benitez knew they were never going to get someone of his ability every season, but they still had plenty of quality local players to work with. Stephen Wright was one of those who showed promise when he broke into the side, but Houllier later sold him to Sunderland, replacing him with Abel Xavier. I can understand why that annoyed the Academy staff. Wrighty was one of those who'd give you that extra 10 per cent commitment, and with the right coaching and quality players around him he could have stayed at Liverpool for a lot longer. Replacing him with Xavier was nonsense from both a football and business point of view, precisely the kind of decision that has been and is being replicated across England: a promising English youngster makes way for a foreigner with a reputation (not all good) and plenty of experience but who's no better. Houllier also sold Matteo, another youth product, to Leeds so he could buy Christian Ziege – another expensive flop. He later admitted he'd been too quick to accept a good bid.

Of all the youngsters to make their debut under Houllier, none started as well as Jon Otsemobor, who was tipped for stardom throughout his Academy career. After two man-of-the-match performances at full-back, he was subbed during the first half of a game at Manchester City and never played again. It seemed to me that some were almost relieved he didn't succeed after their arguments with Heighway. They'd decided Heighway wasn't finding the right players and nothing was going to convince them otherwise.

You could say many of these players moved elsewhere and did nothing to prove Liverpool's decision to offload them wrong. I reject this as a foolproof theory. Had they stayed at Anfield, they'd have played at a consistently higher level and inevitably improved. They were denied the same opportunities to develop their game as the rest of us. In 2007–08 I watched Danny Guthrie perform well for Bolton and often thought he could do a job for us, but he just wouldn't have had the same chances at Anfield.

Even if this line of reasoning was valid, for all those who weren't considered good enough, I'd suggest the ones who were more than made up for it. As a football club, we should have spent less time arguing with Heighway about what we didn't have and been more appreciative of what we did have. This was the argument Heighway was ready, willing and able to throw back at people whenever his methods were questioned. He was no shrinking violet. When you've delivered at least two of the greatest strikers in Liverpool history and arguably the best central midfielder in Europe, all within the space of a few years, you don't expect to have to justify yourself.

Both Houllier and Benitez would talk to me about their frustrations with Heighway. Maybe they were seeking confirmation I agreed with them. Perhaps they were trying to convince me of their responses. Then I'd look around the training pitch and see teenage 'gems' such as Djimi Traore, Sebastian Leto, Anthony Le Tallec, Gregory Vignal, Carl Madjani, Alou Diarra and Gabriel Palletta.

I have to admit it. Had I been forced to pick sides in this squabble, I'd have been standing alongside my former youth coach.

The longer I've been at Anfield, and the more I've seen teenagers come and go from abroad, the angrier I've become at hearing Heighway's work under so much attack. Throughout the last two decades, more than any Premier League team,

Liverpool's best players have been homegrown. Only Manchester United can compete with us on this score. Imagine the last decade and a half without Owen, Fowler, McManaman and Gerrard. And yes, I'll add my name to the list. Think about our greatest triumphs – the FA Cup wins, the Champions League, the League Cups. Who were the heroes that day? Of course both Houllier and Benitez made good signings who played a crucial part, but no one's going to tell me we'd have had the same success if it hadn't been for the Academy boys who cost nothing.

Had Heighway brought through just one world-class player in ten years he'd have deserved congratulation. To find at least five, and plenty of others who were sold for a good price, is a track record deserving of far more respect. I'm not going to say the success or otherwise of our youth policy was all down to him, or that some mistakes weren't made. Whether Heighway was at Liverpool or not, I'm 90 per cent certain I'd have made it with or without his assistance. But then it stands to reason that if he doesn't deserve all the credit, he certainly doesn't warrant all the criticism either.

I don't blame him for the shortage of local talent in recent times. If the players aren't there, what's an Academy director meant to do about it? I don't care how good a coach is, there's one absolute certainty in football: no one can turn a bad player into a good one. You've either got what it takes, or you haven't. If it's there, good coaches will nurture it, draw it out of you, and your own personality can influence how capable you are of taking your skills on to the pitch. Heighway was probably instrumental in adding 10 per cent to my game, and that could have made all the difference. But if there's nothing to work with, it's a hopeless cause.

Liverpool, like many top clubs, have suffered because it's impossible to guarantee world-class youngsters breaking through on an annual basis. Where are the North London boys emerging through the Arsenal or Spurs ranks? How many Salford lads have made their debut at Old Trafford since the mid-1990s? Or Geordies at Newcastle? Some of the best youngsters 'produced' by the biggest clubs have been stolen from other parts of the country, or shipped from abroad. Which part of Manchester was David Beckham born in? How good did Arsène Wenger's scouts need to be to spot Cesc Fabregas in the Barcelona youth team and offer him huge wages to emigrate at the age of sixteen? I've seen similar tactics at Liverpool recently. Our scouts bring a new member of the Spanish Under-18 side for a trial every month. I won't lie – I don't like it. We're behaving like Pied Pipers, enticing children to England with the promise of wealth, even though there's no certainty too many will make it at such a tender age. The way it's going, you'll soon be seeing Premier League scouts hanging around maternity wards in Madrid, Barcelona and Paris waiting for the next prodigy to be delivered by a midwife.

I understand why we've jumped on board, recruiting foreign teenagers by offering their families huge financial incentives. We've no choice to avoid being left behind. But it's an issue which should be stamped down on. I'd rather the authorities took action to ensure everyone followed the same rules and stopped stealing young talent from elsewhere.

Our record in terms of bringing in overseas teenagers is, at best, dodgy. Houllier pinned his hopes on Traore at seventeen, and later Florent Sinama-Pongolle and Le Tallec cost the club £7 million. None could be described as a success. Benitez took the philosophy to a new extreme, and it looks as though it might finally be working to the club's advantage. Last season we won the Reserve League with a mix of foreign and youth-team players, and there's a chance one or two will be promoted into the first team. I fully expect signings such as Spanish striker Dani Pacheco and Hungarian Krisztian Nemeth to play regularly for us at the highest level. At the time of writing this book, however, we've had ten years at Anfield without a single top young foreign player being brought through our ranks, and despite their potential there's certainly no indication those who are rated today will have the impact of a Fowler, a McManaman, an Owen or a Gerrard. I'm eager to see the outstanding local boy who was a key part of our last Youth Cup win, Jay Spearing, get the opportunity he deserves, and also Stephen Darby and Martin Kelly.

Yet, even if one of our teenage recruits is a triumph, morally I'd say it's wrong. If Liverpool have the next Gerrard coming through and Real Madrid decide to buy him when he's fifteen, how will we feel?

I spend a lot of time in Kirkby working with the coaches and I'm often asked to get involved in the recruitment process if Liverpool identify a nine-year-old with potential. It's disturbing to hear some of the arguments made by parents who say they may send their child to Everton instead, simply because they're not seeing our local boys get a chance. If we don't put this right, when the next Owen, Gerrard or Carragher comes along, he may not want to come to Anfield. I'd urge all youngsters to head to Liverpool as their first choice, of course. Our facilities are as good as any in Europe, and the rewards if you do make it are overwhelming.

I have to believe class will tell in the end, that if you're good enough you'll make it, but the warning signs must be heeded. We must encourage our local boys to believe it's possible not only to follow the instant route to superstardom of Owen, Fowler and

Gerrard, but also to come through the ranks and develop as I did. The Academy system at Anfield today is unrecognizable from ten years ago, and flooding the clubs with foreigners who are no better will never sit comfortably with me, but I'm not going to join the anti-foreign crusade others are leading. Having said that, common sense must prevail to preserve our own traditions. We want to recruit the best to help us become better, not the mediocre who stop us from playing and developing at all.

It's thrilling to see so many of the world's top players coming here and raising standards and entertainment levels. The moment Fernando Torres walked into Anfield was when I believed we had a striker who could help us compete with United and Chelsea again. The good overseas players help English players. John Terry couldn't have wished for a better tutor at Chelsea than Marcel Desailly; Manchester United's youngsters were assisted by the years they spent alongside Eric Cantona. It's the foreigners lower down the scale that bother me. There are average and poor players joining our league on the cheap simply because they've more experience than the English youngsters.

I'd favour a new rule where at least six of every club's eighteen-man squad hail from the country in which that club plays its football. You'd soon see a greater priority placed on developing and blooding local talent. It wouldn't stop the top clubs buying the best internationals from Spain or France, but it might make them think twice about purchasing so many fringe players from abroad.

English football as a whole needs to rethink how quickly players are judged, how to ensure those with the potential to step up get the opportunity to do so. The history of our game is littered with examples of world-class performers who peaked in their late twenties. Look at John Aldridge, or Ian Wright. How many lower-league players get plucked from obscurity these days?

It's a European problem, but as the wealthiest and most attractive league in the world, it's starting to affect England more than others. And within that, because of our reputation, I often feel a more critical glance is directed at Anfield whenever another year passes without a local graduate, even though no one has produced as many internationals as Liverpool within such a short space of time. The reason the flow has temporarily stopped at Liverpool is a combination of luck and unforeseen circumstances.

For a start, it was a mistake to separate The Academy from the first team geographically. The new complex should have kept us all together. The more astute watched and learned, picking up invaluable tips from the professionals. The hunger burned inside to follow in their boot steps while we did our jobs, whether it was cleaning the players' boots, collecting the police cones after a day's training, or washing down the showers. This has all changed with the introduction of Academy football. Traditional 'apprentice' work is a thing of the past. Even the nine-year-olds have the smartest white boots and kits. I know twelve-year-olds who have their own agents. Youngsters are already preparing for a Liverpool career before they've any experience or grasp of the hard work required to achieve such an ambition. Some are being misled into believing they have a better chance of making it than they actually do. It's cruel.

I don't begrudge their better quality of life. Every generation thinks the latest has got it easy when it comes to material possessions. My dad thought we were lucky because we had four TV channels and an inside toilet when we were growing up. In years to come, my children may laugh about the days when they had only a few hundred channels to watch. I've used the benefits of my career to make sure my kids want for nothing. It's a natural reaction. But you do wonder what impact it has on the drive of youngsters to push on and fulfil their ambitions.

I was never motivated by money, but I appreciated a successful football career would change my life. How many of those at The Academy today truly want it as badly as I did? I've seen plenty of 'nice' lads playing for the youth side, but not enough of the working-class scallies I played alongside at the same age. If you're from what's considered an 'underprivileged' background, perhaps the longing to better yourself is stronger. I see this in the African lads now. They understand what real poverty is, and their desire to change their future may add that extra 5 or 10 per cent some of our lads are lacking. I've heard both Houllier and Benitez argue it's the lack of desire, character and strength of players arriving from Kirkby that is worrying as much as concerns about technical ability.

That's when they'd repeat this annoying sentence: 'It's not the next Owen or Gerrard we expect, but another Carragher.' That's supposed to sound like a compliment, but it's hitting me on the arse with a backhand. I'm presented as some kind of example of a player who isn't world-class at a young age, but with the right guidance and coaching can take his game to an extra level. To some extent I accept this evaluation of my career, but I also feel insulted by the implication I wasn't an outstanding player when I was sixteen. I made my debut in the senior side just two years later, so it shouldn't be such a surprise I'm still here twelve years on. To suggest there have been a lot of other players out there who could have been as good as me but for weak Academy coaching is not only offensive to Steve Heighway, it's disrespectful to me. I'm not an average player who suddenly became good enough to play for Liverpool. I was in the elite group at

Lilleshall, so I had every justification for believing I was one of the best players in the country for my age. I wasn't in Mo's or Stevie's class (who is?) but I was no 'average joe' either. I resent the notion that I've achieved in the game despite my limitations rather than because of my strengths.

I'm prepared to give credit where it's due to the likes of Heighway, Houllier and Benitez, all of whom did their job to get the best out of me, but I'm also prepared to dent my ultra-modest reputation to make this point: with or without them, I was good enough to play for Liverpool throughout the modern era, and quite possibly in previous ones too.

Throughout my career, my reputation has been one of a no-nonsense physical type of player. At sixteen I was a striker praised for my technical abilities. My passing, control and understanding of the game were my best qualities. Heighway always believed I'd play for the first team, but I was a slow developer. I was smaller and less muscular than many of my team-mates, and I didn't have the electrifying pace of Mo or the strength of Stevie, but I'd always been thought of as a potential first-teamer. I lived up to my expectations rather than defied them. As my career developed, it became obvious to me that if I had been from Bologna rather than Bootle, playing for Italy rather than England, I'd be rated higher.

Naturally, there was no instant success, and there were times when I doubted how I'd cope with the step up. My first games against older professionals were especially challenging. My debut for Liverpool's 'B' team ended in a 4–1 defeat to Manchester United. 'Welcome to the real world, lad!' the football industry seemed to scream at me. I was now playing big boys' games with big boys' rules. I was sixteen and taking on League players in their twenties. It was like being back at primary school and being thrown in against the seniors. My body needed to develop before I could cope.

When I was later promoted to Liverpool's 'A' team, the side below the reserves, I noticed another leap in class. My debut ended at half-time. I was subbed against Everton because the pace of the game was beyond me, but I never felt down about this, knowing once I filled out my natural capabilities would stand me in good stead. One of my enduring qualities has been my capacity to adapt. None of these early experiences made me doubt my ability, only how I'd adjust to the physical demands.

By the 1994–95 season, I'd forced my way into the reserves. My first appearance for them was against Blackburn Rovers at Southport's Haig Avenue, and although again the transition took time, positive signs were there. I was man of the match that day.

Had I been judged on those 'A' team displays, I might have been written off instantly or sent out on loan. I needed more than one chance at reserve level to fine-tune. It took me a full season before I felt comfortable. The difference then was that manager Roy Evans and Ronnie Moran were in constant contact with Heighway, monitoring my progress. There seemed less pressure or inclination to make instant verdicts, and you also felt everyone from the manager down was willing you to get there and making assessments with an open mind. Players were given time to bed in and develop physically before decisions were taken on their future.

In my case, by the time I was seventeen I'd turned the corner, assisted by a pivotal change of position. My days as a striker were over.

As a schoolboy, the further up the pitch I played, the more impact I had. As I edged closer to the first team, I began to retreat further towards my own goal, until eventually I was established as a defender. The 'A' team and reserve games made me realize I wasn't a forward. I didn't have the speed to stay upfront. Initially I was moved into a central midfield role, but during the FA Youth Cup run of 1996 a series of events gave me a taste of a different future.

Through the course of that competition I played in the centre of the park, keeping a younger and not quite up-to-the-mark Steven Gerrard out of the side, before finally being used at centre-half. By the time we met Manchester United in the quarter-final, the forward role I'd once made my own was earmarked for another.

'We've a player returning from Lilleshall to play in the game,' Heighway explained. 'His name is Michael Owen.'

I didn't know much about Mo other than his impressive schoolboy reputation. Ninety minutes later I came off the pitch believing I'd seen one of the best strikers in England, and he was still only sixteen. United absolutely battered us that day, playing us off the park in every area except one. Mo tore their defence apart single-handed. It wasn't just his blistering pace that caught my attention, but the ferocity of his tackling. He was an animal. For a small, slightly built lad, his strength was phenomenal. I'd never seen a striker tackle like him. When he suffered injuries later on, he toned down this aspect of his game.

Mo scored a hat-trick in a 3–2 victory, assisted by the iron will to win of what I'd call the 'team of scallies' around him. In fact, I have no shame in describing that 1996 Youth Cup winning side as a team of little fuckers. Whoever we came up against knew they were going to have the fight of their lives to beat us. We looked like a gang of street urchins from the toughest areas of the city, and we mixed our Sunday League nous with the professionalism and coaching the School of Excellence training drilled into us.

Even those who didn't go on to make it at Liverpool have forged careers elsewhere – striker Jon Newby played for a succession of Championship clubs, and Gareth Roberts was a success at Tranmere Rovers – but it's fair to say it was a team packed with more character than skill. I was part of a foursome with David Thompson – Little Thommo the Birken-head-the-ball – Jamie Cassidy and Lee Prior. 'This is a team which has got spunk,' Heighway would tell us. We were as tight a unit off the park as we were on it.

Lee was from Scotland (Scotty) Road, one of the most famously tough and charismatic areas of the city. 'If you want any knock-off gear, go and find Lee,' was often heard around the training ground. He's the only player I've worked with who forced a coach to fine himself. Sammy Lee gave him a clip round the ear one day on the pitch, and twenty-four hours later apologized for losing his rag. I dread to think what would happen if a similar incident happened now. If Sammy had hit a foreign lad, he'd probably have spent the next week in crisis talks with the player's agent. We simply got on with such matters, considering it a part of growing up. Prior got stick from the lads for a day or two, and then it was forgotten. It was character-building.

I saw Cassidy and Thommo as certainties to make the grade, but both were victims of the fragile nature of our profession. Injuries halted their otherwise inevitable rise. Like me, Thommo would never tell anyone he was injured, so determined was he to feature in every training session. I remember him playing one practice match using one foot for the whole game. I'd often do the same if I felt a hamstring strain. The competition was so intense, we'd never want to allow others a chance to push ahead of us. In Thommo's case, the price was paid longer-term. A knee injury he suffered as a teenager caught up with him in his mid-twenties and he was forced to retire early. That was the end for 'Beardo' – my nickname for him. It goes back to a game against Sunderland in the late nineties. We were warming up when one of their fans shouted, 'You look like Peter Beardsley!' Thommo was gutted. I couldn't contain my laughter and sprinted back to the dug-out to let the other subs know. Suffice to say, the more it wound him up, the more it stuck.

Gérard Houllier's arrival at Liverpool in the summer of 1998 led to Thommo's departure from the club. Whereas some of us compromised, Thommo's character never fitted in with the new boss who couldn't understand the ultra-Scouse sensibilities and characteristics. As a teenager, Thommo would walk up to first-team players like Jason McAteer and brazenly inform them, 'I should have your place.' It was seen as lightening the mood, not causing tension, but Houllier was looking for maturity and responsibility on and off the pitch. Thommo became expendable. He was given one final warning too many.

In 1996, however, he was still a symbol of everything that was right about Liverpool Football Club. With Mo as our lethal weapon, there was no stopping us in the Youth Cup, even though United and West Ham, who we beat in the final, were technically superior.

We beat Crystal Palace over two legs in the semi-final to set up that meeting with West Ham, whose stars were Frank Lampard and Rio Ferdinand. During the course of those games my career took another twist. Our centre-back, Eddie Turkington, was sent off in the second leg against Palace, leaving a hole at the back. Ronnie Moran and Hugh McAuley suggested to Heighway he move me to centre-half for the final. They saw me developing in the same way as Phil Thompson years earlier. He'd also been switched from central midfield, where he'd learned to read the game and see it from different angles before establishing himself at the back.

Moran's intuition set me on a new course. This shows, yet again, the value of having the youngsters mixing with the senior coaches and professionals. Could one of the Melwood staff make such a suggestion today? Would he know the local players well enough, or even be listened to?

Without Michael, we won the first leg of the final at Upton Park 2–0. He returned for the second leg, played in front of twenty thousand at Anfield. Although Lampard struck first, Mo underlined his class to secure a 4–1 aggregate win and a trophy I still rate as highly as others on my Liverpool honours list. The senior side lost at Wembley to Manchester United that summer, so our performance offered consolation and the hope of a new generation of local players to assist Robbie and McManaman in the first team.

We were on £250 a week at the time, but within a few weeks this was increased to a whopping £750. There were no agents or long-drawn-out contract negotiations. Roy Evans called a few of us in, asked us if we'd sign, and we walked out with the ink on our hands. Today, I hear ex-Liverpool players from the sixties and seventies lamenting the passing of simpler days when players weren't multi-millionaires and appreciated what they had at Anfield independent of financial reward. For some of us, those times passed more recently than the older generation might think. As I said, money was and is secondary to me. No matter what Liverpool had put in front of me in the summer of 1996, I'd have signed it.

As Michael, Thommo and I headed off to put a dent into our new wage packets, Steve Heighway must have felt he'd secured a lifetime of appreciation at Anfield thanks to his remarkable success in providing the players who'd flourish in the Liverpool first team. In 2007, accepting the Youth Cup again while announcing his Liverpool exit, I could sense the tears in his eyes. No matter how highly he rated those players he was leaving behind, he knew the odds against his prodigies enjoying similar triumphs with the Liver Bird on their chest were long. Like so much at Anfield during his era, the blame lay elsewhere. The forces of time were undermining traditional aspirations.

4

The Bootroom

The Anfield bootroom is as much part of Liverpool legend as the greatest players or managers. It's become a mystical place, presented as a symbol of the era when the club dominated domestic and European football. Bill Shankly, Bob Paisley, Joe Fagan and Ronnie Moran welcomed opposing managers into little more than a glorified cupboard near the Anfield dressing room, shared a glass of whisky, then sent them packing having seen their team deliver another football masterclass. Supporters still embrace the romanticism of this humble history, and it's easy to understand why. Four or five working-class heroes were the inspiration for eleven others in red, who in turn put the fifty thousand watching spectators into a fiery trance for ninety minutes.

'The Bootroom' wasn't just where the footwear was kept, it was where 'The Liverpool Way' was born and where the modern institution of Liverpool FC formed its identity. Shankly didn't merely transform the football club, he embodied it, creating an unwritten Anfield code of practice that has been stringently followed ever since. He imposed the style in which the club played; the modest but confident manner in which players conducted themselves on and off the park; the mentality of the staff and supporters.

Generations of Liverpool players, managers and fans have tried to follow Shankly's traditions with a sacred passion, myself included. Over the last two decades there's sometimes been confusion because there's a conflict between respecting the past and being stuck in it, but when the big moments arrive, like cup finals or major European nights, we're still able to summon the ghosts of our unprecedented history and be stirred rather than haunted by them.

Every new Liverpool manager is introduced with the shadow of thirty years of unbroken triumph hanging over him. Replicating that sustained period of success is a daunting prospect, but we will always strive to learn from those enduring influences. For all our recent problems, we have maintained the club's stature.

I never met Shankly, but from what I've read I know he was a modernizer and a visionary who challenged old ways to drag Liverpool to the peak of the English game. If he'd been a Premiership boss, I doubt he'd have been looking to the 1960s and 1970s for inspiration; he'd have been thinking up fresh ways to get ahead of the opposition. He'd have been just as much an innovator and forward thinker. More than any other manager, I wish I'd been around to play for him. I'm proud to think I'd have been his type of player.

Such was the strength of Shankly's legacy, Liverpool never had to look outside the club for a successor in the decades following his departure. After his arrival in 1959, every Liverpool manager had some connection with Anfield, either coming through the ranks as a coach in the case of Paisley, Fagan and Evans, or as former players like Dalglish and Souness. It was a policy others

Fan-tache-stic: My dad's parents, Nanny and Granddad Carra, Auntie Ann, Mum and Dad. I think Mum and Nanny Carra are laughing at my dad's bad early-80s muzzy.

Mum and Dad, the biggest influences on my life and career.

Lucky mascot: Getting my hands on my first piece of silverware as Dad's team Merton Villa win the Sunday League in 1983. I'm on the shoulders of Eric Crainey – one of the biggest Blues around – as we celebrated in The Chaucer.

Feeling Blue: A shaky snap taken on holiday at Butlins in 1985. That's my bitter Blue mate Seddo in the grey Everton away kit.

My mum's parents, the Vesallos, celebrate my first Holy Communion in 1985. Notice the cans of mild being used as ash-trays, Royle Family-style.

Holy Communion Day, 1985: Me, Paul and my cousin Joseph with Nanny Carra. (*Right*) With Mum and cousin Joseph.

The Bootle Clampitts! Trips to my uncle Pat's in Formby made us feel like the Beverly Hillbillies. Here's me, John and Paul enjoying his jacuzzi.

Blue blood: Kitted out with my dad and brothers, John and Paul, before heading off for the 1986 FA Cup Final.

The Holy Trinity: Is it Ball, Harvey and Kendall? Or perhaps John, James and Paul Carragher.

Small world: Nicola's and my first photograph together, as part of the cross country team at St James Primary in Bootle in 1986. I'm on the back row, fourth from right. Nicola is on the front row, second from the right. Nicola's brother John is on the back row, first left.

League Division 1 Champions
McDonald Cup Winners

Champions: St James Primary celebrate their title in 1987 under the management of Mr Rourke. I was the skipper, holding the cup.

'I Can Do That': My first taste of fame came on an ITV children's show doing 'keep-me-ups'. That's me on the back row, far right, in my Barcelona kit.

Welcome to Anfield: My first appearance at my future home playing for Bootle Schoolboys in 1988.

WIRRAL v BOOTLE.

Following boys should meet the coach at the usual places at 9.30am.

O'Connor.   Jeffers.   Unfortunately Wirral cannot provide
Cronin.   Sandys.   a 'B' Team for Sat. Therefore there
Hilton.   Rowan.   is only one game. Next B Team game is
Pike.   Lawson.   against Wirral at home on 17th Dec.
Carragher.   Smith.
Ready.   Watts.
McDonald.K.   Palmer.
Jones.

Vernons League

Table at 9.12.88.

	P	W	L	D	F	A	Pts.
BOOTLE	4	3	1	0	17	4	7
SOUTHPORT	4	3	0	1	9	6	6
CROSBY	3	2	0	1	17	5	4
WIRRAL	3	2	0	1	11	3	4
LIVERPOOL	2	1	1	0	11	2	3
WARRINGTON	2	1	0	1	5	4	2
ST HELENS	3	1	0	2	6	10	2
KIRKBY	4	0	0	4	6	22	0
SKELMERSDALE	3	0	0	3	0	26	0

Our next league match is not until 28.1.89 when we play Southport at
home. Lets make sure we stay on top in '89.

Photo orders.

If you still require copies of the colour photos, please let me have
your orders by next weeks training session at the latest. I will be
sending off the order after that date.

Leading scorers.
A
Carragher-28.
Palmer   -11.
Ready   -10.
B
Hoare   -6.
Morgan   -4.
McDonald 4.

Skelmersdale keeper ?

It's the only way we can
stop Carragher scoring!

Favourable treatment: Bootle Schoolboys'
manager, Ian Chapman, applies some
liniment ahead of another crucial fixture
– this one at Goodison Park – in 1988.

My goalscoring exploits were big news in Bootle,
as this school newsletter shows.

We're going to Wembley: My dad (*centre*) followed The Chaucer's flag with the Blues at home and
abroad. Here he's preparing for the 1989 Cup Final.

'I've just sold Everton a circus act': The Everton legend Alan Ball's guest appearance at my dad's pub, The Solly, in 1991, after selling us Peter 'Somersault' Beagrie from Stoke, with (*left*), Jimmy Sanders and my father-in-law, John Hart (*far right*). Richie Porter has the blue hat on, and at the front is Stevie Porter, who tragically died while the lads were watching me play for Lilleshall.

Only England: International recognition arrives in Lilleshall in 1992. I had to get back to Bootle for my barber Mick to sort my haircut.

envied, creating a seamless transition from one glorious decade to the next. Promoting from within has never yielded such consistent results as it did at Anfield during the 1970s and 1980s. As a rule, it's a risky strategy. Players find it difficult to see former assistants as 'the boss'. Liverpool showed the world it could work.

With eighteen titles and regular European Cups, Liverpool justly believed their methods were foolproof. But the ticking clock meant sooner or later the club was going to have to look beyond its past for inspiration in the dug-out. Sadly, this was a lesson we would only learn through painful experience after Dalglish's resignation in 1991, when a period of sterility without a League title began. By the time I made my first-team debut in January 1997, there was a vast gulf between how the club and fans perceived us, and the reality on the pitch. Our claim to be a club based on Shankly's principles and what I insist is one of the most essential commodities in football, 'character', was sounding like an idle boast. Even our fans thought we had too many egos promising much but delivering little.

That this decline should become more obvious under the leadership of Roy Evans, the manager dubbed 'the last of the bootroom boys' when he took the job in 1994, was especially ironic. Evans was seen as the safe pair of hands who could restore the old ways. A thoroughly decent, hard-working and honest man, he learned his trade from Paisley, Fagan, Moran and Dalglish and fitted the bill as a Liverpool manager-in-waiting, coming through the ranks like his mentors. Liverpool were craving stability after Souness's reign, during which he'd tried to impose the more continental methods he'd picked up in Italy but had alienated the players and fans. It was during Souness's reign that the go-ahead was given for the bootroom to be demolished. There was no use for it any more other than for museum tours, but getting rid of it to build a press room was criticized in some quarters like it was an act of sacrilege. Evans would be the link between the past and the future. Less brash and outspoken than Souness, he'd try to use the quiet wisdom of ex-managers to bring the title back. But the pursuit of a 'new Shankly' or Paisley was forlorn. Roy was fighting a losing battle, even though he came closer than any Liverpool manager since Dalglish to winning the Premier League.

Sir Alex Ferguson once said every team reflects the manager's personality, and I agree. Perhaps if Roy had inherited a fantastic squad and was building on solid foundations he'd have had more of a chance, but he had to try to start afresh. Having been at the club so long, it was impossible for him to change the image he had among the older professionals as a 'good guy' but not a tough one, and at the same time he couldn't get a grip on the signings who came in and badly let him down. Between 1994 and 1998, Liverpool were respected and 'nice' to watch, but they didn't have the steel needed to take the step to a higher level. The philosophy that had made the club so strong and proud took a pounding. The new wave of 'celebrity' footballers plagued the club, threatening the most important bond of all – the respect between players and fans.

Our slide didn't begin under Roy, but it reached a point where the dressing room was beyond the manager's control. The responsibility for this fell on the players as much as the boss. A visit to Stamford Bridge sticks in my mind, and throat, more than any other for exposing our strengths and weaknesses under his reign. For me, Roy's management career was depicted in those ninety inconsistent minutes. We were dazzling and then woeful, strolling through with seemingly effortless class when things went well but caving in like gutless cowards if the going got tough.

It was only a couple of weeks after I'd made my League debut, and I was an unused substitute for this fourth round FA Cup tie in London. There couldn't have been a more painful venue to expose where we were going wrong. Chelsea's King's Road is perceived as the opposite to everything Liverpool represents. Recent epic battles between the clubs have been presented as a clash between football tradition and the arrogant rich. While we celebrate our working-class roots, the Londoners love nothing more than to wave £20 notes at our visiting fans. Their players are granted the luxury of behaving like celebrities and superstars. Ours are expected to abide by a different set of values – the Shankly laws – and to show humility in a city where being flash is frowned upon. This tie proved to be a role reversal: our players looked like the prima donnas, Chelsea's the street-fighters.

The first half was an exhibition in 'pass and move' football which lived up to the finest Anfield traditions, and which was common during Evans's tenure. I've never played in a more naturally gifted Liverpool team. John Barnes was pulling the strings in midfield, Steve McManaman was linking attack and defence in his roaming role, and Robbie Fowler was at his clinical best, assisted by the enigmatic talent of Stan Collymore. Liverpool raced into a 2–0 half-time lead with goals from Robbie and Collymore. We were cruising.

Out came the cigars and deckchairs and strutting arrogance our supporters despise. Chelsea boss Ruud Gullit sent on Mark Hughes at the start of the second half. Within minutes he'd pulled a goal back, and the next forty minutes were among the most torturous in the club's FA Cup history as Chelsea ran riot.

The manner of the surrender was worse than the defeat itself.

We were watching a domino effect in full force. Hughes was able to intimidate the Liverpool defence to such a devastating degree that once one wilted under the pressure, the rest buckled. Chelsea played with the character, courage and skill that were supposed to be Liverpool's trademarks; Liverpool looked like the fancy dan southerners we'd seen submit so often on trips to Merseyside – not prepared to go in where it hurts.

After Gianluca Vialli wrapped up a 4–2 win, the vibes from the Chelsea fans' celebrations making our dressing-room walls shudder, furious Liverpool coach Sammy Lee turned to where I was sitting.

'I never want to see you bottling it like some of the fuckers out there today,' he said.

Evans lasted another eighteen months in sole charge, but this was the beginning of the end for him. He saw the values he held so dear being betrayed by players he'd brought to the club. The second half at Stamford Bridge proved there were no leaders and there was a lack of mental toughness. We didn't have enough winners, which was a crime at Anfield. Only the local players like Robbie and McManaman were consistently performing. Every humiliating defeat that followed made calls for a clear-out louder.

It's no coincidence to me that the most successful players since 1990 have been those who've come through the ranks, or who want more than simply being part of the team. Our best buys have always been, and will continue to be, those who share our sentiments. Players like Sami Hyypia, Didi Hamann, Xabi Alonso, Pepe Reina, Javier Mascherano and Fernando Torres have come to Anfield showing the hunger I can relate to, embracing the culture and mentality of the supporters. Plenty of others have walked through the door and I've known within a few months they didn't have what it takes. Many we have signed didn't see a move to Anfield as the beginning of their ambitions but the completion of them. It's as if being a Liverpool player was in itself a winners medal. The process of trying to collect cups often seemed a secondary concern. Too many arrivals turn up and spend the next couple of seasons patting themselves on the back because they've made the 'big time'. Instead of seeing a multi-million-pound move as a stepping stone to fulfil their potential and win titles, they see the extra possibilities of securing advertising contracts or commercial endorsements, of living the celebrity lifestyle. What happens on the pitch is a bonus.

All the top clubs in Europe are vulnerable to this, not only Liverpool, which is why leadership from the top down is the only way to make sure every member of the squad knows the real priority.

To the supporters, it's all about perceptions. If they hear about Liverpool players on a night out hours after a woeful home performance, as often happened during Evans's reign, they're immediately going to question the desire of those they put so much trust in. When our fans are with you, there are none better. Once you lose them, you struggle to get them back.

If I become a manager, I won't just want players scouted properly before I buy them, I'll want to know what they're like as individuals too. That's where Souness, Evans and later Houllier went wrong. I'm sure they did assess every aspect of a player's background, but perhaps not always as thoroughly as they later wished. Signing a player shouldn't merely be a case of weighing up how good he is, but also if he's capable of performing consistently and blending into a club's culture. It should be like a job interview. I had a chat with Clive Woodward once, who told me he not only considered players' performances but their character profiles. He wanted to know the kind of person he was putting into his squad, whether they were disruptive, temperamental and moody or inspirational and intelligent. If Liverpool had taken this approach, they'd have saved a lot of money wasted on players who looked great when they arrived but failed miserably to cope with the pressure. They could also have signed players who were more in tune with the ideas of the club and the manager, or at the very least more willing to learn and embrace them.

No one typifies this more than Stan Collymore, the flagship signing of the Evans era. No sooner had he joined Liverpool in the summer of 1995 than he was given the traditional Melwood nickname 'Fog in the Tunnel' by coach Ronnie Moran. 'That's always the excuse when players are late for training,' Ronnie explained, and Collymore's ninety-mile road trip every morning meant his kit was often still in the dressing room when we were on the Melwood pitch.

I was staggered that Liverpool paid a club record £8.5 million for a player and never asked him to move house, let alone looked further into his personality.

Within a matter of weeks, Collymore was mouthing off about the club not playing to his strengths, which instantly caused tension within the dressing room. At Liverpool, the idea of 'no one being bigger than the club' was being threatened by expensive signings who thought they commanded higher status before they'd kicked a ball.

A few snotty words in *Four-Four-Two* magazine were one thing. Smashing a chair over the head of our popular reserve keeper Tony Warner took matters to a different level.

It was my first pre-season trip with the senior team, in Ireland in 1996. Warner was trying to wind me up, flicking water on my seat after I stood up in the hope I'd sit down and get a wet arse.

I spotted the trick and swapped my chair for Collymore's, who threw a wobbly when he returned, demanding Warner swap seats. When the keeper refused, there was mayhem. Warner reacted to the smashed chair with a couple of punches, the rest of the squad joined in to try to break them up, and once it all calmed down only peacemaker Roy had a blow for his troubles.

Collymore refused to play in that night's friendly. Last year he criticized my decision to quit international football, saying I should have been grateful for every cap I got. Well, Stan, at least I turned up for every game I was selected for. If it wasn't friendlies he was bailing out of, it was a reserve match.

The level of unprofessionalism of certain players as I came through the ranks makes me cringe now. At the time, however, I knew no better. Liverpool had their way which, up until five years earlier, had served the club perfectly well. But it was a wonder the club managed to maintain any kind of position near the top of the table given the attitude of some players. It reached such a bad state that reserve coach Sammy would ask the same question on the morning of every reserve game: 'Listen, lads, can you promise me you'll turn up tonight? If you can't I'd rather know right now so I can organize the set-pieces with the team.' Poor Sammy could never take positive responses for granted.

When the 1997 Grand National was postponed for forty-eight hours because of an IRA bomb scare, Liverpool had a reserve game scheduled on the Monday night. At least six players called in sick to Melwood on the morning of the race, all claiming 'they had the shits'. The coaching staff knew where they were. The only running they were interested in was at Aintree. As one of those who arrived for the match – I'd never even considered missing the game – I earned myself extra respect in the eyes of Evans, and he reminded me of it years later. That showed how mistrustful he had become of the players, and how wary the coaching staff were of their negative influence on the youngsters. It was a situation that should have been nipped in the bud before it reached that stage.

Even when everyone did turn up for the second string, results were abysmal, despite the fact I was part of a reserve side which was probably the most expensively assembled in the club's history. There were certain players I looked upon with admiration, thrilled to be in the same team as them. Jan Molby, Ian Rush and John Barnes would often be alongside me if they were recovering from injury, and they were great characters as well as tremendous players. 'I'm celebrating my anniversary today,' Big Jan told me after welcoming me into the dressing room. 'It's ten years since I missed a penalty.' On another occasion I was reading an article in the *Echo* about Everton's centre-backs Craig Short and David Unsworth. 'Those two wouldn't get the ball off me in a phonebox,' he said. He wasn't joking that time.

Others exposed how the club had drifted. Collymore, Paul Stewart, Mark Walters, Julian Dicks and others didn't do themselves any favours on reserve duty. Stewart welcomed me into the reserve side with a 'What the fuck are you doing here?'

'What the fuck are you doing at Liverpool?' should have been my reply.

A 2–0 defeat at Bolton proved the final straw for Moran, who said to Collymore, 'You'll never get back into the first team playing like that.'

'And I could have played against you tonight,' Moran added to Walters.

Walters responded, 'Why don't you get your fucking kit on then?'

As we sat in the showers, I heard Collymore laughing. 'I can't get the image of Ronnie trying to run around in his shorts out of my head,' he said, sneeringly. In my book, Collymore wasn't fit to share a dressing room with an Anfield legend such as Ronnie Moran, but here he was mocking him.

It's fair to say Ronnie was a traditionalist, which is why there was such a culture clash between him and the high-profile, increasingly wealthy players. Ronnie's view of the game was based exclusively on the Shankly values. He called the first-team squad 'the big heads', which was sadly becoming increasingly less a piss-take and more a statement of truth. So long as you performed well on the pitch, he'd turn a blind eye to any faults you had off it. Respect was earned through hard work and application of talent. He was 'old school'.

When you were one of Ronnie's favourites, the sun shone out of your backside twelve months of the year. Ronnie could get a tan if he stood behind players like Rushie and Barnes, as I often found during my early training sessions. Barnes was majestic in training as well as in games, so it was no wonder he was admired so much by staff and team-mates. If Rushie made a bad pass to me and I lost it, Ronnie would shout at me to do better. Should I ever put Barnes through and he miscontrolled, Ronnie would blame the weight of my pass. But if either of them ever missed a sitter, we'd all hear the familiar line from the coach: 'Happens in football that, son.'

I didn't resent this. It was his form of creating a class system within the squad. If you'd been there, done it and collected medals over many years, it was right you were treated differently from the young upstarts who'd achieved nothing. I'd like to think if I was still working with Ronnie I'd be one of his golden boys now and others would be starting the process of earning his respect.

There was wisdom in his style. If Ronnie had a go at you, you usually deserved it, and you listened. It wasn't for show, it was for your own good. You were getting advice from someone who'd been part of the most successful coaching staff in English football history. He knew what he was talking about.

My favourite day of the week was Monday, when the senior players had the day off and the youth and reserve players took on the staff. It was a free-for-all. There were no positions, no off-sides and no referees. You just played, passed and moved. There was competition, but the coaches would talk to you throughout the game, offering tips and giving you a real insight into how they wanted the game played. I'd always make sure I was near Ronnie on the pitch because he taught me more than anyone during those practice matches. They were stopped once Houllier took over, so the youngsters who've come through since have missed out on what was a major part of my training to become a professional. While later I agreed with many of the adjustments Houllier made to training, I now wonder if we ended up going too far in the opposite direction.

'The game never changes,' Ronnie used to tell me during my early reserve appearances. In some respects he was wrong. Football is much quicker now, players are more athletic, and you can't get away with behaving like a fan off the pitch, hitting the town after every game, and still expect to look like a sportsman in his prime on it. On the other hand, the basics are fundamentally unaltered. It's still eleven men versus eleven men. The goals are the same size, and managers still choose from the same limited tactical formations, most preferring 4–4–2. The game evolves at a steady pace, but I've seen nothing during my years as a professional that has surprised me.

There's still as much to learn from Moran's simplistic view as there is from the analytical scientific approach of modern coaches, which also fascinates me. Shankly said 'football is a simple game complicated by idiots', but the best managers will absorb elements of both modern and traditional methods. You can't just abandon what's worked in the past, but you ignore the changing times at your peril.

The bottom line is this: if you assemble a squad of players with talent and the right attitude and character, you'll win more football matches than you lose, no matter how inventive your training sessions, what system you play or what team-talks you give. But anything that can give you the extra 10 per cent, whether that's through diet, your general fitness or the correct word in your ear, also has merit.

Players like me responded to Ronnie, but new arrivals never held him in the same esteem. I was more aware of the history of the club, of his role in taking Liverpool to European heights. I grew up in Liverpool. I knew who Ronnie Moran was, and what he'd achieved in the game. I loved hearing his words of advice, still do when he visits our training ground every week. There was nothing in football he hadn't seen.

If I was a sub, I'd sometimes be watching his reactions on the bench as much as the game. On the opening day of the 1996–97 season we were away to Middlesbrough when Fabrizio Ravanelli scored a hat-trick. The Boro fans celebrated, and several of them ran towards our bench. As the third goal went in, Ronnie had been squirting the contents of a Lucozade bottle into his mouth. A screaming woman in a Boro shirt raced arms aloft towards where we were sitting, as though she'd just witnessed a cup final winner. Cool as you like, Ronnie aimed the bottle towards her and squirted her in the face. I had to stop myself laughing in case anyone thought I was happy we'd conceded a goal.

That incident showed me it didn't matter if Liverpool

were winning or losing, Ronnie remained unflustered and kept his wits about him. People thought he was a ranter and raver. He was often the calmest man on the bench, taking everything in.

Too many of the younger generation of signings saw Ronnie as a symbol of the past who they could take the piss out of behind his back. Even younger coaches like Sammy Lee couldn't control the situation.

I respect Sammy even more now than I did then, because reserve manager is the toughest position at a club. You don't pick the team or tactics, but you have to work to the manager's instructions. If a player is coming back from injury, you're ordered to play him for the last thirty minutes. You can't drop players or throw the youngsters in without permission. Your influence on the side is minimal, but if results go badly, you get the blame. It's the ultimate no-win position.

I could see how agitated Sammy was as the reserve side went from one shambles to the next. He dedicated himself to the job but got nothing back from the majority of players. As a last resort Sammy started to play himself, even though he was now in his late thirties and clearly nowhere near the player he once was. That didn't work either: we lost 6–0 at Nottingham Forest. As the goals tumbled in, Sammy came off the bench. The first thing he did was lose the ball, and Forest immediately scored. 'At least he can't have a go at us now' was the attitude of the rest of the players.

Liverpool were almost relegated from the reserve league in Evans's last season as we hit an all-time low. We survived by beating Everton in the final game. The *Liverpool Echo* asked for a team photo to mark the occasion. Sammy thought the request was taking the piss. 'You're fucking joking, aren't you?' he asked the photographer.

When I hear players from the time suggesting claims of indiscipline were exaggerated, I can only put this down to their being unable to compare what it was like then to how it is now. I sensed the frustration of more influential figures like Barnes, who was increasingly aware of the difference between our outdated methods and the continentals, and could see how far behind we were drifting. In the summer of 1996 we were invited to a soccer-six tournament in Amsterdam and neither we nor our opponents could believe the contrast in styles. Our warm-up consisted of little more than shooting balls at a wall; the Ajax and AC Milan sides we were competing against went through an intense series of exercises. The match with Ajax went to a penalty shoot out so I asked Barnes if he was taking one. It was as if what he'd seen before the game had hit home. 'No chance,' he said to me, shaking his head in disillusionment. 'We're a fuckin' disgrace.'

At seventeen, even I felt bold enough to confront the senior coaching staff. Evans's assistant manager, Doug Livermore, was treated like one of the lads rather than as an authoritarian sidekick. In one five-a-side training game he disallowed a goal by my team so I reacted in the same way I'd heard so many others and said, 'Fuck off, Doug, it was well in.' He went ballistic. I was given a well-deserved pasting for daring to question one of my bosses.

I thought nothing more of it, treating the incident as Doug's way of pointing out there's a line you can't cross. The next day I was walking on to the training ground when Doug, Ronnie and Roy pulled me to one side.

'You passed an important test yesterday,' Doug said to me. 'You got on with the game as if nothing had happened. You've shown us you've got character.'

People can see, and hear. I'm a talker on the pitch now, and I was the same as a youngster. The ticking-off from Doug hadn't changed my approach for the rest of the training session. I was still mouthing off if I thought it was necessary. Others might have withdrawn into their shell, or hidden. Roy and Doug obviously had years of experience of such incidents and knew what to look for in players' reactions.

Despite their problems, they must have taken satisfaction from the way their youngsters were developing. There was still hope for the emerging local players who were more willing to embrace the club's traditions. They must have hoped that as long as their methods sank into a player like me, there was a promising future.

Some of the older professionals were beyond help. Whenever I arrived at Melwood on the morning after an important match there would be a queue of signings stretching along the corridor to the manager's office, all demanding an answer to the same question: 'Why am I not in the team?' Roy Evans should have sat them all down and played a few reserve videos, although as his reign progressed first-team games offered just as good an explanation.

His squad became known as 'The Spice Boys'. The notorious 'white suits' FA Cup Final of 1996 cemented the sadly justified image of mid-nineties Liverpool as more image than substance. Roy's team is remembered for this more than its performances. Many of the players had a following of teenage girls as much as die-hard Kopites. Modelling contracts and shower commercials did little to enhance their reputation.

Of all teams, Liverpool were playing Manchester United that day at Wembley, which provided another example of how we'd allowed our rivals to invade traditional Anfield territory. We'd picked up the bad habits Alex Ferguson had successfully rooted out of Old Trafford. In the 1980s, it was Liverpool led by a working-class Scot who won the League most years while the brash, arrogant upstarts from Manchester consistently failed to live up to their pre-season promises under Ron Atkinson. Now it was United acting like the old Liverpool while our lads were behaving like those flash United players we used to hate.

The youngsters, like Jamie Redknapp, Robbie Fowler, Steve McManaman and David James, took most of the criticism for those infamous ice-cream Armani suits. They were right to feel offended. The responsibility for the humiliation lay with the older players and staff, who went along with the absurd idea. Put it this way. If one of the young lads in our squad had asked me or Steven Gerrard before the 2006 FA Cup Final to wear a white suit, what do you think our reaction would have been? You're impressionable at a young age. The advice you get from the staff and older players is critical. If someone had been strong enough to say 'You can fuck right off' when the idea of wearing those suits was mentioned, as would happen now, those young lads would have thanked them for it after the game. For the experienced professionals to say it had nothing to do with them won't wash. It's they who should have been showing as much authority as the manager in those circumstances, preventing the more naive players from making a calamitous error of judgement.

I felt particularly sorry for Jamie Redknapp, who had to fight against the Spice Boy accusation for years after. Jamie is one of the few players I've met who shares with me an absolute devotion to football. He was no more a Spice Boy than Robbie and McManaman, but because he was a Londoner and he married a pop star, he was an easy target. Jamie despised the image he was wrongly given. He's one of the most polite fellas you could wish to meet, but it was the one subject that sent him into a rage. Michael Owen's dad gave an interview shortly after his lad broke into the side, and it was headlined 'My Lad's No Spice Boy' with a picture of Jamie alongside. That was obviously nothing to do with Mo's dad, but Jamie went berserk and rang him up to make his point. There was no better professional at the club at the time, no one who took more pride in his performance or worked harder to improve his game. But for injuries he'd have achieved far more than he did at Anfield. Anyone who tries to lump him into the same bracket as a few others at the club at the time is seriously mistaken. That's why Jamie was made captain when Houllier arrived a few years later.

Robbie and McManaman escaped much of the fall-out after the final because their performances were beyond criticism. Everyone knew Robbie didn't buy into the celebrity lifestyle nonsense. He was a normal lad with an extraordinary talent. I became a big pal of Robbie's because we're from the same background, but also because even at the height of his powers he never let it go to his head. While he was banging in thirty goals a season, I was still in the youth side trying to impress. Although I was at Melwood all the time, I'd never spoken to him. He knew me only by my name and appearance. I was walking around town with some friends one day when Robbie appeared, spotted me and simply said, 'All right Carra?' It may seem nothing, three quietly spoken words with a nod of acknowledgement as I walked past. But it made me feel a million dollars in front of my friends, who all worshipped Robbie and now believed he was a mate of mine. I knew after that he was a top lad, so by the time I was playing alongside him it was inevitable we'd get on. He wasn't given the nickname 'God' for nothing. As someone who epitomized how Scousers wanted to be on and off the pitch, his iconic status was deserved.

Steve McManaman was never held in the same regard, but his performances under Evans deserve far more recognition than they're given now. People seem to forget he virtually single-handedly won two cups for Liverpool. The 1992 FA Cup win under Souness was McManaman's tournament in every round, and he inspired the sole cup success under Evans, the 1995 League Cup against Bolton.

His reputation suffered when he moved to Real Madrid as part of the most high-profile Bosman deal of the time. Liverpool have since benefited from such free transfers themselves. Markus Babbel was one of the most respected defenders in Europe in 2000 when we took him from Bayern Munich without paying a penny, but that tends to be overlooked when McManaman is accused of betrayal by some of our supporters. To pin that on him is an unforgiving and inaccurate reflection of what happened. He'd nearly been sold to Barcelona for £12 million in 1996 but the Spanish club opted to buy Rivaldo instead. He played out his contract and accepted a golden opportunity to join Real Madrid, where he won league titles and Champions League medals. McManaman presumed (correctly as it turned out) he'd never get the chance to win the same honours at Anfield. At that stage of his career he faced the genuine prospect of never playing in the Champions League. If he could make the decision again, does anyone seriously believe he should act any differently? Had Real Madrid had to pay for him, they might not have gone ahead with the transfer. Despite being accused of greed, Macca also lost money to secure the move. He was one of the lowest earners at Anfield, despite being the top player, because he'd refused to sign a new contract. Financially he took a big risk, putting his career before money. I respect him for that.

Robbie and McManaman opened the doors for young players coming through on Merseyside. Not so many had made the jump in the years before them, but their progress signalled the start of a prolific period, with me, Michael Owen, David Thompson, Dominic Matteo and Steven Gerrard soon to follow.

It was my intention to follow their lead to give the first team a solid local base. I could hardly wait for that symbolic moment on a Friday morning when Ronnie Moran took the pre-match meal orders. That's when you knew. There was no summons to the manager's office, or grand announcement of your inclusion. A simple question from Ronnie was all you needed, to know you'd made the squad.

'What do you want to eat tomorrow?'

Those seven words started hundreds of Liverpool careers.

It was the question I was desperate to hear. I'd even rehearsed my answer to make sure I didn't ask for the wrong food.

'Chicken and beans,' I told Ronnie when he finally spoke those words to me.

I had Alan Shearer to thank for my response. I'd read an interview with him a few weeks earlier in which he'd revealed his pre-match meal, so thought I was on safe ground following his example.

First I was an unnamed sub, then pre-season friendlies gave me a chance to progress. As if designed by someone above, my first ever appearance in Liverpool's senior team was against Everton at Goodison Park in a practice match in 1996. I was a wing-back, adding another position to my varied repertoire. My dad nearly spat out his Bovril when he saw me running out as I'd been given no prior indication I'd be playing.

I had to wait another six months for my 'real' debut, of course,

which came on 8 January 1997 in a League Cup tie away to
Middlesbrough. I replaced Rob Jones fifteen minutes from time
in a 2–1 defeat. Three days after this I played a full half in central midfield against West Ham at Anfield in a 0–0 draw. Those
appearances were swiftly forgotten by the fans, many of whom
still believe my League debut came a week later on 18 January
when Aston Villa came to town. That was when I made my first
start for Liverpool, promising to forge a career as a goalscoring
central midfielder.

Patrik Berger's dodgy stomach opened the way for one of
those fairytale afternoons you'd lie in bed constructing in your
mind but could never imagine would come true. Typically, I
arrived at Anfield on the morning of the match expecting to play
in one position but found myself starting in another. On the eve
of the fixture Roy Evans told me I'd be centre-half. The club had
just signed Bjorn Kvarme from Rosenborg, but his international
clearance hadn't arrived in time. I went to sleep preparing to
mark Dwight Yorke and Savo Milosevic. Overnight, Kvarme was
given the green light to play, but no one at the club thought this
information important enough to be passed on to me. But for
Berger falling ill, I'd have been on the bench. Instead, I played
central midfield. Everything I'd been planning mentally had to be
disregarded. Now I'd be taking on one of the most experienced
central midfielders in the country, Andy Townsend. He must
have felt confident of running the game against an unknown
Scouse rookie. I was determined to prove him wrong.

The adrenalin rush as kick-off approached clearly affected my
judgement. In my anxiety to get changed and on to the pitch, I
put the wrong shirt on. My squad number was 23, a number I've
stuck with ever since despite plenty of opportunities to move up
the pecking order. I was ready to head out wearing Mark

Kennedy's 22 jersey until someone patted me on the shoulder.

The referee's whistle saw me frantically pursue my first involvement, whether it was a pass or a tackle. I clattered into Townsend with a fearsome late challenge after twenty seconds. He did me a favour by getting up straight away. Others might have milked it, and I could have been in the record books for the quickest sending-off in Anfield history. As it was I was booked, which was the second best thing to happen to me that day. It settled me down for the rest of the game. I began to relax, and the nervous energy was channelled in a more appropriate direction.

I was alongside Jamie Redknapp in midfield and acquitting myself well. Then my moment of glory came. For Stig Bjornebye's corner five minutes into the second half I drifted into the box and headed in at The Kop end, the first in a 3–0 win. Off I went towards the corner flag. Of all the preparations I'd considered, celebrating a goal was not among them. You spend years dreaming of such a moment, visualizing how it will play out and how it will feel. It's a once-in-a-lifetime experience you can never explain or understand. Suffice to say, having forty thousand supporters cheering you is spine-tingling.

My dad was in the crowd, sitting next to Fowler and McManaman's parents. They rushed to him and gave him a hug, he told me later.

I gave an interview to *Match of the Day* after the game, trying to give the right impression. 'I know I'll be out of the team when everyone is fit next week,' I said, eager not to sound like a 'big head'. I thought I was saying the right thing, but Sammy Lee told me otherwise. 'Never say anything like that,' he told me the following Monday. 'Make it as hard as possible for the manager to drop you. Don't put yourself down in that way. You're as entitled to a place in the side as anyone now.'

I headed to The Chaucer on the night of the game to be met by a standing ovation, and several re-runs of the goal were given an airing. The evening ended in Aintree's Paradox nightclub as I began to discover what it felt like to hit the town as a recognizable face. Some players feel the biggest moments pass them by, but I've always tried to pause and soak them up.

I'd made the breakthrough. From then on I wasn't just James Carragher from Bootle, I was Jamie Carragher the Liverpool footballer. But plenty of youngsters over the years have made a blistering start only to end up as the subject of 'Where are they now?' features in *The Kop* magazine. The next challenge was to establish myself as more than a one-goal wonder.

And before you get accepted by the fans, or even the manager, you have to become 'one of the lads'. As Collymore found to his cost, this isn't as straightforward as it may seem. There are all kinds of trials and tribulations to undergo, all of which provide as much a test of your personality as ninety minutes against a top striker.

Steve Harkness was responsible for many of my sternest examinations off the park as he pushed my tolerance to the limit with his 'pranks'. He is a good mate of mine, and was a great source of banter in the dressing room. He welcomed me into the squad on away duties by wiping shit all over the door handle of my room. Not the kind of welcome gift you'd wrap up. Harky was also put in charge of looking after me during the soccer-six trip to Amsterdam, which was a good way of ensuring I ended up in the kind of establishments I shouldn't have been in. In one pub at about two a.m. a bouncer the size of a sumo wrestler ordered us to leave.

'Ay you, yer fat bastard,' was Harky's response to the breaking news of an imminent bar closure.

The bouncer towered over Harky, ducked down and fixed a cold stare on him before replying in a Dutch accent, 'Are you talking to me?'

Harky didn't fancy the odds if he continued the conversation.

'No, I was talking to him over there,' he said, pointing behind the Dutchman.

I'd already made my way to the exit, and by the time the bouncer looked back we were both halfway down the road.

The sense of indiscipline may have been frowned upon, but there was no shortage of laughter in that squad. Much as I agreed with many of the decisions that were taken later, there's no doubt the sense of humour was lost when disciplinary measures were taken to a new extreme. 'Banter', as we footballers like to call it, can be a source of team spirit. The more players enjoy one another's company off the park, the more they'll be prepared to help one another on it. The best managers get the balance right between working hard and playing hard, in every sense.

My expectation of returning to anonymity after that goalscoring arrival proved sadly accurate. Whatever the manager's reasoning, my fantastic introduction to the top flight didn't trigger a prolonged run in the side. I'd hoped for at least a ten-minute sub appearance here and there, but Liverpool were in contention for the title. I had to wait until the following season, 1997–98, for my next appearance, by which time Evans had drastically reshaped the team and shipped out some big-name players such as Barnes and Collymore.

There was always a missing piece of the jigsaw with Roy Evans's side, as if a final magical signing would transform us from hopefuls into champions. This was wishful thinking. Whenever one area was strengthened, another was weakened. Collymore's departure to Aston Villa was offset by Mo's emergence and the signing of Karlheinz Riedle, though it wasn't long before the fans were demanding a new target man. Barnes moved on to be replaced by much-sought-after ball-winning midfielder Paul Ince, and with Barnes went the fluent passing game that had been so eye-catching.

Throughout 1995–96 and 1996–97, with Barnes at the centre, it was acknowledged Liverpool played wonderful football but were defensively vulnerable. Those two campaigns are symbolized by the 4–3 wins over Newcastle in April 1996 and March 1997 – the first of which is replayed countlessly on Sky TV and described as 'the greatest game in Premiership history' and underlines why it was Manchester United who won the League. Neither side could defend resolutely. In the long term, even though Liverpool won, they effectively handed the title to United that night. Ferguson must enjoy watching re-runs of that match even more than Liverpool fans. Psychologically, Newcastle were damaged beyond repair, while Liverpool's capacity to self-destruct wrecked hopes of a revival. Having put themselves back in the race for the title with a last-minute Collymore winner, Liverpool lost away to Coventry, 1–0, four days later.

This was a side that couldn't be trusted. The fans said they knew the solution. 'We need a midfielder like Graeme Souness or Steve McMahon!' The topic dominated the airwaves. It was the 'rotation policy' or 'where should Steven Gerrard play?' issue of its day, becoming an obsession for media fed by growing agitation in the stands. The 3–5–2 formation Evans introduced after his appointment was dismissed as too negative, and the more traditional 4–4–2 was viewed as the obvious remedy. Evans heard the complaints and changed tack for his final full season, recruiting Ince to replace Barnes and reverting to a 4–4–2.

This proved to be a mistake. Ince was a tremendous player, but his aggression wasn't enough. Liverpool needed seven or eight players prepared to put their foot in, not one. Expecting him to arrive and transform a physically vulnerable side into a powerful unit was optimism bordering on delusion. The fans never took to him either. There was an instant contradiction between someone playing for Liverpool and calling himself 'The Guv'nor'. As well as being an ex-United title winner, he was also someone who gave the appearance of considering himself an England player first and a Liverpool midfielder second. The Kop was never comfortable with that.

Changing the side to suit Ince's strengths had an impact in other areas. In 1997–98, the new recurring issue was 'when are Liverpool going to buy two decent centre-halves?' The squad was more suited to 3–5–2. The defenders weren't strong enough to play in a flat back four, and McManaman was more effective in his free role.

My first appearance of that campaign was the second match, at home to Leicester, which we lost 2–1. The season was a struggle to the end after this, but the enduring troubles gave me a chance to establish a position in the side.

The game where I 'came of age' was thirteen months after my goal against Villa, on 23 February 1998. Derby day.

Playing against Everton was in itself of monumental importance to me. The background to the game made it even more significant. Five days earlier we'd lost 2–0 in the League Cup semi-final to Middlesbrough in a game where I felt responsible for both goals. I conceded a penalty after a minute and also made a mistake in the build-up to Boro's second. We went out 3–2 on aggregate. The imminent appointment with the Blues – my first derby – wasn't just a test, then, of my capabilities against Duncan Ferguson, whose reputation for performing against Liverpool was well established at that time, I also had to prove I could recover from setbacks. I'd go so far as to say if I'd failed in the derby doubts would have been raised about my capacity to survive at a club of Liverpool's stature. At the very least the fans would have started asking questions.

We didn't beat Everton. We fought out a 1–1 draw in a match remembered most for the horrific cruciate injury suffered by Robbie Fowler, a knock he struggled to recover fully from in the years that followed. Ferguson scored for Everton, but it was acknowledged I'd played him well considering my inexperience at centre-half. No one could doubt I had character after that game. The manager knew he could rely on me if I was needed again.

Roy Evans wouldn't get many more opportunities to do so. He must have known his days were numbered towards the end of that 1997–98 season, although given his overall League record he hardly merited being regarded as a failure. Judged against the managers of the time, Evans did a good job. Unfortunately for him, Liverpool managers aren't simply compared to their peers but to their predecessors, whose achievements speak for themselves. Being good is not enough at Liverpool. You've got to be exceptional.

Roy never finished outside the top four and pushed United harder for the title than Gérard Houllier or Rafa Benitez. He also won one trophy, reached the FA Cup Final, and made a European semi. To claim he didn't make brave decisions would also be wrong. The 3–5–2 system worked well for a couple of years and was correctly seen as an inventive solution, breaking with tradition to bring the best out of skilful players. Despite the accusations he was too weak to be a manager, he proved he was capable of making tough calls at certain moments. He dropped every member of the squad at least once, including his captains, with only one exception: Steve McManaman was the only player to avoid the axe, which is no criticism or surprise given his form throughout that period. High-profile stars such as Julian Dicks, Don Hutchison and Mark Wright were all bombed out at some point. Collymore was sent packing after two seasons.

The manner in which Ince was handed the captaincy ahead of Wright was especially ruthless. Our first game of Roy's last season was away to Wimbledon. There had been rumours Ince would get the armband, but Wright, who had been vice-captain behind Barnes and captain in previous years, still wasn't told of any decision. Evans made the announcement in the Selhurst Park dressing room. There was no explanation, just a firm, matter-of-fact revelation. Ince was captain. Nothing to discuss.

Despite these incidents, overall it wasn't enough to make examples out of players now and again. Players needed to know who was the boss every day, not occasionally. The Anfield environment had to change for every existing and new player to alter his attitude. For Liverpool to transform their image completely it was going to take an outside influence. Someone new had to come in and put everyone on their toes, make them more wary of how they handled themselves, more prepared to knuckle down.

That man was Gérard Houllier.

Rumours had been circulating of a possible change, but most were expecting a new assistant manager. I arrived for pre-season training in the summer of 1998 and immediately noticed the absence of Ronnie Moran. This was unheard of. Ronnie was the first to arrive every morning and the last to leave at night. Evans told the players he'd been given a few extra days off. The next thing we knew, the club was unveiling Houllier as part of a 'joint management' set-up, which was doomed before the pair began the job. Ronnie, it was announced, had retired.

It was a classic fudge by the club. You can't have two managers. Within a couple of days you could see tensions were developing, and from a purely operational point of view it wasn't working. It can be hard enough to keep some players' attention for one team talk, but two? Our heads were spinning as we were bombarded with different information from each manager. As each of them tried to assert his authority, they succeeded only in undermining each other. Roy would give his speech, then Gérard would begin talking while his co-manager was anxious to get us on to the training pitch.

And not only did we have two managers, we had several assistants. If we'd had coaches versus players games they'd have had more reserves on the bench than us. Gérard brought in Patrice Bergues, who had a lot of fresh ideas he wanted to establish quickly, while Doug Livermore remained as Roy's assistant.

Any notion that Liverpool old and Liverpool new would form some powerful alliance was madness. A political battle ensued, and the players' loyalties were tested: those sympathetic to Roy would always speak to him, while those of us fascinated by the new arrivals and their opinions would feel guilty asking for advice. I admired Roy, but I was fascinated by Houllier and his ideas. Maybe some players, particularly those who'd been at the club for a lot longer, felt more allegiance to Roy which made them less trustful of Gérard. I saw them both as my manager, and was as happy listening to the new boss as the old one. I didn't buy into all the anti-foreign coach hype which a few Anfield traditionalists were spouting. Those of us who'd gone through the previous few seasons recognized a figure like Houllier could sweep away the debris. I can say without any sense of guilt the mistake the club made was not ending Evans's reign in the summer of 1998. It wasn't fair to drag his inevitable departure through the torturous sham of a marriage with a manager he'd never met before.

As results continued to deteriorate at the start of the 1998–99 season, a swift divorce was the only answer. A 3–1 League Cup defeat to Spurs at Anfield on 10 November was the end for Evans. We were called for a meeting the following morning, at which he tearfully announced his resignation. It was impossible not to sympathize with him on a human level. He'd dedicated his life to the club, and for all the evident problems, he'd only narrowly failed to deliver the title.

I glanced around the room as Roy left. Most of the lads had their heads bowed. A few of them should have been feeling guilty about their own role in his downfall. To my horror, a couple of players began to laugh, apparently finding the emotion of the occasion funny. I guess you find out who your real friends are in those situations.

Rightly or wrongly, the media announced the Spice Boys' era was over, and Houllier got to work enforcing a new sense of discipline and professionalism.

Evans's failure to repeat the glories of the past confirmed fears that a forty-year period of unparalleled success had come to an end. When he departed, Liverpool were not just saying goodbye to one of their favourite sons and greatest servants, they were acknowledging the passing of time. Against their wishes, the modern world was finally catching up with Liverpool FC.

Even then, the club refused to wholly abandon its traditional Anfield links. Former captain Phil Thompson, who'd left under Souness, was appointed assistant manager, ensuring the spirit of the Shankly boys could be passed on to a new generation of players. Something had to change at Anfield in the late 1990s, but the presence of Thompson, a man who'd learned his trade under the Godfather of Anfield, meant there was still a comforting familiarity to the new regime.

Thommo could now rightfully claim to be 'the last of the boot-room boys'. Once he left a few years later, as the sole survivor of Evans's team I'd like to think it's a title that was justifiably passed on to me.

5

Houllier

Gérard Houllier spoke my football language. He just did it in a foreign accent. His critics dismissed him as 'the Frenchman', but Houllier was the best 'British' manager I've worked with.

Liverpool's revival under him came as a result of updating conventional English principles, not by imposing trendy, unfamiliar continental methods. Hard work, strict discipline, mental and physical toughness and team spirit were at the heart of his philosophy. This was how he delivered on a promise to bring winning times back to Anfield. He collected major trophies and led us into the Champions League by rigorously modernizing Liverpool traditions. He's judged as a failure because he didn't win the League. That's the only area he fell short in, but he's not alone in recent Anfield history.

Illness cruelly deprived him of the sharp judgement that had led to swift early progress, but for three years he was a great Liverpool manager. This statement could once be delivered without controversy. Now, there are Liverpool fans prepared to question how good he was. My memory isn't tainted by the last two appalling years of his reign. I appreciate what he did for me and Liverpool before his heart operation intervened, prior to those dark days when Michel Platini advised him to sign Salif Diao, and Houllier put his neck under his own guillotine by insisting Igor Biscan was a centre-half. Sadly, the message on his tombstone will read 'Here lies the man who bought Salif Diao, Bruno Cheyrou and El-Hadji Diouf'.

Football is an unforgiving business. He deserves more than that.

I owe much of my success to him, so whenever I hear supporters dismiss his reign, I'm ready to dive into the argument. Try to remember where the club was when he took over in November 1998 and how many finals we'd won and European nights we'd celebrated six years later. Then compare this to the grim eight-year spell before he arrived. Our recovery began under him.

There was good reason for me to instantly like Houllier. The words 'Jamie, I'm going to get you a new contract' always sound agreeable, and Houllier mouthed them a month after taking full control of the side. Not a bad way to secure my support. 'You're exactly the type of player I like,' he told me. 'I wish I had more like you.'

We discussed Liverpool's weaknesses and I'd nod in agreement. They were the same conversations I'd have with friends after every game. We weren't aggressive enough; not enough players got their shirts dirty; some of the lads didn't like a tackle; Sean Dundee was not a Liverpool footballer. Such observations weren't new to Melwood. Ronnie Moran, whose departure when Houllier arrived saddened me most, made the same point about the team's lack of aggression. Ronnie always told the players they were too much of a soft touch. No one paid attention, brushing off the comments as the ramblings of an old man. The generation gap couldn't be bridged, even by a legend such as Ronnie. By 1998, it seemed English players were prepared to cut foreign managers more slack, whereas poor old Ronnie paid the price of the continental revolution. When Houllier arrived and made identical comments, everyone listened as though he was an enlightened football philosopher. I didn't care whether he was from Bootle or Bordeaux, he was just talking sense, and that's what mattered now.

Since the formation of the Premier League there's been a willingness to regard overseas coaches as more knowledgeable, especially when it comes to the tactical and technical areas of the game. It's a media myth created by the brilliance of Arsène Wenger. He joined Arsenal in September 1996, and within two years they were Premiership champions and FA Cup winners. Every top club wanted to go down the foreign route to repeat his success, and British managers have been struggling for the biggest jobs ever since. But for every class foreign manager like Wenger, there's been an Alain Perrin.

Liverpool copied Arsenal by opting for Houllier, but I was instantly struck by how English he was in his approach, so it wasn't difficult to adapt. People expected me to enjoy a closer relationship with Roy Evans, given our backgrounds. I didn't work long enough with Roy for such a bond to develop, but from the start I always felt close to Gérard. We shared an obsession with football. He would return home after an evening fixture and watch the match twice on video so he could tell each player what he'd done right or wrong at training the next day. I'd have private meetings with him at Melwood when he'd go through the tapes and pick out my errors. Some players hated it, but I enjoyed it. The painstaking attention to detail was weird yet inspiring. If I played well in my next game and showed the manager how much I'd taken his advice, he'd make me feel ten feet tall with his congratulations.

Houllier's man-management skills were his strength. He could be severe – witness his ban on mobile phones at the training ground, one of many rules introduced to create a more strict working environment (it didn't bother me: at the time, I didn't have one) – and generous in equal quantities. No matter how good a player, whether a Michael Owen or a young reserve, a word of praise in the ear puts an extra spring in the step. Houllier recognized the importance of polishing a player's ego when needed, while at the same time condemning those who weren't performing. Paul Ince can vouch for this. He was the unwitting victim of the most brutal exhibition of management I've seen at Anfield.

Manchester United cast a shadow over Liverpool throughout the 1990s and beyond, and for me they inadvertently thread the two halves of Houllier's story together: my faith in him grew following a heartbreaking fixture against United in 1999, and evaporated on the eve of the short trip to Old Trafford five years later. Reputations can grow or die on the basis of trips to Old Trafford. Score the winning goal or play a blinder and you'll be remembered for ever; endure a nightmare and you can irreversibly lose the fans' and manager's trust. Houllier arrived with a plan to confront what he perceived as the strongest, most disruptive personalities at the club. Not even the captain would be free to assert his authority any more. By the time he left, his position had been undermined because our inspirational new skipper was brave enough to speak on behalf of everyone at the club and question his judgement. In both instances, meetings with United were the catalyst for a symbolic shift in power.

The first of these pivotal fixtures was a fourth round FA Cup tie in January 1999. I've mentioned this was a key date for personal reasons. Professionally it was equally significant. Halfway through the second half, with Liverpool leading 1–0, Ince limped off with an injury. United fought back to win 2–1. Our season was effectively over.

A week later, a team meeting was called during which Houllier tried to keep our heads up and set objectives for the final difficult months of a traumatic campaign. Ince had some issues of his own he wanted to raise, and as club captain he decided it was time to take on Houllier.

'We're not training properly,' he said. 'The strikers haven't been doing enough finishing practice.'

Houllier's response was furiously impressive. In an instant he reeled off the dates and times the strikers had been called in for shooting exercises. Michael Owen and Robbie Fowler confirmed the accuracy of Houllier's memory. Then he turned to Ince.

'Since the day I arrived, how many five-a-sides have you won?' he asked. 'I'll tell you. It's four in six months.'

Ince was bewildered, as we all were, by Houllier's memory and grasp of detail. Most players wouldn't remember how many five-a-sides they'd played in training in a season, let alone how many they'd won or lost. And the manager wasn't finished.

'Now, maybe you'd like to explain to all the lads what happened to you at Manchester United last week?'

If you think the atmosphere at Anfield on a European night is electric, you could have lit the stadium floodlights with the vibes in that team meeting.

'When my Liverpool team is 1–0 up at Old Trafford in a cup tie, I don't expect my captain to limp off with an injury,' Houllier continued. 'If he has to come off the pitch, I expect it to be on a stretcher because he needs to go to hospital in an ambulance.'

Incey had no response.

As Mo and I left the room, he turned to me and said what I was thinking: 'What a manager we've got here.' We were both in a state of shock.

Ince was one of those sold before the start of the next season. To me, it was a sign of a gifted manager that he was prepared to sacrifice a star player for what he perceived as the greater good of the team. I liked Incey and looked up to him. I saw him as a mentor because we'd played in the same position, me for England Under-21s and he for the senior national side. But even the regard in which I held him couldn't prevent me being impressed with our no-nonsense new boss.

This was the first but by no means last occasion on which Houllier pulled players when they were out of line. He didn't care about their reputation. In Ince's case, the fact he was such a strong personality gave Gérard the ideal opportunity to show who was in control. But there was no favouritism or honeymoon period for any recently signed player either. Our German full-back Markus Babbel was once summoned in front of the squad to explain remarks he'd made in a newspaper claiming he was being played out of position and should be a centre-half. Babbel had just arrived from Bayern Munich with a huge reputation, but he knew within a few weeks Houllier wouldn't let him get away with any misdemeanour.

'Respect your team-mates when you talk to journalists,' Houllier told him. 'How do you think Sami Hyypia and Stéphane Henchoz felt reading this rubbish?'

It was precisely what the club needed. The joint-manager experiment had failed. We knew there was only one boss now.

Pre-season was especially inspiring under Houllier. He'd detail the plan for the year over a series of days in our Swiss training camp. No player could have been left confused about what was expected on and off the pitch. Team meetings were Houllier's forte. He was a charismatic speaker. One day he'd lecture us on the type of football we'd play; the next, discussion would focus on our behaviour off the park and how we looked after ourselves. Then there would be long speeches about what we should and shouldn't say to the press. When Gary McAllister signed in 2000 he said he was amazed by this meticulous preparation. That was a considerable compliment from such an experienced player.

On the training ground it was a less hands-on approach. When I describe Houllier, the word 'manager' is crucial. The difference between Houllier and Benitez is Rafa is an out-and-out coach while Gérard oversaw a management structure. Whereas Rafa handles every training session and all aspects of how his side plays, Houllier delegated coaching responsibilities. He would be on the training pitch, but observing rather than instructing. I'm not sure what a technical manager or director of football is, but I suspect Houllier is the ideal fit for the term.

I recently read Clive Woodward's autobiography where he talked about how he led the English rugby team to World Cup victory. I could see similarities in how he and Houllier worked. As long as the right people were around him, Woodward could bring out the most from their talents. We too had a series of specialist coaches who reported directly to the manager. At first Patrice Bergues was the chief coach, with Sammy Lee assisting him; Phil Thompson looked after the defenders and Joe Corrigan was our goalkeeper coach. Later, Ian Rush was appointed specifically to work with the strikers.

The problem with such a system is the manager is at the mercy of the quality of his staff. How they perform reflects well or badly on him. Bergues was a top coach, but when he left to manage Lens in 2001 his replacements, Jacques Crevoisier and Christiano Damiano, never commanded the same respect. This impacted worse on Houllier than on the individuals concerned when public judgements were made.

At the top of the structure, Houllier was the organizer, man-manager and inspiration, casting an all-knowing eye over every strand of Liverpool Football Club. While his backroom staff kept their side of the bargain on the training pitch, he was free to rebuild the club and get into the minds of his players. For a while, his gaze appeared firmly fixed on turning me into a model professional. If players such as Ince were beyond salvation in Houllier's eyes, others were treated more like prodigal sons if they stepped out of line, as long as they were prepared to learn their lesson. Youth and inexperience were on my side when I made mistakes, but the warnings were clear, particularly when it came to one recurring touchy subject.

Alcohol was a topic close to Houllier's heart. He was determined to keep it away from our livers. 'If you drink too much you'll be finished by the time you're twenty-six,' was his message on the bottle. He was appalled by what he perceived as a drinking culture in England. He saw my career as an alcohol-related accident waiting to happen. He provided me with lists of players who'd peaked in their early twenties but he felt hadn't looked after their bodies in the right way. Paul Gascoigne was the example he'd use most, but Robbie Fowler was never far from Gérard's thoughts when discussing the perils of the demon drink. Niggling injuries, Houllier argued, were a consequence of over-indulgence and poor diet. He even named Roy Keane as a victim of excess drinking, arguing he'd be an even better player if he stayed in the right condition.

I once turned up for training stinking of stale beer and he demanded to know where I'd been and who I'd been with.

'I just went for a few bevvies with my dad,' I told him.

He was outraged.

'Your dad?' he screamed. 'I can't believe that!'

Gérard, who hadn't met my dad yet, could not grasp the idea of a player drinking not only with his family's permission, but with their encouragement. After this, he took a peculiar interest in my personal life.

Most youngsters get teased by their mates or their mum and dad about finding a girl. In my case it was Houllier who was fixated with getting me hooked up and settled down. His theory was the sooner I had a steady girlfriend, the less likely I would be to go out on the lash with the lads. 'Have you met anyone yet, Jamie?' he would often enquire. I'm surprised he didn't go as far as trying to set me up. Sometimes I'd lie and say I'd been on a date so he wouldn't think I'd been out drinking after a game, only to tell him the mythical female 'wasn't my type' a few weeks later. He must have been thinking I'd gone through more girlfriends than Georgie Best by the time I met my wife Nicola, but it was all to cover my tracks.

In his defence, I gave him plenty of reasons to be worried.

The Liverpool players' Christmas party of 1998, for instance, took me from relative national obscurity to the front page of the *News of the World*. The tabloids presented it as another example of professional footballers abusing their wealth and fame. Naturally, this was hugely overplayed. It wasn't much of a story when you broke it down. A twenty-one-year-old Scouser gets bladdered on a festive work night out and ends up getting caught in a compromising position with a stripper.

OK, throw in some of England's World Cup heroes and it becomes a bit juicier.

The pictures of me in a Quasimodo costume working my way through a variety of angles with the naked woman in question didn't exactly help. And the hump wasn't just on my back, unfortunately. Overall, though, I think the newspaper's editor must have been gutted they caught only me with my pants down. Had it been Michael Owen or Paul Ince, it wouldn't have been the first five pages of the paper covering the story but the whole edition.

In fact, Mo had been concerned on my behalf within minutes of the 'incident'.

The venue was a pub called the Pen and Wig in Liverpool city centre. It has since made the most out of the notoriety of that evening by turning itself into a lapdancing bar, probably because the punters thought the stuff we got up to was a weekly occurrence. I'm surprised they didn't put a plaque up on the spot where I made my mark. Mo spotted an elderly couple in the corner acting suspiciously and figured they were either reporters or perverts – or, as is often the case with those covering such stories, both. When he went over to speak to them he found a camera. He went berserk and smashed it, but it wasn't the lucky escape we'd hoped. The paper had their spies.

'This is a set-up,' Mo said to me. He was right, and there were a few casualties as a result as suspicious fingers were wagged all over the place.

Houllier tried to pin it on my friend Willie Miller, a well-known comedian and radio DJ from Liverpool who organized our Christmas parties, but there was no way he was responsible. Willie wouldn't have done that to the lads, and if there was one player more than any he wouldn't stitch up, it was me. He could have earned far more over many years by targeting bigger names, but he never has. I felt really sorry for Willie because Houllier wouldn't allow him into Melwood for a while afterwards.

On Boxing Day we were heading back on the coach from an away game in Middlesbrough when one of the lads received a call from a mate that they had who worked in the media. It was the news we'd all been dreading. The player had heard every line of the article due to appear in the *News of the World* from his journalist friend.

'What's the story?' I asked him.

'Sorry, mate, it's all about you,' he replied.

I waited at a garage until midnight for the first edition of the Sunday papers so I could check the damage. It was bad, but also funny.

I warned my mum and dad about it, but I wonder what kind of elaborate excuses the lads used on their wives that Sunday morning. I expect every copy of the *News of the World* on Merseyside mysteriously disappeared. Though the cameras focused on me, in one shot you could clearly see another player in fancy dress lying on his back with a semi-naked girl and a smile on his face . . . in that order. Part of the article also referred to a player dressed as Ainsley Harriott getting it on with a stripper in a corner of the bar. I bet the lad responsible spent hours convincing his wife more than one of us was dressed as a big black celebrity chef. My mum, who was working in a pub the next day, took far more stick about it than I did. I felt sorry for her more than for myself, though I'm sure it was all good-natured banter.

I was still just about single at the time. Fortunately my future wife Nicola, who I'd been on a few dates with, and her family saw the funny side. It was the kind of stunt every young footballer has been 'forced' into by senior players for fifty years and more, and I can assure you such rituals still go on, even if the Christmas party at Anfield was a more sober occasion for a while afterwards.

I was dreading going into training the next morning. Predictably, Gérard and Thommo called me straight into their office at Melwood.

Any worries I had were swiftly eased. Both were laughing.

'Don't worry, son,' said Thommo, 'I've been there.'

For the sake of Phil's wife Marge, can I add at this point I don't think he meant this literally.

Houllier then told me he'd give me a lift to Anfield, where we were training. Thommo walked out of the office and the smiling stopped. In the car to the stadium, Houllier gave me one of his prepared sermons.

'There are six players at this club who I rate and who I want as part of the team next season,' he said to me. 'You, Michael, Gerrard, Berger, [Vegard] Heggem and Redknapp will stay. If you're going to be with me, you've got to be more careful.'

I'd like to say I listened to Houllier and never stepped out of line again, but it didn't quite work that way.

Privately, I was concerned a previous incident with a stripper might come to light. A couple of months earlier I'd been in a pub on the Dock Road in Liverpool with my friends Gary 'Siggy' Seagraves, John 'Pritch' Pritchard and a couple of exotic dancers. Pritch was all over a stripper with a face like a smacked arse when he decided to take off his jacket, revealing one of my 'Carragher 23' Liverpool shirts. It was funny at the time, but it wouldn't have been such a laugh if it had come to light immediately after the infamous party. I lived in fear for months that another old couple had been sitting in the corner with a hidden camera that night and were biding their time before providing the Sunday papers with a tasty follow-up. God knows how Gérard would have reacted.

Although my performances on the pitch throughout that 1998–99 season won me the club player of the year award, trouble followed me off it. When Paul Ince organized a thirtieth birthday party for his wife in the leafy suburb of Heswall on the Wirral, he didn't cater for the arrival of the lads from Bootle. We'd been watching the England versus Poland European qualifier in town and had been drinking all afternoon. I turned up worse for wear with Siggy and Pritch and instantly caused mayhem, for some reason believing it was a good idea to act like a pisshead. Inevitably we were thrown out, at which point one of the guests' luxury cars paid for our frustration and was given a bit of a kicking. The police arrived quicker than an LA SWAT team and instantly pounced on me and Siggy, but Pritch managed to do a runner.

'Name?' asked the policeman.

'Paul Carragher,' I replied.

As I spoke, Pritch reappeared, having decided bluffing was a better escape route than hiding behind a bush in the hope the police dogs wouldn't sniff him out. He approached the policeman and, for reasons only he can explain, decided to speak in the worst fake posh Wirral accent I've heard.

'Hello, officer. I hope there isn't any trouble here. I was dropping off my girlfriend and heard quite a commotion.' Unaccustomed to this new vocabulary he stumbled through his words while trying to stop his legs wobbling.

The copper didn't need to be Columbo, or the help of one of his tracker dogs, to smell the bullshit.

'Where do you live?' he asked.

As interrogations go, this wasn't the most intense in

Merseyside criminal history. It didn't need to be. Unfortunately, when you've taken a taxi from Bootle to Heswall but you're under the misapprehension you're somewhere else, even this question can finish you off.

'I just live around the corner . . . in Chester,' said Pritch.

'Get in the car,' replied the copper.

Pritch wasn't finished.

'I'm not speaking to anyone else until I've seen a solicitor,' he said.

'Who do you want?' asked the copper.

'Can you get me Rex Makin?' blagged Pritch, demanding the attention of the best-known legal man in Liverpool.

We woke up with bad heads in a Wirral police cell a few hours later.

'You've got Rex Makin on the phone,' Pritch was told.

'Ah, forget it,' he said.

By now the coppers had realized I wasn't my brother. I had some explaining to do the following Monday, not only to Houllier but to the club's chief executive Peter Robinson. The club solicitor, Kevin Dooley, was an expert at keeping stories out of the papers. 'I've just come from Everton,' he told me. 'One of their star players has been caught with his pants down again. I've managed to stop the press running it.' He didn't have the same luck with me, although he tried to convince the club the story was exaggerated as part of an anti-Liverpool agenda in the national papers. Not quite. My biggest concern was explaining to Houllier why I hadn't taken my latest non-existent girlfriend to Ince's party, as promised. 'She was there but left early,' I lied.

Houllier's patience had its limits. In November 1999 he dropped me from the squad away to Sunderland in the

Premiership after a fan rang the club to say he'd seen me drinking with Robbie Fowler on the afternoon of the England v. Scotland European Championship qualifier.

We were hardly inconspicuous.

We'd headed off to watch the match in the Bureau Bar with our mate James Culshaw. James had a unique party piece he liked to show off with after a few pints which ensured we'd stand out in a crowd: he'd take off his mechanical leg and put it on the bar. Given the right encouragement he would use it to kick everything in sight, including any passing lamppost. From our perspective it was an hysterical scene, but I suppose a few Liverpool fans found it all a bit too much to see two star players encouraging a disabled lad to kick streetlights, especially if they didn't know he was our friend.

'But Gérard, I wasn't the one who was legless,' I pleaded.

For Houllier, these incidents were becoming too frequent. One of my closest friends in the Liverpool squad at the time, David Thompson, was getting the same warnings as me. The more scrapes he got in to, the more he was edged towards the exit door. Eventually he was pushed through it. The implications were obvious. I was bailing myself out by performing well on the pitch, but if I lost form I was giving the manager a ready-made excuse not only to drop me but to move me on.

In February 1999 I was suspended after a harsh sending-off at Charlton, and the way the fixtures worked out I wouldn't play for forty days. Houllier was so concerned I'd hit the booze he ordered me in for double training sessions, morning and afternoon. Forty days and forty nights deprived of first-team football and drink – an appropriate number, you might say, for my period in the wilderness.

I'm sure Houllier would have sent me to a desert to keep me

away from temptation at that point in my career. 'Don't go to nightclubs while you're a player,' he'd plead. 'Buy one when you've retired.' (I'm sure he's proud to know it's a healthy-eating sports café I've bought instead.) But any fears he had about regular drinking were exaggerated. I'm a social drinker only, although there's never been such a hobby as 'going for a couple of drinks' in my world. If I say I'm going out, it's for the full pelt. When I hit the ale, it's not for the taste of it, it's to wind down and get bladdered. I had a reputation as a drinker when I was younger because of the skirmishes that made the papers, but that's because when I did go for it there were no half measures, so to speak. If a supporter saw me on a genuine night out, there was a good chance I'd had too much to drink. It only needed a couple of incidents like this to create an impression, but you won't find any alcohol in my house, nor will you ever catch me having a glass of wine with a meal. I'm not a heavy drinker. Nights out on the alcohol have become increasingly rare, and I never touch a drop in the week of a game. I'm not going to say I never drink during a season, of course I do, but I'm far more sensible in my attitude to alcohol these days. Doctors may say otherwise, but it's far better for a player to go on the lash properly a few times a season than to hit the drink casually every week.

I believe I'm one of the most professional players in the Premier League. I've become addicted to looking after myself off the pitch as much as on it, determined to add as many days to my playing career as possible. That's Houllier's influence. His words of advice have been carried out, and I'd pass them on to fellow professionals. I have regular massages and take more ice baths than any other player I've worked with. Some of my team-mates think I'm obsessed about staying in shape, but the speed with which I've returned from serious injuries shows how it has worked for me.

Undoubtedly I owe much of this healthier lifestyle to Houllier, but he was preaching to a young pupil who was easily converted. I learned my lessons under his spell, and on those occasions when I tried to kid him, he was never fooled. The last time I drank within a few days of a match was in November 2000, after we lost 4–3 at Leeds. Mark Viduka scored four, but I actually had a good game. I went out that night and had a terrible hangover the next day. The following Thursday Liverpool were playing in the Czech Republic against the mighty Slovan Liberec in the UEFA Cup. My performance was disgraceful and I was hooked off ten minutes into the second half.

'Are you ill, Jamie?' Houllier asked.

I reckon he was checking my breath to see if he could still smell beer, I was so poor.

He said nothing else, but he knew. He didn't need to drag me into his office to deliver another warning after this. I never again wanted to experience such a feeling on a football pitch, and it was clear to me as much as it was to Houllier what had caused it. My habits changed, and I began to feel the benefits physically. I became far better prepared for games when I didn't celebrate victories with drink, or drown my sorrows after defeats.

I'd often hear former Liverpool players slaughtering Houllier for stressing his anti-alcohol stance, but I came to recognize their views were outdated and lacked credibility. The fact that the Liverpool teams of the 1960s, 1970s and 1980s still produced great football while getting drunk every Saturday night ignores a key fact: all their opponents behaved in exactly the same way. You had twenty-two players all of whom had probably been on the ale a few days earlier, so it was a level playing field. Liverpool had the best players and they got away with it. In the 1990s Liverpool were too slow to change this culture, until Houllier took control.

I'm sure he saw me as a challenge. If he could make me change my ways, he knew others would follow my example. Within a couple of seasons, the days of me threatening to be on the front rather than back pages had long gone. I grew up under Houllier; he guided me down the right path. He cleaned up my act and ensured my long-term future at Anfield.

On my birthday in 2004, I asked Houllier for a round of applause before training.

'What for?' he said.

'I'm twenty-six today. Not finished yet, am I?'

But sorting my and the other players' lifestyles out was one thing; revolutionizing the club and bringing the title back was going to be tougher. Whenever I'm asked what Liverpool need to challenge Manchester United, Chelsea or Arsenal, my answer is always the same: 'Better players.' Every manager is judged on his signings. When Houllier bought well, he enjoyed good results, the team radically improved, the fans trusted him and so did his squad. There were a couple of duds during his early years, but he got more right than wrong, recruiting some of the most consistent performers in the club's recent history.

Centre-halves Stéphane Henchoz and Sami Hyypia, two of the seven signings in the summer of 1999, were spectacular successes. Sami was originally bought as a gamble, Houllier expecting him to cover for me. We began the 1999–2000 season together in central defence because Stéphane arrived from Blackburn with a groin injury. Henchoz, who cost £4.5 million, was seen as the more significant arrival; Sami, a £2.5 million Finnish defender from a Dutch side no one had heard of, wasn't carrying great expectations. I believed Stéphane would eventually replace Sami and we could form a long-term partnership.

Yet again, Manchester United intervened to send my career in a new direction. I scored two own-goals in our defeat at Anfield to United early in the season. Any faith Houllier had in me as a centre-back was gone for good.

There was nowhere for me to hide the night of that game, so I headed out of the city to Formby. I found a suitable pub, far away from supporters who wanted to discuss my rare double, sat down and called my dad.

'Where are you?' I asked.

'I'm in The Grapes in Formby, lad. Where are you?'

Call it the Carragher sixth sense. We'd both escaped to the same pub.

I knocked back a few ales like a condemned man. It would be five years before I was a central defender again.

I still find the haste with which Houllier changed his mind about my best position puzzling. My contribution the previous season seemed to be written off on the basis of one nightmare half. I'd won rave reviews at centre-back throughout 1998–99, despite having to cope alongside numerous defensive partners. I also played most of that campaign in pain after fracturing my wrist. I needed an operation which would keep me out for six weeks. After he heard the diagnosis, Houllier called me at home begging me not to have surgery. It was no hardship agreeing with him. Today, I still can't bend my wrist properly because the injury wasn't dealt with, but when the manager says you're the only centre-half at Liverpool he can rely on, you don't want to disappoint him. How quickly this was forgotten. I spent the next couple of years fighting for a place at left- and right-back.

I had few complaints at first because of Sami's immediate impact, which no one, including Houllier, had anticipated. It was a formality he and Stéphane would form a new partnership. But in later years when there were injuries or suspensions, I still wasn't considered a centre-back. Houllier would select Salif Diao, Igor Biscan or Djimi Traore ahead of me in the position, and just before he left the club he wanted to buy Jean-Alain Boumsong, and then Philippe Mexes from Auxerre, to play alongside Biscan. Phil Thompson would plead with Houllier to give me a chance back in the middle, but he was stubborn right until the last month of his reign, claiming I was a couple of inches too short for the role.

Another major player for us, arriving with Sami and Stéphane, was Dietmar Hamann, although his signing owed much to luck. While Didi was planning to sign for Arsenal from Newcastle, Houllier was targeting Marc Vivien Foe as Ince's replacement. The move broke down, and in Didi we ended up with one of the best holding midfielders in Europe, as well as a top man in the dressing room.

The signing I didn't rate was Sander Westerveld, who replaced David James. He wasn't my type of fella and we didn't see eye-to-eye. I thought he was an average goalkeeper who seemed to think he was Gordon Banks. A lot of Dutch players had a reputation for fancying themselves, and he lived up to it. Whenever he made a howler – and they became more frequent the longer he was at the club – he'd provide a strange excuse. One mistake at Middlesbrough was put down to ice on the ball, but his worst indiscretion was being out-jumped and out-muscled at a corner by little Dennis Wise at Chelsea. He claimed he was fouled. None of us was appealing for a free-kick.

Westerveld's missus wasn't shy to express her opinions when they weren't wanted, either. Shortly after my two own-goals against United, the players and our wives and girlfriends organized a meal at the Blue Bar on Liverpool's Albert Dock. Westerveld's wife suddenly decided she was some kind of spokesman for The Kop.

'You're a disgrace,' she said to me. 'The way you're playing I'm surprised you're happy to be seen out in public. You shouldn't be in the team.'

I gave her my sternest Bootle boy scowl and snarled, 'Fuck off back to Holland.'

If she thought I was bad, she and her husband must have been arguing constantly when he started throwing them in. Westerveld played his part in the treble season, but our defence was so good it wasn't difficult for him to look decent. There were games when he had nothing to do. It was no surprise to me when he was unceremoniously dumped by Houllier a couple of months after we won the cup treble. Many fans sympathized with him. I couldn't see why. A weak link had gone, but not quietly. When his replacement Jerzy Dudek endured problems of his own a year later, who was the first to run to the press to rub it in? Sander was at it again, which wouldn't have been so bad if his mate Markus Babbel wasn't still sorting him out tickets for the players' lounge after our home games.

'Markus, a word,' Phil Thompson said to Babbel. 'Tell your mate Sander he's not welcome at Anfield again.'

Certain signings concerned me because I thought they were useless, others because I was worried they'd keep me out of the team. Much as I respected Houllier, and despite his positive influence on me, I began suffering a recurring nightmare. I was convinced he'd force my future children to grow up without a Scouse accent. I'd wake up in a cold sweat at the prospect of young Carraghers returning to Bootle sounding like woollybacks or cockneys. Every summer for five years it seemed my future was in doubt. Full-backs came and went but I was never 100 per cent sure I'd survive the arrival of the next cross between Cafu and Paolo Maldini the fans were screaming for. Leaving Liverpool would have been bad enough, but the wider implications bothered me too. I'd think about which clubs I'd join, not in terms of their stature, more in terms of whether I'd have to abandon my Merseyside roots. Michael Owen has my sympathy, not only because he ended up at Newcastle but because he had to make his children go to school there. They might have Geordie accents, for God's sake. I couldn't handle that. I love home too much.

Managers like nothing more than talking about togetherness in a team, but there's no solidarity when a threat to your position arrives. Any manager expecting me to help someone he's bought to take my place is kidding himself. Every time Liverpool bought a full-back or central defender, my initial response was to make them look as physically and psychologically inferior to me as possible. They were my sworn enemies. There wasn't a hope they were going to walk off the training pitch having played better than me, or having beaten me in five-a-side. It's still the case. I've got to overshadow them by any means. If there's a fifty-fifty challenge to be had, I don't give a shit about that either, no matter how much they've cost. This is my Liverpool shirt we're talking about. No one is waltzing into Melwood and taking it off me without a fight.

The same applies the other way, of course. Several players have arrived believing they could undermine my position.

After I established myself at right-back, our African defender Rigobert Song found himself out of the team and our previously healthy relationship instantly deteriorated. One morning in training he was told I'd been called into the England squad after performing well at full-back. There was a look of astonishment on Song's face, a bit like the one I used to give him when he claimed he was only twenty-one. He might as well have blurted out he thought I wasn't good enough for international football. He strolled off to his French-speaking friends and began talking to them. I could see him pointing towards me while everyone was grinning. It was clear what he was saying, and the rage inside me simmered.

Later, Song walked on to the training pitch with a smile on his face. He was limping off it with a grimace an hour later. The first chance I got, I did him. Never have I hunted down a fifty-fifty tackle with greater appetite.

'You're not fucking laughing now are you, you soft twat?' I said as he hobbled away.

Did I care if he had a knock? No way. I don't remember him, or anyone else in the squad for that matter, trying to take the piss out of my ability again.

As I said, new rivals for my position arrived every summer. The closest I came to leaving was in 2003 when Steve Finnan joined the club. I joked in the papers I might have to send the boys round to Steve's house if he took my place. The fans presumed I was joking. I was, but only partly. I was genuinely worried I'd be left out, and I wasn't prepared to stay at Liverpool as a sub. Supporters think because you love a club you'll hang around as a squad player. I wouldn't. I love playing football first and foremost. I'm not the type to have sat on the bench regularly during my peak years. I'd have left. Absolutely.

The list of full-backs Houllier brought in as direct competition was endless. I'd seen off Song, Babbel and Christian Ziege, but still the manager was looking for an alternative. John Arne Riise signed from Monaco with a reputation for goals. In one of his most surprising deals, Houllier even bought Abel Xavier from

Everton. For a very brief spell I wondered if I could be bothered to prove myself any more. It became tiresome heading into every new season with the same cloud hanging over me, fighting a constant battle for security. Finnan, who later proved a great signing for us even if I didn't welcome him at the time, nearly broke my resolve by doing nothing more than walking into Melwood.

I was aware of interest from other clubs, though it went no further than that, fortunately. I doubt the club would have accepted any offer for me had one been made, but I was getting so demoralized I might have taken the decision for them, simply to get a bit of appreciation elsewhere. Some of our own supporters were contributing to my despair. They were watching Arsenal with their rampaging full-backs and expecting me to transform myself into Ashley Cole. They pigeonholed me as a limited player, and it's a reputation that stuck.

These myths start early, and even ten years at the top can't shake them. I've heard for over a decade how Rio Ferdinand is an elegant passer of the ball who starts attacks from the back. He must have hit a sixty-yard pass when he was seventeen because I haven't seen much evidence since. Ferdinand is a top defender, but he's been served well by his friends in the media continually describing him as some kind of modern Franz Beckenbauer.

It works the other way too. What image do you have of Roy Keane? A tough-tackling midfielder? I also rated him as one of the best passers of the ball in the game. No one emphasized that, but there weren't many times I saw him give it away.

I had one big weakness whether I was playing left- or right-back, and that was my crossing. People said my all-round distribution was poor, but I resented this. You can't play for years at full-back if you can't pass. You get exposed. Full-back is the one position on the park where you've so much time in possession your passing has to be of a good standard. There's no hiding place. Numerous players have been used in the role over the years who were shown to be dreadful passers. Look at Stéphane. He lasted a game in the position. What about Josemi? He struggled to find a team-mate six yards away. Djimi Traore had the same weakness. How many players have moved from centre-half to full-back and then become an England international? I wasn't getting the credit I felt I deserved at my own club.

One fan wrote to the *Liverpool Echo* every week for months with the same criticism of me, claiming I was a weak link. Eventually my dad had read enough and was determined to find the culprit.

'I'm sorry, we're not allowed to give out that kind of private information,' a reporter informed him during his first attempt.

Time for plan B.

My dad called the paper again and said he'd been living in Australia for the last twenty years and wanted to meet up with his old school friend. He said he'd seen his name in the *Echo* in a letter about Jamie Carragher and needed his phone number so he could make a surprise call. The paper agreed, gave him the details, and a few minutes later my critic got the biggest shock of his life. Suffice to say, the letters stopped after that.

I've endured some bad times during my Liverpool career, but I haven't felt much worse than I did during a home game with Fulham in April 2003. I'd asked Houllier if the rumours we were signing Finnan were true, and he fobbed me off by denying it. The fans obviously didn't believe him because Finnan was given a warm reception when he arrived in a Fulham shirt. He took a throw-in by The Kop and they stood up and applauded. That was fair enough. If he'd played any other position, maybe I'd have reacted the same way. When you know a player is joining, you want to show him support. From my perspective, however, it was a personal slight. I'd been determined to outshine Finnan that day, and I was named man of the match. I wanted to hear supporters saying we don't need another right-back because we've got Carra, but the enthusiasm for Finnan suggested no one was worried about my future at the club.

By then I was getting tired of hearing about how Liverpool's weakness was a lack of attacking full-backs. On the day Finnan signed, it seemed even Houllier was putting the boot in. 'In the modern game, it's important for a full-back to be able to attack,' he said at the press conference.

'You cheeky bastard!' I shouted at the television.

His observation was right, but we'd done nothing on the training ground to improve my attacking capabilities, even though I was desperate to work on this side of my game. If Houllier wanted me to attack more, why was 100 per cent of my practice focused on defence?

After all the hype surrounding Ziege, Riise and Finnan as 'modern' full-backs, I stormed into Houllier's office.

'Do you want me to go forward more?' I demanded to know.

'No, Jamie, I want you to continue to focus on what you do best, which is defending.'

He was contradicting himself, telling me one view and the press another.

The supporters and players knew we lacked width, but it was too simplistic to point the finger at the full-backs. The problem wasn't simply my lack of natural attacking instinct, it was the imbalance in our side. Under Houllier we used a series of wide men who preferred to play in-field. Danny Murphy, Vladimir Smicer, Patrik Berger and Nick Barmby all began as central players who were asked to move to the flanks. Each of them would have loved a rampaging, overlapping full-back. What I wanted was an out-and-out winger I could feed the ball to and watch running up and down the line for ninety minutes. The combinations were wrong, not just the players. Harry Kewell arrived from Leeds United at the same time as Finnan and it was hoped the problem of lack of width would be solved. What did Houllier do? He played the left-winger on the right, so instead of staying on the flank Kewell would cut inside on his favourite foot.

Playing week in, week out, you get a sense of where the problems in the side are, but often you get an even greater insight when you step away and watch the team from the sidelines. It's not an option I'd ever choose, but in 2003–04 circumstances dictated I had more time than I wanted watching rather than playing for Liverpool. And I had Lucas Neill to thank for that: my leg was broken following his horrific tackle at Ewood Park on 13 September 2003.

People often claim I tried to play on with the injury, but I hate that. I wasn't being courageous. I genuinely didn't know how serious the knock was until hours later. I thought I could run it off. My problem at the time was that Milan Baros had snapped his ankle a few minutes earlier, so by the time I was carried off our brilliant club doctor, Mark Waller, wasn't around. I had to be treated by a physio from Blackburn who seemed more interested in telling jokes than dealing with my pain. My dad knew I wouldn't come off the pitch unless there was a serious problem, although by the time he reached the treatment room he was as concerned about getting his hands – or his fists – on Neill.

Houllier and Thommo were as angry on my behalf, but the argument that followed between Liverpool and Blackburn got out of hand. I'm sure the existing bad blood between the respective coaching staffs – a consequence of Thommo's sacking by Souness years earlier – contributed to the ferocity of the attacks on Neill. I didn't want to be used as an excuse to have another go at Souness, who was entitled to offer as much support as he could to his own player. Besides, I like Souness and have a lot of respect for him. Neill, on the other hand . . .

I didn't contribute to the animosity in the press, but my mates were ready to hunt him down if I gave the go-ahead. A few weeks later, I received a phone call.

'You won't believe this, Jay. We're in the Trafford Centre and Lucas Neill is walking straight towards us. What do you reckon?'

Did I really want Neill to take a crack?

'There's only one problem,' added the voice. 'He's got little Davey Thommo with him.'

That was that. I could hardly let one of my best mates, David Thompson, now a Blackburn player, become a witness to an assault; besides, he'd have recognized the attackers. The impromptu mission was aborted, and I sent a text to Thommo telling him Neill should be giving him a hug of thanks. As word got back to Blackburn about the near miss, or should that be hit, their coach Terry Darracott – a Scouser – appealed to one of my friends to 'call the boys off'. I agreed, so the Australian never felt the full force of a Bootle revenge mission.

Neill almost had the last laugh when Rafa Benitez tried to sign him twice during the 2006–07 season. Our interest in him annoyed me. We only pursued him as a squad player. He wasn't the type who'd be able to turn Liverpool into a Premiership-winning side, and of all the defenders available I couldn't understand why we were chasing him. Neill had the cheek to turn us down for West Ham. I was pleased.

Unexpectedly, the spell out of action improved my game. While the leg was mending I had time to rethink my style of play, and I returned a much more attacking full-back. This was no consolation to Houllier. The injury came at the worst possible time for him as speculation surrounding his future grew.

I was never appreciated more by the supporters or the manager than when I wasn't available. My reputation improved. The fans began to see how much I added to the defence. Houllier offered me a new contract while my leg was in plaster, and spoke in glowing terms about me in the papers, underlining how much I'd be missed. It must be said, this didn't go down so well with other players. John Arne Riise said he felt undermined hearing how the defenders weren't coping without me. I'd have felt the same way, but from a personal point of view I'd never felt more secure at the club than when I was injured.

I was determined to return as soon as possible, and formed something of a private duel with Baros to beat him back into action. Four months later, on 21 January 2004, I made my comeback against Wolves at Molineux, a month quicker than the Czech forward. Sadly, I was jumping back on board Houllier's rapidly sinking ship. The positivity of his first years in charge had started to fade, and he was now desperately trying to save his job.

It was a tragedy for him. If Houllier hadn't fallen seriously ill he might still be Liverpool's manager today.

The turning point of his reign was 13 October 2001, when Liverpool met Leeds United in the Premiership. Early in the second half I looked towards our bench and noticed he wasn't there. The seriousness of the situation only became apparent in the dressing room later. Houllier had been rushed to Broadgreen Hospital for heart surgery after collapsing at half-time. For twenty-four hours none of us knew if he'd survive. The prospect of him continuing as manager was secondary to him returning alive.

The way Phil Thompson and Sammy Lee handled the crisis in the days and months that followed remains one of the most underrated periods of this era. They were admirable, Thommo especially impressive after he was thrust into the limelight after three years in the background. There was a faultless changeover when he stepped up and took the reins, even though it was only temporary. The circumstances were appalling, but I could see he was enjoying the new responsibility. I know many of the lads preferred Thommo in his role as a caretaker manager.

I liked Thommo and was thrilled when he walked back into Melwood following Roy Evans's departure. He was a Scouser, he was a centre-half, and I knew we'd share similar views on how the game should be played. His introduction wasn't welcomed in some parts of the dressing room as much as it was by me. There were one or two lads who'd played under Thompson for the reserves before he was sacked by Souness, and when they heard news of his return they reacted as if they'd suffered a family bereavement. Thommo's reputation under Souness wasn't so good, but he proved a lot of doubters wrong in the years that followed, particularly during those five months as caretaker boss. As a former player, issues that might have been difficult for other coaches were no hassle to him. If a player was left out, he'd explain the reasons. Just like Houllier, he wouldn't think twice about slaughtering anyone who deserved it in private, but publicly he wouldn't have a bad word to say about us.

This public support was often needed, especially following the 'magic coin' scandal at Highbury in the FA Cup that season. An Arsenal fan threw a coin at me as I was taking a throw-in, so I picked it up and threw it back. There were about thirty-eight thousand fans in the crowd that day, but I think only five of them failed to make an insurance claim. Every day a new supporter was in the paper pointing to the bruise I'd given them as the coin bounced off one head on to another. Thommo backed me up, but I had to apologize and take my medicine.

It wasn't only opposing fans he had to protect me from. Danny Murphy and I took abuse from the crowd during a home game against Southampton in January 2002, and Thommo instantly stepped in on our behalf. I told someone in the Main Stand to fuck off, which earned me a rap on the knuckles behind the scenes, but Thommo willingly supported us in the papers. Houllier did the same, calling us to make sure we kept our heads up. A few days later we beat Manchester United 1–0 at Old Trafford, and Danny grabbed the winner, so their pep talks worked.

There was little hint things would go so badly wrong at this stage, especially not so rapidly. Houllier was on the mend, and increasingly dictating events from his hospital bed. Early in March 2002 he was smuggled into Anfield on the morning of a match with Newcastle and gave another inspiring team talk. 'We're going to win the League,' Didi Hamann said to me after the stirring speech. Houllier made us believe it.

Maybe he could see the impact his return had on us, particularly on an emotional evening against Roma on 19 March, when he officially made his comeback and sat in the dug-out. We needed to beat the Italians 2–0 to reach the quarter-final of the Champions League. Houllier was introduced to a crescendo of noise at Anfield, and from that point on the result was never in doubt. His brash statement declaring we were 'ten games from greatness' prior to our next European meeting, with Bayer

Leverkusen, backfired terribly when we unexpectedly crashed out, but we were bidding for a Premiership and European double, and he wanted us to believe.

This was only a mild error. Even though the 2001–02 season ended without silverware, we finished second to a brilliant Arsenal team and seemed to have made giant strides in the League, closing the gap and finishing above Manchester United for the first time in ten years. We felt tantalizingly close. The serious mistakes were still to come.

In the summer of 2002, Houllier told me about two exciting new signings from Senegal, urging me to watch their opening World Cup match with France. The names El-Hadji Diouf and Salif Diao now make the legs of the toughest Liverpudlians shudder in fear.

Their reputation at Anfield was never greater than when Senegal beat France 1–0. Diao outplayed Patrick Vieira in midfield, while Diouf led the forward line. For the rest of the summer Liverpool fans were hailing a transfer coup – but not as much as Houllier himself.

I arrived for pre-season training much anticipating my first glimpse of the players who'd turn us into title winners. I returned home the same evening in a state of depression.

The first concern I had with Diouf was his pace. He didn't have any. He was signed as an alternative to Nicolas Anelka, who'd been controversially released after a successful six-month loan spell. I didn't disagree with this. Anelka was excellent, but too similar to Mo for my taste, especially for his price. I wanted a striker who'd play deeper to complement Michael. After a few training sessions with Diouf, however, I'd have walked to Man City to get Anelka back.

Do you remember being at school and picking sides for a game of football? We do this at Liverpool for the five-a-sides. Diouf was 'last pick' within a few weeks.

'You paid ten million for him and no one wants him in their team,' I shouted to Gérard. 'Says it all.'

He didn't react. He knew he'd made a mistake.

I asked Houllier why he'd bought him and he trotted off a story about Patrice Bergues, our former assistant manager, recommending the player. Bergues was now at Lens, the club that sold him to Liverpool for £10 million. Was I alone in thinking Patrice might have been thinking more about the transfer fee than Liverpool when he told his mate to sign Diouf?

In all my years at Anfield, I've never met a player who seemed to care less about winning or losing. An FA Cup defeat at Portsmouth in February 2004 effectively sealed Houllier's fate months before his sacking, and there was a desolate scene at Melwood the following day. No one was more distressed than Mo, who'd missed a penalty at Fratton Park. As he arrived at the training ground with his head down, Diouf drove in with his rave music blaring out of his car, then danced his way across the car park into the building. You'd think we'd won the cup the way he carried on.

His attitude disgusted me.

If Diouf was a disappointment, Diao was a catastrophe. He couldn't pass, was a liability when he tackled, and never looked capable of scoring a goal. And they were his good qualities. A few years into his Anfield career he was jogging around Melwood with me when he piped up with some bombshell news.

'What do Liverpool fans think about Everton?' he asked.

I thought it was a bit strange given he'd been with us a while.

'Why?' I asked.

'They've been in touch with my agent. Do you think the

Liverpool fans will be upset with me if I sign for Everton?'

So excited was I by this question, I even convinced myself the rivalry between the Reds and Blues was over-hyped in a forlorn bid to talk him into the move.

'Not a problem,' I told him. 'If you go to Everton they'll love you for turning your back on Liverpool and the Liverpool fans will wish you every success. You should go for it, mate. Go on. Sign for them. It would be a big mistake not to. You will, won't you? Promise me you will. Go on. Please.'

Sadly, I wasn't as convincing as I'd hoped, and Diao never made the magical move to Goodison.

But even he wasn't the worst arrival of this hideous summer. Houllier also signed Bruno Cheyrou, which left me scratching my head for months. Yet again, Liverpool signed a central midfielder who didn't have the athleticism, strength or quality to play in this position in English football. He would end up on the flanks, where he lacked the pace to make an impact. Of all the signings, Cheyrou baffled me most. And the more Houllier tried to talk him up in the press, the more embarrassing it became.

Cheyrou and Diao were perfectly decent lads around the training ground, and I felt sorry for them as they struggled on. The issue I had was they should never have been signed, and that was the manager's fault.

I started to compare Houllier's record in the transfer market to Wenger's, and it became clear the Arsenal manager had much more success, particularly with French players. Houllier paid £10 million for Emile Heskey when Wenger paid the same for Thierry Henry. While Liverpool were dividing Merseyside to snatch Nick Barmby from Everton for £6 million, Robert Pires was arriving at Arsenal for the same money. Liverpool paid

£500,000 for Djimi Traore while Wenger spent half a million on Kolo Toure. Had our scout reports been mixed up?

An impressive opening to the 2002–03 season papered over the cracks. Our purchases had weakened not strengthened us. After nine wins and three draws we were on the verge of beating a Premier League record. All we had to do when we travelled to Middlesbrough for our thirteenth game of the season was avoid defeat and we'd be rewriting a small piece of history. I should have been thinking we were at the start of a title-winning campaign. Instead, I was more convinced than ever the downward slide was beginning.

Houllier's team at the Riverside demonstrated how much he was losing sight of the main objective. For the first time in years, Danny Murphy was asked to play in 'the hole' behind the striker in a negative 4–4–1–1 formation. We didn't have a shot all match, and lost to a late Gareth Southgate goal. Had we drawn 0–0 I'd have been livid, but I'm convinced Houllier would have been celebrating the Premiership record. That mattered to him more than the three points.

We were still capable of turning over the top sides on our day, but consistency eluded us. The 2003 League Cup Final, when we outplayed Manchester United to win our fourth major trophy under Houllier, proved a temporary stay of execution. It probably bought the manager an extra season, which in retrospect was a mistake. Our League form was dismal, and even lesser European sides were beating us in the Champions League and UEFA Cup. This was accompanied by an increasingly worrying proneness to denial by the manager, who refused to appreciate the seriousness of our slide. 'Why has Houllier started to talk so much shite?' Liverpool fans began to ask me after each press conference. After once believing everything he said, privately even I couldn't defend him now.

The illness was the biggest factor in Houllier's demise, but he also reached a stage where he became curiously obsessed with the team's press coverage. I once caught Houllier sitting with a pad and paper trying to name a team of eleven ex-Liverpool players working in the media.

'Can you think of any I've left out, Carra?' he asked me.

I walked away, thinking there were far more important issues to grapple with than what the papers and former players were saying. After several years during which every decision was vindicated, Houllier felt untouchable, so he dealt badly with media criticism. Unfortunately for him, the Liverpool fans would not be fooled. They watched wretched performances and felt even worse when they heard interviews talking about shots on goal or the number of corners the team had won. We were all sick of being told bad signings who were clearly never going to improve would eventually come good if the fans were patient. As for trying to convince everyone Igor Biscan was a centre-back ... The supporters didn't know whether to laugh or cry.

By the time I returned to the line-up after my broken leg, the nails weren't yet in the coffin of the Houllier reign, but the undertaker was on standby. The team gatherings which had been so enthralling were now tiresome and repetitive. He'd call a summit the day before a game, another in the team hotel on the eve of the match, a third instantly after we'd played, and then a fourth at the training ground a day later. A psychologist was even appointed to change our dipping fortunes.

By this stage, the Gérard Houllier in front of me was a pale imitation of the man who'd strolled into Melwood and taken on the most powerful player in the club. He'd seek the opinions of Stevie and Michael to reassure him his team selections were right. He knew he needed their support if he was going to survive. Mo was asked to write out what he considered to be Liverpool's strongest eleven. Houllier was shocked when it was so different to his, mainly because Vladimir Smicer wasn't in Michael's line-up.

Just as his clash with Ince after that FA Cup game in January 1999 demonstrated Houllier's power, an encounter with Stevie and Mo prior to a massive game at Old Trafford in April 2004 underlined his weakness. He told them his team included Cheyrou and Baros rather than Murphy and Heskey. Stevie and Mo were asked their opinion on the selection, and they said they didn't agree. Houllier changed his mind, included Murphy, and dropped Cheyrou and Baros. Danny scored the winner a day later. It was a great victory which effectively secured our Champions League spot for 2004–05, but I had a hollow feeling inside. I knew the manager had to go. This wasn't the Houllier I knew. This was not the man who'd taken on Ince so impressively in that team meeting. In 1999 he'd never have put the opinion of any player above his own. He was no longer speaking my or anyone else's language. The man needed a break, and the end, when it came, was unavoidable.

A few days after the final League game of the 2003–04 season, against Newcastle, the rumours began to gather pace. I suspected he'd gone, but public confirmation wasn't immediate.

'What do you think is happening?' Phil Thompson asked me.

'The silence is deafening,' I replied.

Rick Parry, our chief executive, told us an announcement would be made shortly, and it was clear what that meant. Houllier was sacked five days after the end of the season.

I sent him a text message thanking him and wishing him success in the future. Only the English players in the squad bothered to get in touch. The French players didn't care as much as we did about Houllier losing his job.

It was the end for Thommo, too. He was keen to stay, but the new manager, Rafa Benitez, wanted his own backroom team. The link with the famous Anfield bootroom was being cut.

My emotions were mixed. I was personally sorry for Houllier, but I knew it was the right decision. The club needed a fresh start. The supporters now perceived Houllier as a manager who bought poor players and talked rubbish. Their view of him had been contaminated by his final two seasons. For me, he'll always be the boss who did everything except win the title at Anfield. I'd rather think about the good times than dwell on his mistakes. I'd rather remember the medals we won together, and none was more satisfying than the bundle we picked up in 2001.

6

The Treble

'Go out there and make yourselves fucking legends.'

Phil Thompson's plea bounced off the dressing-room walls as we headed into the Westfalenstadion in Dortmund.

The UEFA Cup Final of 2001 was the climax of our sublime trinity. The League Cup and FA Cup were already rubbing ears in the trophy cabinet. Now we were ready to complete the set. In doing so, we knew we'd achieve what Liverpool had never done before: play every game possible in a season and win every knockout competition entered.

After 120 minutes in Germany during which we contrived to drop the cup four times but grabbed it five times, we returned to the changing room clutching our winners medals and reflecting on the uniqueness of our deeds. Mentally, physically and emotionally we were too drained to celebrate. I threw off my kit, kicked off my boots, dipped myself into a bath that was bigger than a swimming pool and stared blankly at my team-mates, breaking the surprisingly restrained atmosphere with a few mutters about what had happened. The pace with which each triumph had overlapped the next meant none of us had had a chance to pause to absorb the scale of our accomplishment. There was no evidence of the ecstasy you'd expect in the winners' quarters. The party had been left on the pitch and was heading into extra time on the streets outside; sober consideration was the dominant vibe in the dressing room. Cloud nine wasn't all it was cracked up to be. We were too exhausted and bewildered to appreciate the view.

We'd achieved what had seemed impossible so soon into Gérard Houllier's reign. It remains my triumph above all triumphs, the one I recall with most fondness, even though time hasn't been generous in its appraisal of our efforts. Ask Liverpudlians to list the most iconic moments at Anfield and they'll need reminding about this peculiar season as they plough through the various other accolades on the honours list. Fans hail the great Shankly teams of the 1960s, Paisley's European Cup trio of the 1970s and 1980s, Kenny Dalglish's double winners, or his 1988 title-winning team. Istanbul leapfrogged many of these. Club historians will eventually recognize how unlucky Houllier was to find himself at a venue that could afford to be blasé about this exceptional campaign. If he'd done this anywhere but Liverpool, Arsenal or Manchester United, he'd have been given a new ten-year contract on the spot and the freedom of the city, and had a statue immediately erected in his honour. Instead, he finds himself sandwiched between an era of unprecedented regular success and a season that ended in the most extraordinary Champions League Final of all time. Regardless of what we won under him, his period at Anfield is still perceived as a bleak spell. The three years that followed the treble led to a re-evaluation of his work, and then Rafa came along and stole everyone's hearts by eclipsing him within twelve months.

Shankly, Paisley, Fagan and Dalglish never found themselves in a situation where such a high was followed by underachievement. Shankly left as manager having won the FA Cup. Paisley was a League title holder on his retirement day. Fagan was only the boss for two years, but won a treble of his own and reached consecutive European Cup Finals. Dalglish left Liverpool as champions. These managers peaked early and sustained their success. All were able to bow out with their reputations intact. Houllier initially upheld this tradition, but then broke with it. He was damaged goods when he was sacked. That corrupted fans' memories of what had gone before as they lingered on the sense of what might have been in the immediate aftermath of 2001.

With every year that passes I feel more sympathy for Gérard for the way his reign has been tarnished. The medal haul in my house, and the collection of cup final wins on DVD, underlines his bad luck. For all the traumas of frustrating Premier League campaigns, the glory years have never stopped for me at Liverpool. Houllier not only triggered the revival of our good fortunes, he activated the beginning of mine. I've won every honour except one, and I've not given up on the League title yet. I've had more ups and downs than a trapeze artist during my time in a red shirt, but there's been nothing unrewarding about my Liverpool treasure hunt. Trophies have arrived with the same regularity as they did for my illustrious predecessors, and at certain times with greater frequency.

The 2001 treble topped the lot. Istanbul was my finest hour, but 2001 was the result of a whole season's work, making it more satisfying and more worthy. For all the pleasure holding aloft the European Cup brought, I didn't join an exclusive group in winning it. Every May, new sets of players join the club saying they've won the Champions League. To this day, only the few of us who contributed to every minute of the three cup finals in

2001 can say we achieved something rare. This particular treble had never been done before by an English side, and may never be done again. I doubt any feat has been overlooked and underestimated more at Anfield. Lifting the UEFA Cup, FA Cup and Carling Cup within the space of a few months would be enough to merit reunion dinners every summer at most clubs. At Liverpool, it's the underplayed 'forgotten treble'. It's packaged up and left on the shelf as one of numerous jubilant campaigns the club has enjoyed. Few would rank it as a peak now.

You start each season with the aim of winning one trophy. The fixture list arrives pre-season and you imagine gaps appearing after a cup exit or two. To look back after nine months and realize every weekend and midweek slot has been filled – that's special. We didn't just win three back-to-back trophies, we emerged victorious from the ultimate test of football endurance. As now, we didn't appreciate it as much as we should have at the time. The sweat was still dripping from my brow in Dortmund when supporters and journalists were asking us about the League title the following season. Even as we were parading all three trophies around the city centre in May 2001, our thoughts were drifting towards the seasons to come.

The obsession with pursuing the Premier League can sometimes blur a player's sense of the present. I now know the value of savouring a triumph rather than thinking too much about the consequences down the line. My advice to any footballer or fan is this: the hour of glory itself should be enough; relish it while it lasts. You must always strive for more and plan ahead, but too often recently I've heard Liverpool supporters redefine our greatest nights and victories because they didn't lead to the League title later on. But a cup final win is in itself a pinnacle. Those trophies had no less value because they were the zenith of our achievement under Houllier. When we were dancing and singing around the Millennium Stadium and the Dortmund pitch with those cups it didn't feel possible he'd be so scarred by future events. On those glorious days when we beat Arsenal and Alaves, it should have been all about living for the moment. Houllier had led Liverpool back to where they belong, among the cream of Europe.

I was involved in fifty-eight of our sixty-three fixtures in 2000–01, the last ten stretching my stamina to its absolute limit. Had those fans who turned up at Anfield on 19 August for our first League game been told what was to come, they'd have reacted with disbelief and excitement. When I took my place on the substitutes' bench that day, I too could never have imagined I'd be so involved in a career-defining campaign: German full-backs Markus Babbel and Christian Ziege had signed from Bayern Munich and Middlesbrough, prompting fears I faced a prolonged spell learning the full definition of a rather undesirable new phrase that had invaded the English language – 'rotation policy'.

That first match at home, to Bradford, when I spent most of the game on the touchline warming up, did nothing to ease my concerns. Fortunately for me, it needed only one nippy run from the opposing right-winger to expose how Ziege was a more accomplished attacker than defender. He was uncomfortable in 4–4–2. Our left flank became leaky, so he was swiftly moved into a midfield role.

Ziege arrived with an unblemished reputation, but before he joined it was well known he was a left wing-back rather than an out-and-out defender. Houllier rarely played three at the back, so it was a strange signing. To be blunt, Ziege couldn't defend. I wondered what our scouts had been up to recommending that

Houllier sign him, and I later heard many had advised him not to, especially given the controversy surrounding his so-called 'tapping up' (Liverpool were fined for an illegal approach). Ultimately, it worked in my favour. If he'd been that good, I wouldn't have been in the team as much as I was in 2000–01.

With Ziege not up to it at the back, after a brief return to central midfield, Houllier shifted me to the role I'd make my own for the next few years – left-back. We were away at Newcastle in November and hit with injuries when the decision was taken. On the eve of the match, Steven Gerrard and I agreed one of us would be the square peg filling the round hole. I got the nod and played well enough to earn a second chance, even though we lost 2–1. I stayed in the side for an 8–0 midweek demolition of Stoke City in the League Cup. This triggered a run of ten games where we had eight clean sheets. It was enough for Houllier to recognize he'd stumbled upon a winning formula in defence. I was staying put.

Houllier's much-respected and clever assistant Patrice Bergues spent extra time on the training pitch with me to guide me through the perils of my new role. It was invaluable advice, and pretty soon no one was questioning my right to stay there. I had a lot to work on in an attacking sense, but we were rock solid where it mattered.

I'd been everywhere but in goal now, but I wasn't complaining. Securing a place in that team was tough, and having already spent my brief career reinventing myself, it was no hardship. The 2001 side remains the best I've played in at Anfield. You had to scrap to get into it, and it was even harder to stay in. There was plenty of talk at the time, as there has been ever since, of the manager changing players too much, but Houllier's selections were largely consistent in the key areas. The back four never changed, unless there was an injury or suspension. Continuity in defence was the foundation for our success.

We weren't a flamboyant side, but you had to play out of your skin and battle to beat us. We had that elusive quality I've emphasized so often – character. We were a team in tune with my Marsh Lane principles: resilient, honest and uncompromising. I glanced around the dressing room before a game and knew I was standing alongside players I could trust. We were powerful, experienced, hungry for success, and expertly organized. I can't remember a fixture during that season where each of us didn't go out comfortable with what we had to do. I was always confident we'd deliver a performance. The bottom line is that across all areas of the pitch we had players who believed we would produce the goods.

To one side I had big Sami and Stéphane Henchoz, who'd drip blood for a clean sheet. Babbel played sixty-one games that season, which may have contributed to the exhaustion he suffered later. His career was cut short by a freak illness in the summer of 2001, which was a devastating blow to the squad given his outstanding contribution until then. Upfront we had Mo, who you could always depend on to grab a goal when you most needed it. Emile Heskey had the season of his life, scoring over twenty goals and forever promising to get the best out of his formidable talent. Steven Gerrard was maturing into the world-class midfielder he's become, Danny Murphy, Nick Barmby and Patrik Berger were a constant goal threat from midfield, and Houllier's masterstroke was to add the nous and experience of Gary McAllister to guide the younger players and provide an extra creative spark in the middle.

The lynchpin of the midfield was Didi Hamann, who'd glide effortlessly across the area protecting the back four, destroying enemy probes. He came to the fore and became an integral part of our success, finding his form at precisely the right time, because Houllier was seriously considering selling him. At the end of 2000 he added Igor Biscan to the ranks amid suspicions he'd lost faith in Hamann. Didi instantly raised his game and sustained a level of performance over the next six years to qualify for legendary status.

In the summer of 1999 Houllier thought he was signing the ultimate professional who lived like a monk off the pitch.

'Look at Didi,' he'd say. 'I never see him without a bottle of water in his hand.'

We'd walk away laughing. 'That's because he's dehydrated,' we'd say to one another. 'When we're on a night out we never see him without a pint in his hand.'

There are some players who can enjoy a night out on a Friday and give a man of the match performance on a Saturday. Didi comes into that category. It's a quality that endears him to fellow players and supporters, but it never helped his cause with managers. If ever a player defied your expectations of German footballers, it's Didi. Houllier and later Rafa Benitez couldn't cope with him because he's the opposite of the kind of robotic, characterless ideal modern coaches want. He'd be awful on the training pitch, but he'd consistently give eight, nine or ten out of ten performances when it mattered most.

We knew we'd signed a guy with charisma the day he joined the club. We took him out for a night in the city centre, expecting to be out with a quiet, shy German bloke. By the end of the evening such preconceptions were well and truly quashed. As we left a club, Didi announced he knew the perfect way to get us a taxi. We watched in horror as our £9 million midfielder lay in the middle of Liverpool's lively Castle Street in the hope or expectation a motorist would slam on the brakes rather than kill him.

Thankfully, a bemused driver obliged.

'I'll give you forty pounds to take me home,' Didi said to the shocked target.

'Where do you live?'

'I haven't got a clue,' Didi replied. 'I've only just arrived here.'

To this day, I've still no idea how he got to his flat that night, or where he told the driver to take him.

An altogether different influence, but equally inspirational on our treble run, was Gary McAllister. Unlike Didi, Gary Mac was a manager's dream. There was uncertainty when Liverpool signed him at the age of thirty-six, and no one was more surprised than me. There were no clues from Houllier as to his intentions. The previous season, when Liverpool played Coventry, Houllier had even singled out Gary as a potential weak link in their line-up. He pitched me against him in centre midfield, saying, 'You're running on petrol, he's running on diesel.' Six months later Gary was signing for the club. It proved to be one of the most astute purchases Houllier made. There couldn't have been a finer role model for any young player. Some older heads when they offer advice can sound too preachy and make you want to switch off rather than listen. Gary Mac wasn't like that. When he had something to tell you, it always made sense. I'm sure the two years many of us spent working with him had a huge influence on all our careers.

If ever a player was born to play for Liverpool, it was him. He fitted the bill as someone the fans could relate to, classy and cultured on and off the pitch and reminding the club of the working-class Scottish heritage that has been so influential in our history. No player has been at a club for such a short period but made such a lasting impression. It's a tragedy for Liverpool they didn't sign him ten years earlier. I'm sure the club would have won a lot more trophies during that time.

The competition in midfield was intense. If 2001 was an underrated season, Danny Murphy was one of our most under-valued performers. He'd score around ten or twelve goals in a good year but never entirely won the crowd over. Houllier came to trust Danny after inheriting him from Roy Evans at a time when it looked like he'd have to leave the club. Danny is the first to admit he's a player who needs to be in 100 per cent shape to produce his best, and Houllier brought that out of him. Unfortunately, as soon as Benitez arrived he accepted a bid for Danny and he moved on, not prepared to stay where he felt he wasn't wanted. I know he's regretted it ever since. Had he fought on, I'm sure he'd still have played a lot of football for Liverpool.

And then there was Michael Owen, by now my room-mate and best friend in the game, who ended the season in the sort of form that led to his being named European Player of the Year. Mo seems to have spent his entire career proving critics wrong, and even then it was the same old story. Each season would follow a similar pattern: he'd score goals aplenty, have a mini dip when his fitness and sharpness would be questioned, and then when the biggest games came round he'd be the hero.

There's no one who can match Mo for self-belief or tempera-ment, no matter what the occasion. Some players get anxious when the pressure is on. It always seemed to make him find an extra yard. At his best he could go eighty-nine minutes feeding on scraps, then get half a chance in the last seconds and bury it. There could be no finer example of this than the 2001 FA Cup Final.

Michael and I became friends because we shared a passion for the game and, despite our different public images, we had a lot in common, in that from the moment we could kick, football was our life. Our dads brought us up to be footballers. While I was being educated on the fields of north Liverpool, Mo was receiving a similar upbringing in North Wales from his Merseyside born and bred parents.

For a variety of reasons, Mo never had the same rapport with The Kop as his strike partner at the time, Robbie Fowler. It's too simplistic to say this was because of Robbie's Toxteth roots. The 'problem' for Mo was he became an England legend before a Liverpool one. He won the hearts of the nation before he won those of The Kop. It was the 1998 World Cup, in particular the goal he scored against Argentina, that catapulted him to superstar status. At eighteen he was described as the future of English football and was immediately linked with the top Italian and Spanish clubs. Liverpudlians, unconcerned about England's fortunes and uneasy about their players being seen as others' property, felt distant towards Michael. First they never related to him, then they never wanted to try. It wasn't Mo's fault he was so good so soon, and it was his brilliance for Liverpool which so swiftly earned him an opportunity for his country, but the supporters remained suspicious of his priorities. When he left for Real Madrid in 2004 some said it proved their misgivings were fair, but that's too cosy an argument. They never appreciated the Michael I know so well, who for as long as he was my team-mate was one of those I knew would never give less than 100 per cent, and who was as devastated by defeats as I was.

He's more of a character off the park than the fans imagine too. Away days are the most tedious in a footballer's life as you're stuck in a hotel room wondering how to fill the hours before a training session or match. You can't go out, you can't have a drink, you can't do anything without the permission of the manager. Pranks become the only major source of amusement, and there are plenty of tales I can reveal about Mo, but I wouldn't want to ruin his chances of becoming the next face of the Persil adverts, or whatever other product he's endorsing nowadays.

I've often felt Mo would have benefited from revealing his true character more often off the pitch. Football nowadays is as much about image and being presented in the right way by agents and representatives as it is about the game itself. At international level that's very important, but at a club like Liverpool, sometimes not being seen as perfect makes you more popular. Flawed genius is revered on Merseyside.

While Michael fought a constant battle for The Kop's fullest affections, Robbie could do no wrong, despite his increasingly tempestuous relationship with the management.

Even during the treble season, the tensions that would eventually lead to his first departure were visible. Houllier hated the idea of personalities dominating more than the 'team ethic' that was his fixation. When determining whether or not to pick Robbie, he often felt he had to consider more than football issues.

We had four top-class strikers that season: Heskey, Owen, Fowler and Jari Litmanen. Heskey's form made him a certain starter, and he was the ideal foil to the other three. Mo was up and down but ruthless towards the closing months, Robbie had injury problems, and Litmanen, it was hoped, would be the missing link to play in the 'hole' behind the strikers.

The fans thought the new Dalglish and Beardsley had finally arrived in the shape of Jari. He was the type of player we'd been crying out for, slotting in behind a more advanced striker. All the greatest sides have such players. United began to win titles when they bought Eric Cantona, and now Rooney or Tevez can play in this role. Arsenal had Dennis Bergkamp. Every summer I hoped Liverpool were going to be in the market for a similar forward. Steven Gerrard was given the role in 2007–08 and played it successfully behind Fernando Torres for most of the campaign, even though he'd still see himself first and foremost as a central midfielder.

Litmanen was undoubtedly a brilliant footballer, but he lacked essential attributes for the English game and didn't fit our style. Away from home he was a passenger, but when the fans saw his skills at Anfield, where we dominated possession, they'd demand his inclusion. His vision and passing ability were a joy to watch, capable of transforming us from a methodical outfit into one more pleasing for the purists. This is what we were craving longer term under Houllier, but his resistance to Jari was emblematic of his reign. Physical power was preferred to flair. The fans' pressure to add panache annoyed Houllier more than it should have done. He stood his ground where Litmanen was concerned, but it was one of those occasions when his stubbornness got the better of him. Jari was correctly fourth choice, but he should have been called upon far more in specific circumstances against less demanding opponents, especially at Anfield.

Whatever attacking combination Houllier picked, he'd be criticized the following day as the fans chose their favourites. It shows how fickle we all are that there was a home match against Ipswich earlier in that season for which Heskey was 'rested'. We lost 1–0 and there was nearly a riot afterwards, the supporters demanding to know why Emile hadn't been picked. That's hard to believe now. Fowler and Owen were the favoured partnership that day for just one home game, and The Kop wanted Heskey instead. That shows how good Emile was, and how badly he dipped before he was moved on.

When Robbie wasn't selected and we didn't win, it was a similar story. Although he was joint captain with Jamie Redknapp, who missed nearly all of the season with injury, you always sensed the tension between Robbie and Houllier would lead to a final, inevitable outcome. Over the Christmas period in 2000 Liverpool accepted an offer from Chelsea, but Robbie opted to stay. After we'd won the treble, he'd finally had enough and moved to Leeds.

People expected me to be firmly in the camp of those disagreeing with his sale. Robbie is one of my best friends, but I thought Houllier was right to let him go. The Leeds bid was acceptable to all sides, especially given Robbie's recent injuries, and the private fall-out had been played out in public too often. He was effectively competing with Michael for the 'poacher's' role in the side, and the game was becoming increasingly about pace and athletic fitness as much as finishing prowess. Mo had all this, which gave him the edge. Houllier's judgement was unquestioned by the majority of fans by then, so there was only one winner.

I believed Houllier would use the money from Robbie's sale to buy a striker with different qualities. I was hoping for a younger, physically stronger Litmanen. Had I known then how he'd squander the transfer kitty, as well as how much I'd miss Robbie's presence and banter in the dressing room, I would have taken a different view.

When I re-evaluate those months, Robbie's contribution throughout the treble season was greater than Houllier or I gave him credit for. He wasn't the player he was when he broke into the side – and that was part of the problem between him and Houllier, who kept hearing about this striking prodigy but who'd never had the chance to work with the younger Robbie – but compared to most strikers in England and Europe he was still one of the best. In 2001 he was cruelly denied the chance to be the hero of the hour twice: but for two last-minute equalizers he'd have scored the winning goal in two major finals.

The first ought to have been the most satisfying of all. Birmingham City stood in our way in February as we pursued Liverpool's first major trophy in six years. We headed to Wales determined to outclass our Championship opponents. Instead, I left Cardiff after the League Cup Final feeling relieved rather than exhilarated by the experience of my debut showpiece occasion.

We were awful. A goal up early, thanks to Robbie, we should have eased our way to victory. Instead we toiled, allowed Birmingham back into the game with a last-minute penalty, and almost self-destructed in extra time. I was troubled that we needed a penalty shoot-out to claim the cup, and it soiled my view of the victory. The spot-kicks were the only point in the game when anyone could notice the gulf in quality. Birmingham dispatched just two.

I was eager to take one, virtually demanding I be put on the list, despite the concerns of the coaching staff. 'I don't fancy Carra scoring his,' Phil Thompson confided to Danny Murphy. I was so angry as I made the walk from the centre circle I didn't care about any personal consequences. The venom with which I struck the sweetest of right-footers let out all the frustration of the previous 120 minutes. Emotionless, I walked back to my team-mates and said nothing, neither expecting congratulation for scoring nor commiseration had I missed.

People talk about the sense of guilt when players fail during penalty shoot-outs, but I've never felt any. If I'd ballooned it and we'd lost the cup, I wouldn't have blamed myself for our defeat. We botched it as a team. Had we played to our potential, we'd never have put ourselves in that situation. That's why I've never shied away from penalties. I felt the same during the World Cup. Those who tried to thrust responsibility on me in 2006 – Tord Grip, if I want to name names – were overlooking the overall performance of the England side. Once you get to pens, neither side deserves to win or lose, and no individual player need feel responsible for the outcome.

Sander Westerveld made the final decisive save to capture Houllier's elusive first piece of silverware, but my outward jubilation was balanced inwardly by a nagging sense of unfulfilment with our performance. Still a youngster in the side, I had no intention or expectation of seeing this day as the highlight of my career. That's why I didn't delight in our success as much as I'd imagined. Just like my earlier honour, the FA Youth Cup, I sensed this was another step in the pursuit of a greater goal. We were still in the FA Cup and in Europe, and I wanted us to learn from our mistakes in Cardiff and ensure we improved.

A win in any competition is special, particularly your first major trophy, but at Liverpool you're always going to strive for more than the League Cup. Although we received the credit we deserved from our own fans for taking the silver back to Liverpool, deep down all of us knew we hadn't won over many doubters with our sub-standard performance. So when we returned to the Millennium Stadium three months later for the FA Cup Final, we were keen to make amends.

We'd overcome some tough opponents to reach Cardiff for the second time, most notably Leeds at Elland Road in the fourth round. Still a top-five Premier League outfit in those days, they were our closest rivals in pursuit of the Champions League places, so to go there and win as convincingly as we did, 2–0, gave us the momentum we needed to go all the way. We also emerged victorious from a 'derby' against Tranmere Rovers at

Prenton Park in the quarter-final. That may seem an easy tie on paper, but bearing in mind their form – they'd knocked out Everton at Goodison Park and turned round a 3–0 deficit at home to Southampton in the fifth round – it was a really taxing encounter. A year earlier countless giant-killing acts had led to a place in the Carling Cup Final. Their manager, John Aldridge, fancied his chances against us that day, but Houllier had his wits about him, fielding the most 'English' team he could muster. Eight British players started that match, with only Westerveld, Babbel and Hyypia representing the continentals. I doubt those percentages have been repeated in a Liverpool starting eleven since. We won 4–2, but plenty of other Premiership teams would have come a cropper given the way Tranmere bombarded us in the second half. Once more I reflected on the guts we'd showed throughout the competition. We survived bruised but unbeaten. We still had enough English players in our squad to bring such characteristics to the fore when needed.

If our semi-final win over Wycombe was a formality, there was no hope of an easy ride in the final. The Carling Cup Final might have been a lesson in how to win a cup without playing well, but the FA Cup took it to a new extreme. The game against Arsenal was embarrassingly one-sided. The best team didn't win, and we were fortunate Michael stepped up to change the game. I'd like to say he did so single-handed, but the fingers of Stéphane Henchoz, who made a couple of great saves he thankfully didn't get credit for from the referee, also helped. Two goals in the last ten minutes stole it from Arsène Wenger. The gods smiled upon us, but unlike after the match against Birmingham, I felt no guilt about our manner of victory this time. Arsenal had it coming against Liverpool. Those fans who remembered losing the League title in the last minute in 1989 saw this as a mild form of

revenge. Even the Gunners had to admire our never-say-die attitude. They could outplay us, but they never outbattled us.

Under Wenger, Arsenal have consistently been the most complete football side I've faced. You can talk about Barcelona, AC
Milan, Chelsea and Manchester United all you like, but the
Arsenal team that featured Thierry Henry and Patrick Vieira at
their peak was the most daunting of all. They had skill, pace,
stamina and flair. Some of the times I faced them I came off the
pitch certain I'd played against the best team in the world. Henry
was the one player who persistently gave me problems. Every
defender has one rival like this, and he was mine, simply because
there's no response to raw pace. When it's allied to the close ball
control he possessed, it's virtually unstoppable. There were times
he ran past me with the ball seemingly glued to his boots. Their
only weakness was a frequent inability to finish teams off. This
happened once or twice at Anfield when they played us off the
park but we somehow nicked a draw. In Cardiff, Michael made
them pay the ultimate price for their wastefulness, breaking their
hearts with a classic smash and grab.

We hailed our victory, acknowledging Mo had carried a get-
out-of-jail card on to the pitch. This was 'The Michael Owen
Final', just like we'd enjoy 'The Steven Gerrard Final' five years
later. Stevie later admitted he learned more from Vieira's performance that day than he had from any opponent in previous
years. He recognized the jump in class he still had to make in
order to dominate a midfield. Like all great players, he analysed
where he needed to improve rather than simply savouring the
victory, and this gave him the confidence to get the better of
Vieira in future meetings.

Did we deserve victory on the day? No. But sometimes you
win trophies for a season's work, not just ninety minutes' worth.

We were always hearing how lucky we were as we scrapped our way to one win after another. I defy any side to play sixty-three games in a season, win three cups, and not have the run of the ball once or twice. Look at United's treble in 1999. They deserved everything they got, but they saw everything bounce their way, beating us and Arsenal on the path to winning the FA Cup, and Bayern Munich in the Champions League Final, on each occasion scoring the winner in the last minute. I've never begrudged that. Just like United in 1999, we had to make our own good fortune on plenty of occasions, playing some robust, uncompromising and class football to put ourselves into a position to benefit from our breaks. Had we not won all three cups, I'd have been arguing how unlucky we'd been to concede two last-minute equalizers in two major finals.

If we weren't being accused of relying on good fortune, we were being told how dull we were to watch. This allegation plagued us. For eight months of our UEFA Cup run we sent the nation to sleep, only to rouse everyone with one of the most exciting finals ever.

The comparisons with Arsenal's and Manchester United's style of play weren't favourable, but the criticism was harsh. We were a developing side and, first and foremost, Houllier was right to make us hard to beat. After years of analysis of Evans's side and complaints about a lack of spine, now the club was being targeted for being too reliant on discipline, structure and organization. Considering the speed with which we'd gone from being a 'soft touch' in that notorious FA Cup tie at Stamford Bridge in 1997 to heading to places like the Nou Camp and grabbing a clean sheet, some of the punditry at the time was foolish and uncharitable. Part of the problem was that all our European games were screened live on BBC1, and you can understand their hoping for a more entertaining brand of football to sustain viewing figures and justify rescheduling *EastEnders*.

It's the classic contradiction in the modern game. To us and the fans, winning is entertaining. We saw each victory that season as part of a building process. We hoped in the years to come we'd develop a more fluid style, but at that point of our development, at a club that had only a League Cup win to its name in the previous eight seasons, any win would do.

I remember saying at the time the history books would never record how we got those fantastic results on our way to the UEFA Cup Final, only that we got them. We kept a clean sheet over 180 minutes against Barcelona, and won 2–0 in the Olympic Stadium in Rome. Fabio Capello was their manager and they won the Italian league that year. We also beat the Porto side that went on to win the UEFA Cup and Champions League in 2003 and 2004 respectively, as well as Olympiakos, who are regularly in the Champions League. It was in fact the strongest UEFA Cup competition in years, packed with Champions League level sides (this was before the number of clubs from the major leagues was increased to four). They were colossal scalps for us, and although they weren't achieved by adopting adventurous tactics, we played to our strengths and did ourselves and the club proud.

So to get back home and find the BBC telling everyone how boring we were was, to say the least, a bit irritating. I've never been one to get too prickly about media criticism, but I think this undoubtedly sowed the seeds for what followed with Houllier. He could brush off attacks on his team when we were winning, but when things started to go wrong later he became more insecure and bitter about how underrated he'd been.

The last-sixteen tie with Roma encapsulated how the

competition went for us. Clearly we were underdogs heading into it, but we combined our organization, our spirit and our skill to get through. We also had things fall our way at a crucial time.

Ahead of the first leg on 15 February, Bergues's importance as Houllier's assistant became apparent again. Gérard told us he planned to go with an attacking formation, with Litmanen playing behind Robbie and Heskey; Michael, who'd been in and out of the side after returning from injury, wasn't going to play. Bergues influenced a rethink, and on the day of the game Emile pulled out with an injury. Michael was back in. On such details seasons are defined.

In that game Michael began the goalscoring run which led to him becoming European Player of the Year. It also demonstrated the difference between a player like Michael and someone like Emile. If the roles had been reversed, there's no way Michael would have stepped aside to allow Emile to play in such a massive game. Emile possessed the ability to be a Liverpool player, but not the mentality. There was a spell during the course of that season when he was unplayable. Even Michael was telling me he thought Emile had become one of the best strikers in Europe, as he battered defenders and began to score regularly. We hoped he'd matured into a striker who'd dominate English football for the next decade. Unfortunately, he didn't sustain it at Anfield. His unavailability in Rome, the sort of fixture you fantasize about as a youngster, offers, to me at least, a possible hint as to why Heskey's career has drifted.

Michael reaped the benefits in Italy. He scored twice to set us up for the controversial second leg a week later, remembered for a penalty award that wasn't given. We'd missed our own spot-kick with the score at 0–0, and after Roma went ahead it seemed they'd won a penalty for a Babbel handball. The referee appeared to award it, and had Gabriel Batistuta not run off towards the corner flag to take a quick set-piece, I'm sure the decision would have stood. Instead, the official seemed to change his mind. Naturally, our rivals feasted on the Italians' sense of injustice, but we deserved to win over the two legs.

The same applied to the semi-final against Barcelona, where we were condemned for refusing to allow their best players the time and space to play. Rivaldo was their star man at the time, but we kept him quiet and won, thanks to McAllister's penalty in the second leg.

'You have betrayed football, Mr Houllier,' the Spanish press told the gaffer in the after-match press conference.

At that time in his management, he'd always have a clever response. 'They kept the ball, but we kept the result,' he said.

He'd have the last word in the final, but the more I think about this much-used statement from Houllier, the more I understand why the fans ran out of patience later on. Liverpool's traditions are based on keeping the ball and the result. They tolerated this philosophy in 2001 because we were achieving fantastic results in only his second full season in sole control. A couple of years later, when we were still reverting to this defensive, negative style, our supporters saw no likelihood of him ever changing.

Nobody cared so much when we sent Barca home to face their white handkerchief brigade. By this stage I was describing each win as the highlight of my career, although with games arriving thick and fast there was no chance to join the fans' celebrations. The atmosphere inside Anfield on the night of the semi-final was, up until that point, the loudest I'd known.

Those games were the first stirrings of our reawakening on the European stage. After so many years reading about Liverpool's

European nights, finally we were creating history for ourselves. Since that 2000–01 season, the classic Euro ties have been re-established at Anfield. They've become an annual event again. Eight years ago we'd waited fifteen years for a chance to recreate the atmosphere and images of the past. The club that is obsessed with revisiting former glories now had an opportunity to do so. A new generation of us had a chance to experience what the players before us had gone through. Of course, some of them would never allow us to suggest our success matched up to theirs, but for those too young to be a part of the magic of the 1960s, 1970s and 1980s, this naturally meant far more.

The 2001 UEFA Cup Final has since been eclipsed, but at the time it was the highlight of many Liverpudlians' lives, especially those, like me, in their early twenties who'd only seen the old finals on DVD. My friends and younger members of my family had heard all the old stories about travelling to Europe, the nights out in foreign bars and invading town squares, decorating every club or café with the wittiest banners that could be dreamed up. For over a decade no Liverpool fan had had the chance to relive those sensations. We should never forget it was Gérard Houllier who first brought those times back. The sides of Roy Evans and Graeme Souness competed in Europe, but Houllier lived up to Anfield traditions by conquering it.

Of all the trophies we won that season, the UEFA Cup meant most to him. Modern coaches value European competition more, partly due to traditions in their own country, but also because they're pitting their wits against different managers and tactics. There's an obvious vanity issue there. You can imagine them all at their UEFA coaching conferences, smiling at one another as they chat about their encounters, and privately recalling the games when they got the better of one another. In 2001, Houllier was rightly seen as one of the best coaches in Europe, and winning the UEFA Cup underlined it.

Dortmund's Westfalenstadion was the perfect venue for us to announce our return to the European elite – an open ground, with a Kop-like stand behind each goal. Our fans took over the stadium and made it feel like home. There were blankets of red banners across all the stands. On walking out, none of us felt we'd let the fans down.

Our opponents, Alaves, were an unknown quantity. They'd beaten Inter Milan earlier in the competition, but we knew we were much stronger. We should have overwhelmed them on and off the pitch, and for a while it looked as though we would.

We raced into a 2–0 lead, but our usually tight defence was unbelievably shaky on the night.

After all the emotion and adrenalin in the build-up to the match, at some point during the first half a horrific realization dawned on me.

I was knackered.

The toil of the last nine months had caught up. My mind was giving my body instructions, but it wasn't able to act upon them. I've never felt so vulnerable and exposed when an opponent attacked. Most of us felt the same way. Alaves came from behind four times to take us into extra time. Their full-back, Cosmin Contra, played so well he earned a transfer to AC Milan. We made him look better than he was.

An own-goal by Delfi Geli a minute before the end of extra time won us the cup, 5–4. Gary McAllister floated another perfect free-kick into the box, and the defender unintentionally took his place in Anfield history. It was the most golden of golden goals. Yet again the 'lucky' jibes were showered on us. Yet again I ask anyone to watch that final again and try to convince me the best team didn't win.

'This was the greatest UEFA Cup Final of all time,' everyone agreed. The BBC finally had the entertaining football they'd been crying out for. I'd certainly never played in a fixture like it, and was sure I'd never do so again. Cup finals aren't meant to go that way. They're cautious, tight, usually settled by a single goal. 'If we ever reach another European final, it'll be nothing like this,' we told ourselves.

Over the course of that competition, as in the League Cup and FA Cup, we got our just rewards, even if we made it more difficult for ourselves than it should have been. There was always a sense we didn't get the credit we deserved, and we could never allow the extent of our achievement to sink in. No sooner had we won the UEFA Cup than we had a crucial League fixture to prepare for. It was a relentless grind of a season. We were like marathon runners, pausing to grab an energy drink every few miles before dragging ourselves another extra mile. This led to a strange, incomplete sensation following all our cup wins. We were never allowed to bask in the glory or share the full post-match euphoria of our fans. Each Cardiff success was acknowledged by no more than a team meal, a celebratory speech from the boss which ended with the message 'keep going', and an early night ahead of preparations for a pivotal game days later. We'd simply take a deep breath and start running again.

As young lads, I can't deny a certain level of resentment towards the manager for refusing to allow us to over-indulge on the nights of our victories, even though he was right to do so. Other coaches would have been tempted to allow us one night out, but Houllier was adamant we should wait. Usually you can prioritize certain fixtures during the course of a season and find time for a break. You find yourself out of one of the cups, or struggling in the League, and players subconsciously turn their focus on the trophies they know they can win. There was never a time to stop and reassess priorities during that 2000–01 season. Cup semis and finals were instantly followed by huge European ties or League games that would determine what for many at the club, especially the manager, seemed the most important task of all: qualification for the Champions League for the first time since the Heysel ban.

It had been sixteen years since Liverpool last competed for the European Cup, but we knew it was only a matter of time before we returned. Financially, it was crucial we did so. The silverware brought instant rewards, but as the separation between football's elite and the rest became more apparent, the longer we missed out on the Champions League the more we risked being left even further behind United and Arsenal.

We should have been playing in the tournament instead of the UEFA Cup in 2000–01. Stupidly, we'd failed to win any of our final three matches of the 1999–2000 season, against Leicester, Southampton and Bradford, and lost third spot to Leeds by two points. Had we beaten Bradford in the last game of the campaign we'd have pipped David O'Leary's men and deprived ourselves of the UEFA Cup. That loss in Yorkshire must therefore rank as the best of my career. There was a sense of disbelief at Valley Parade at our failure, but unlike many of our most traumatic defeats under Houllier, this really did prove to be a blessing in disguise.

We had no intention of making the same mistake a year later, but the cup competitions were in danger of distracting us. This is when Houllier's management and organization shone. He was criticized for changing too many players – usually one or two a game – but it ensured we were fresh during the finale to the season. As Manchester United, Arsenal and Chelsea have proved over the years, rotation can work when you're changing the right players and replacing them with ones of similar quality. We were also changing like for like. The spine of the 2001 side didn't alter. The defence and Didi remained intact for the last three months. It was the 'flair' players who were kept guessing, as Steven Gerrard and Gary Mac alternated in the middle, or Stevie moved to the right, while the strikers fought for two spots.

After a demoralizing defeat at home to Leeds on Easter Monday, we won six of our last seven League games while winning two major cup finals. It was an astonishing run, assisted by our most influential players delivering when it mattered most. We didn't just rely on one player as a match winner; throughout that spell different elements of the side grabbed the headlines.

Against Everton at Goodison Park three days after losing to Leeds, Gary McAllister was the difference. This was the derby to beat all derbies. I think my celebrations at the end were even more manic than at Cardiff. We'd gone ten years without winning at Goodison, and how my Blue mates loved to remind me. I still believe had we not won that day we'd have had too much to do to finish third. But it was the manner of victory that was most satisfying. With the score level at 2–2, a thirty-five-yard free-kick in injury time allowed Gary Mac to beat Paul Gerrard, tricking him into thinking he'd be drifting the ball into the box instead of shooting. My Evertonian friends are still moaning about it, claiming Gary stole an extra five yards before he took the set-play – as if scoring from thirty-five yards is so much easier than from forty. I was too busy celebrating to hear their boos. I've never felt such delight at winning a Premier League fixture. Only claiming three points to win the title could ever top it. The spirit in our side must have been as thrilling to Houllier as the result itself.

If anyone was to blame for our enforced abstinence following each trophy win, it was the fixture schedulers. In normal circumstances the UEFA Cup Final would have been the last game of the season. For whatever reason, and it was certainly the first time I'd known it to happen, a League game followed both the FA Cup Final and UEFA Cup Final. This denied us a more fitting, traditional homecoming after Dortmund and explains the sense of anti-climax in the German dressing room.

Our epic journey ended at The Valley, home of Charlton Athletic, on 19 May. Only a win would secure our Champions League place, but at half-time we should have been at least 2–0 down. Then Robbie stepped up with a couple of goals and we romped to a 4–0 win. The Champions League spot was ours. To the money men at the club, this was as much a relief as the three trophies. I looked towards Houllier and Thompson, and there seemed to be an even greater sense of satisfaction etched on their faces than I'd seen in Dortmund. The coaching staff were hugging one another and indulging in a tub-thumping, fist-clenching celebration.

Houllier must have felt untouchable then, and who could have blamed him? Regardless of his reputation today, that was a season when the Liverpool manager got everything possible from his players. It was impossible to have achieved any more than we did. Belatedly, all of us could now enjoy the moment and allow an alcoholic influence on the party.

It felt like a career's worth of pinnacles was being condensed into three months. The climax to this campaign was one dizzying high after another, but I was so fatigued that much of it passed me by. Thousands lined the streets when we paraded the three cups on our return from London, although I was so tired I just wanted to escape from my team-mates and coaching staff, go home and reflect on my triumph with my family.

This was on my mind as I looked across the sea of red and

picked out a banner that read 23 CARRA GOLD – FROM MARSH LANE TO DORTMUND. There it was again, the enduring reminder of where I'd come from and where I was at. The pride in my achievement intensified. It also contributed to making sure I never changed the number on my shirt. I was offered a more conventional jersey when others were sold in the summers that followed. Had I taken it in 2001, it would have been an appropriate conclusion to a season that had begun with my annual worries about being sidelined but ended with a feeling I'd cemented a permanent place in the club's history. I rejected the proposal. Being 23 was more distinctive. Only Robbie Fowler had worn it before me, and I saw no reason to change, especially as the lads had gone to such a grand effort with that flag.

Maybe this was a sign of my growing confidence. As a youngster you pursue the opportunity to be one to eleven, but it was a trivial matter now. I may have been in the team for a while by then, but it underlines how that was the year I truly felt I'd arrived, established myself, provided all the confirmation I needed to of how good I was. I'd proved myself domestically, but now I'd gone to the Nou Camp and won man of the match. I'd gone boot to boot with Rivaldo, Totti and Deco and never flinched or looked out of my depth. I'd spent years knowing who the best players in Europe were, and now a few of them would remember me when our paths next crossed.

Many of the lads had taken souvenirs of our foreign conquests, swapping shirts with those great names. I never bothered. I've always kept my own jersey, unless specifically asked by an opponent, as I've never felt obliged to show a rival how much I respect them. I'd never want anyone I was facing to think I was somehow in awe of their talent. To me, it's a contradiction. I spend ninety minutes committing myself to beating them into submission. Win or lose, I don't want their shirt afterwards. I'd feel too embarrassed to ask. Perhaps this was another indication of how I'd matured as a player.

Breaking into the Liverpool side had forced me to step up a level. The arrival of Houllier and regular European football pushed me to take another jump in class in order to survive. I could never guarantee my long-term future at a club of Liverpool's stature, but now I was confident enough to believe there weren't many out there worthy of joining and taking my place. I felt I belonged on those big stages.

Those three winners medals aren't simply a souvenir of an astonishing few months. They represent the season when we reserved our place in Anfield folklore, and when I began to carve out my career as a one-club man.

'Make yourselves fucking legends,' Phil Thompson had said.

Do you know what, Thommo? I think some of us must have been listening to you.

7

England

Sitting on the England coach as it prepared to drive us away from the World Cup in Germany, I received a text message.

'Fuck it. It's only England.'

I'd just missed a penalty in the quarter-final shoot-out against Portugal. Around me were the tear-stained faces of underperforming superstars. England's so-called golden generation had failed. Again.

An eerie depression escorted us on the short trip back to the hotel, but as I stared at my phone and considered the implications of the comforting note, I didn't feel the same emptiness I sensed in others.

There's no such concept as 'only England' to most footballers, including many of my best friends. Representing your country is the ultimate honour, especially in the World Cup. Not to me. Did I care we'd gone out of the tournament? Of course I did. Passionately. Did I feel upset about my part in the defeat? Yes. I was devastated to miss a penalty of such importance. Had I really given my all for my country? Without question. I've never given less than 100 per cent in any game.

Despite this, whenever I returned home from disappointing England experiences one unshakeable overriding thought pushed itself to the forefront of my mind, no matter how much the rest of the nation mourned.

'At least it wasn't Liverpool,' I'd repeat to myself, over and over.

I confess. Defeats while wearing an England shirt never hurt me in the same way as losing with my club. I wasn't uncaring or indifferent, I simply didn't put England's fortunes at the top of my priority list. Losing felt like a disappointment rather than a calamity.

The Liver Bird mauled the three lions in the fight for my loyalties.

I'm not saying that's right or wrong, it's just how it is. You can't make yourself feel more passionate if the feelings aren't there. That doesn't make me feel guilty. If people want to condemn me and say I'm unpatriotic, so be it. I played for England because it was my country of birth, I was eligible for selection, and a series of managers thought I was good enough for the squad. It was another chance to compete on the international stage. Playing for Liverpool has been a full-time commitment. What followed with England was an extra honour, but not the be all and end all of my purpose in the game. I saw wearing a white shirt as a chance to represent my city and district as much as my country.

We all hear about the importance of 1966 to the country. For my family, the most important event at Wembley that year was Everton winning the FA Cup. If anyone referred to the glorious images of 1966 in my house, they weren't talking about Geoff Hurst scoring a hat-trick or Nobby Stiles dancing along the touchline with the Jules Rimet trophy, they were recalling Eddie

Cavanagh running on the pitch, Mike Trebilcock's two goals against Sheffield Wednesday, and Derek Temple's winner. 'Yes, 1966 was a great year for English football all right,' I'd be told. 'We came from 2–0 down to win the FA Cup. You can't get much better than that. England? Oh yeah, they won the World Cup as well.' Liverpudlians feel the same way about the season as Bill Shankly won his second League title at Anfield. That year's Charity Shield saw players from both clubs parade the World Cup before kick-off, but it was their own silverware that meant more to the fans. That's how we've been brought up to feel, and playing for my country didn't change it.

There was nothing nationalistic about my pursuit of caps. I'd never bellow out the anthem before a game. I don't know what message it's trying to send out. 'God Save the Queen' doesn't get my blood pumping. We sing 'You'll Never Walk Alone' at Anfield, and everyone understands it. It's a rallying cry for standing by one another through thick and thin, wind and rain. Football, or any team sport for that matter, is about togetherness once you cross that white line.

Our nation is divided, not only in terms of prosperity but by different regional outlooks. For some of us, civic pride overpowers nationality. A lot of people in Liverpool feel the same way. I'd stand side by side with supposed rival Mancunians Paul Scholes and Gary Neville in the England line-up, keeping our lips tightly shut as the camera glided along, poking the lens in our faces to see who knew the words to the anthem. I don't know if they felt the same as I did, but a lot of their fans do. For all our differences, this is one area where most Liverpool and Manchester United supporters agree.

Whenever I wore an England shirt, I was colliding with a different culture. There's a split between followers of successful northern clubs such as Liverpool and Manchester United, and the London lads I've played with over the years. If you're born near Wembley, it's a more natural aspiration to play there. It's bred into you. On the streets of Liverpool we have a different view. The clubs represent the lottery numbers and the country is the bonus ball. Playing at Goodison and Anfield was the objective of the lads I grew up with.

I'm sure there are a whole range of social reasons for this. During the 1970s and 1980s, Merseysiders became increasingly alienated from the rest of the country. The 'us' and 'them' syndrome developed, and it's still going strong. I've heard The Kop sing 'We're not English, we are Scouse'. There's no affinity with the national team. While Liverpool as a city suffered economically during the eighties – unemployment was a major issue – our football clubs were the best in Europe. It was the one area where Margaret Thatcher's Conservative government couldn't hurt us. Football was our way of showing the southerners we wouldn't be trampled on. The identity of our clubs is connected to the reputation of our city, so Liverpool and Everton always came first. We were revelling in our region's glory, not sharing it with the rest of the country.

I identified subtle but confusing differences between international and club football as I was growing up. As an Evertonian I was certain I was watching the best players in Europe week in, week out, but international honours seemed unevenly distributed. That didn't just apply to England. It puzzled me how Peter Reid, Paul Bracewell and Trevor Steven weren't acclaimed in this country, but I was equally baffled that Graeme Sharp wasn't Scotland's number one striker. And why wasn't Kevin Sheedy regarded as one of the Republic of Ireland's greatest players? If I could see as a seven-year-old how much better the

Everton midfield was, why couldn't the international managers?

Only after Ray Wilkins was sent off during the 1986 World Cup, the first major international tournament I remember, did Reid break into the England team, and they started to play well. My support was for the player rather than the team. I celebrated when Everton's Gary Lineker scored, but when Diego Maradona knocked England out in Mexico, ten minutes later I was outside playing with my mates copying the handball goal. If it had been Everton losing an FA Cup quarter-final, I wouldn't have wanted to speak to anyone for the rest of the day.

Going to Wembley to watch England was unheard of in Bootle. The thought never occurred to us. I considered England in the same way I did Arsenal or Spurs, as a London club for southern football fans. Wembley might have been the stadium we went to for cup finals, but it still seemed a distant, foreign place, inhabited by a different type of supporter.

I discovered this to be correct when I started playing for England. Although I never had the opportunity to play at Wembley before its redevelopment, even stadiums such as Old Trafford or Villa Park felt unfamiliar on international night. You get this strange, largely subdued atmosphere that only comes alive when England score or attack. There's always a slightly sinister edge, too: you know the mood can shift from euphoric to vicious within the space of a few minutes. If England win, some players still get booed. Over the years, top-class performers such as John Barnes, Frank Lampard and many Manchester United players, all tremendous servants for their country, have suffered, even when the team was comfortably ahead. I dread to think what reaction I'd get from the 'loyal' Wembley faithful if I reversed my controversial decision to retire from international football and answered an SOS.

England internationals are a magnet for fans who are a bit inexperienced, dare I say clueless, when it comes to top-class football. For followers of teams with limited success, particularly in the lower divisions, the national team matters more than for supporters of the top Premier League sides. It's their only chance to travel to Europe and see the best players in action in major competitions. They feel empowered by their opportunity to tell the stars what they really think of them. There's probably an element of club rivalry in the stands too. When Lampard was booed, it was more than likely West Ham supporters, still upset over his move to Chelsea, leading the jeers. 'You'll Never Walk Alone' could never be sung at Wembley during England games because it would be a contradiction. Many top-class England players must have felt lonesome in front of an intolerant eighty thousand crowd.

A superiority complex has also developed. It's presumed England should go close to winning every World Cup and European Championship; failure to live up to this inevitably generates more criticism. But there's no historical justification for it. England's sole success in over a century of international competition is the World Cup in 1966. That was a tremendous achievement inspired by world-class players like Bobby Moore, Geoff Hurst, Gordon Banks and Bobby Charlton, but for all their efforts we're not the only country to win as hosts. Without demeaning their justly legendary status, home advantage was clearly a major factor.

Since 1966, every time we've played a quality side at the business end of a tournament, we've lost. There isn't one team England has beaten in the knockout stages of a World Cup or European Championship we shouldn't have beaten. More relevantly, there isn't a game where the odds were stacked against us when we defied expectations. Go through the record books and it's there in black and white. In the World Cup, England lost to Germany in 1970, to Argentina in 1986, to Germany in 1990, to Argentina in 1998, to Brazil in 2002, and to Portugal in 2006. There's no shame in those defeats, but where are the upsets? Where are the kind of results we've seen our rugby union side achieve at World Cups, when they turn over the likes of Australia when everyone anticipates defeat? It remains the case for those World Cups when the side's efforts were acclaimed: in 1990, only the 'mighty' Cameroon and Belgium had to be beaten to reach the semi-final. England's European Championship record makes for even grimmer reading. Since a third place in 1968 (that World Cup-winning squad again), in those finals we actually qualified for we've only won one solitary knockout match, against Spain in 1996 – on home soil, and on penalties.

Our overall record places England in a third tier of world football, and that will only change with the help of a radical mental rethink. We'll never be as technically gifted as the South Americans, who learn their football on the streets of Rio and Buenos Aires, yet there are those who still believe we should aspire to play in their style. We're also behind the French, the Italians and the Germans, whose greater nous means they consistently produce in the major events, where it really matters.

France have benefited in recent years from the number of African immigrants who arrived in their country as youngsters, and whose natural athletic gifts they've been able to develop in their academies. Italy and Germany are the countries we should be emulating; their success has more in common with the kind of football I've played at club level, especially in Europe. The will to win at all costs, in players and fans alike, is worth an extra

10 per cent in knockout football. This game is as much about 'knowing' how to win as it is about natural ability.

On the surface, there's no reason why England can't match Italy and Germany. Our league is superior, and no one is going to convince me the Italian side that won the World Cup in 2006 was technically better than ours. We've never mastered the methodical, tactically disciplined approach that is the foundation of their achievements. Crucially, we lack the shrewdness of our European neighbours. I've noticed throughout my career how, in general, the top foreign players think much more deeply about the tactical side of the game. They can see how a game is progressing and instinctively recognize the right time to drop the tempo for a spell, often to walking pace, to keep possession. Then they'll speed it up and go for the throat when the time is right. With England, there's a demand to play in one robust 100 mph style. We're always looking for the killer pass, and there have been occasions when no matter how much the manager tells players it's important just to keep the ball, even if it means the game goes through a quiet patch, the supporters demand it goes forward as quickly as possible, which usually means we give it away. At international level, you can't be successful unless you vary your style, usually in the same match. It's the ultimate test of playing with your brain as much as your feet, and we've failed too often to do so.

I could also be controversial and say the foreign lads know how to cheat better than us, but that makes it sound like a negative. What some call 'gamesmanship', others call 'cunning'. I've seen Liverpool teams adopt the 'winning is the only thing' attitude in Europe, just as the Italians and Germans do so expertly in World Cups, but I've never seen it in an England team. We're not cute enough upstairs, and some of our players and coaches are probably terrified of changing our ways. If one of our players hits the deck when he's only been slightly touched and wins a penalty, or gets another player booked or sent off, we declare a state of national emergency and instigate a witch hunt. I can remember Glenn Hoddle being castigated prior to the 1998 World Cup for daring to suggest our players need to go down more. He was spot on.

We consistently suffer from such antics. Remember Beckham against Argentina in 1998, and Rooney against Portugal in 2006? Both saw red because of minor altercations. Their opponents overreacted, our players took the blame. Had the roles been reversed and we'd gone on to beat ten men, I'm not sure the conduct of our lads would have been applauded in the same way. Diego Simeone and Cristiano Ronaldo were heroes in their homeland, where the boundaries between what some call dishonesty and others applaud as craftiness are blurred. Our players are damned either way.

We'd have more chance of winning if we took the same cynical approach, but every fixture is accompanied by this irrational belief the country has a divine right to be the best in the world by playing 'the English way', whatever that is. We're supposed to behave like 'gentlemen' on and off the park. That's a worthy principle if you can get the rest of the world to follow suit. In the absence of such a fantasy, I'd much prefer us to become more ruthless, collect some medals and let the arguments about the morality of our methods be discussed after our post-final celebrations.

The psychology of our international game is wrong. England ought to be embracing the idea of being the underdog on the world stage, ready to do everything and anything to win. We should be revelling in the image of the plucky outsider trying to unbalance the superpowers of Argentina and Brazil, while matching the French, Germans and Italians. Rather than booing players, the fans should be recognizing how creating a vibrant, supportive atmosphere can bestir a flawed team. The greatest nights of my Liverpool career have been spent upsetting the odds. In recent years we've beaten Juventus, Chelsea, Barcelona and AC Milan in the Champions League, despite having inferior players. What we did possess was the desire and wit needed to get a result, no matter what it took.

The Liverpool crowd has been credited with dragging us across the winning line. I've never heard the same said of England fans at Wembley, who are more likely to help the opposition by turning on their own. Supporters of Liverpool, Manchester United, Chelsea and Arsenal rarely boo their own players during a game, and they're more accustomed to success. That's why some of us prefer club football to internationals.

I was never in love with playing for England in the first place. By the time I stopped, I felt a huge weight lifting. I took criticism for my decision, but when I look over my international record, I believe I was more sinned against than a sinner. I never ducked out of a call-up, never pulled out with a slight twinge, and never looked for an excuse to swerve a meaningless friendly. If the cap fitted, I wore it with pride. I know players who've deliberately got themselves booked and suspended because they didn't fancy going on the next unattractive foreign trip. Not me. If fit, I was always available when called upon. And, despite being continually seen as a deputy for others, I never complained. Wherever Sven-Göran Eriksson or Steve McClaren asked me to play, I stepped up with no fuss. I've even cancelled summer holidays to join England squads as a late call-up. For a while, I held the record for Under-21 caps. That was because I was so committed, turning up for every squad.

Having said that, I was no worshipper at the altar of St George. My international career almost ended at Under-21 level as swiftly as it began.

When the England Under-21s, the supposed cream of up-and-coming talent, get together, the rivalry is intense. Nothing is more competitive than the sight of the most impressive defenders, midfielders and strikers fighting it out to be seen as the thirstiest drinkers and horniest shaggers in the country. At the peak of immaturity, respect on the field is secondary to the admiration you earn through your capacity to be 'one of the lads' off it. The Under-21 manager's job must be one of the most demanding in football. You're dealing with twenty-two rough diamonds many of whom need a regular polish.

Not surprisingly, given my earlier reputation at Lilleshall, I tended to find myself involved in most disciplinary mishaps. I wasted no time consolidating my position as a trouble magnet.

The first lapse arrived shortly after my introduction to Under-21 duty, in 1997. With manager Peter Taylor's permission, I went drinking in the hotel nightclub, accompanied by Jody Morris, then at Chelsea, and Sheffield Wednesday's Lee Briscoe. I found to my cost that when the manager said we could have 'a drink' after the game he meant in the singular sense. Our interpretation differed. Taylor caught me taking a piss against the wall of our Swindon base, and grabbed me by the scruff of the neck as I was finishing off. I staggered back to my hotel room, struggling to keep my balance. 'No matter, plenty of strike-outs left,' I thought, Taylor's growls still ringing in my ear. My presumption was wrong. The manager's patience was wearing thin.

The next fixture coincided with England's final World Cup qualifier in 1997, when Glenn Hoddle's side secured an heroic 0–0 draw in Rome to book the trip to France. We'd shown similar battling qualities a day earlier, winning 1–0 in Rieti despite being down to ten men for eighty minutes. Kieron Dyer scored. It was traditional for the Under-21s to head to the senior game twenty-four hours after their own. They did, except for the rogues gallery of five forced straight to Rome airport as punishment for yet more indiscretions the night before. Rio Ferdinand, Frank Lampard, Ben Thatcher, Danny Murphy and I watched events unfold in an airport lounge, banished for breaking a curfew after our match.

Thatcher's performance in Italy had been especially impressive. Not only was he the player sent off early in the game for elbowing, I then watched in awe in the bar a few hours later as he managed to keep hold of a pint and continue to take swigs while being grabbed by the neck from behind by his manager. This after he'd already knocked back ten lagers. My respect for such a manoeuvre didn't cut it with Taylor, whose rage with Thatcher rubbed off on the rest of us.

'You're finished with England,' he told me.

The *Sunday People* splashed with our 'shame' the following week, but any fears of a backlash at Anfield were ill-founded. Roy Evans and Ronnie Moran thought it was funny. Had the incident occurred under the next Liverpool manager, I'd have been training with the Academy players for the next month.

Taylor's promise to end my international career was hollow. Far from being sent to the wasteland, I was soon threatening appearance records. Twelve months after my debut, my transformation from demon to angel was set to be confirmed with the Under-21 captaincy. It was an honour I'd set my heart on the more I contemplated the possibility.

Taylor was considering me and Lampard for the role. We were room-mates at the time, and although I got on with Frank, privately I believed I'd get the nod as the older, more experienced player. The manager called us into his room separately, but as soon as I looked into his eyes I felt deflated.

'Sorry, Jamie, you've missed out this time,' he said.

I didn't agree with Taylor's decision, but I respected it. I rated him as a manager and had grown to like him the longer I'd worked with him. The sense of disappointment didn't fester, although I didn't relish having to return to my room to face the elated Lampard. I was pleased for him, but anyone who tells you private battles between team-mates aren't important is kidding. The 'team first' ethic doesn't always apply. We both wanted the armband and I was hurt to be overlooked.

My wounds didn't bleed for long. My personal setback was put into perspective when Taylor left as part of the Hoddle controversy a few months later.

Taylor was dismissed for no other reason than short-sighted FA politics – typical of the illogical decisions that have plagued the organization for decades. Howard Wilkinson, then the technical director, had been eyeing the Under-21 post. Hoddle's departure led to Taylor following him out the door in what seemed to me at the time a nonsensical decision.

Taylor was respected by the players and had nurtured us well since those misdemeanours in Swindon and Rieti. I reckon his treatment was shameful. Taylor's twenty-three matches included fourteen victories, six draws and three defeats, only one of which was in a competitive fixture. Those he brought through the ranks gave credibility to the view that the next generation of England players had the potential to end our trophy drought. Lampard, Dyer, Heskey, Ferdinand and I were linchpins of the team, all capable of serving our country for the next decade. All we lacked was a prolific striker, and that was because Michael Owen had bypassed the Under-21s and headed straight into the seniors. We won six out of six in qualifying for the 2000 Under-21 European Championship – quite a foundation on which to lose your job. Training sessions were inventive and enjoyable, and there was a focus on developing the technical side of our game. This disappeared when Wilkinson – Mr Functional – took over.

Taylor broke down in tears during a team-talk prior to his last game in charge. All the players felt for him. I don't know anyone involved in the Under-21s at that time who understood why he was told to go.

The FA must accept responsibility for the drop in standards since. 'If it ain't broke, don't fix it' the saying goes. Not only was the structure that brought players like me from Lilleshall through the Under-21s not in need of repair, it seemed to be operating successfully. Since Lilleshall closed, and Taylor's first stint with the Under-21s ended, the conveyor belt of talent hasn't created the same results. Perhaps it's a coincidence. I'm convinced my route through the system helped turn me from a very good Premier League player into an international-class one.

Wilkinson was in charge of the Under-21s when we arrived at the finals in Slovakia and wasted no time enforcing his reputed disciplinary techniques. Lee Hendrie was grabbed by the throat at half-time during a group game for what Wilkinson called 'shitting out of a tackle', which goes to show the new man wasn't as bad as some suggest. There were parts of Wilkinson's approach I liked, but the enjoyment Taylor instilled into our game was gone. A successful era was ending, and those of us who'd played our part were ready to move on – some quicker than others. I'd won my record-breaking twenty-seventh cap for the Under-21s against Slovakia in our final match of a sadly typical unfulfilling tournament. The step up beckoned.

My first taste of senior international action had actually arrived a year earlier. Kevin Keegan suffered a series of injury withdrawals prior to a trip to Hungary at the end of April 1999. I wasn't in the original squad, but was drafted in as a replacement. Midway through the second half I received the call, and in a move of irresistible symbolism given what would follow over the next ten years, I replaced Rio Ferdinand at centre-half. The game finished 1–1.

There was a lengthy delay before my second call-up, which was the first time I was named in the original twenty-two-man squad on merit. It turned out to be an especially significant occasion: the home World Cup qualifier with Germany in October 2000.

My promotion shouldn't have come as a surprise. It was a natural progression from the Under-21s, and at the time Liverpool were rapidly improving under Gérard Houllier. But it wasn't as though I was banging the door down to be called up. There wasn't a great clamour for me to get my chance. Because I was no longer eligible for the Under-21s, there was a sense I had nowhere else to go but to get fast-tracked into the full squad. If I'd drifted into the international wilderness having been such a solid member of the Under-21s, it wouldn't have reflected well on the system. But the way I've progressed since suggests they made the right call.

Hopefully it wasn't my presence at Wembley that tipped Keegan over the edge, because he quit immediately after the game. I'd been in the stands thinking about how I'd cope with the stick my German mate Didi Hamann would give me at Melwood after he scored the winner – the last goal at the old Wembley. By the time I made it to the dressing room Keegan had already made his announcement to the players. The

Adams family, Tony and Crozier (then FA chief executive), were desperately trying to talk Keegan into a rethink. It was a surreal introduction for me.

Keegan later accepted he might have overestimated his capacity to cope with the pressure at that level. From a personal perspective, I didn't work with him long enough to assess how good a coach he was. All I can remember from my time under his management is him telling me how much I looked like Robert Lee. Certainly his team-talk before his final game made what followed unsurprising. I was sitting near Paul Ince when Keegan fatefully announced Gareth Southgate was preferred in central midfield. Ince wasn't even on the bench. Keegan didn't need a resignation letter. His teamsheet did the job.

The timing of his quitting was amazing, though. You don't leave three days before a World Cup qualifier. I faced a similar situation when I quit internationals as I reached a definite decision while with England between fixtures prior to a key Euro 2008 match. Because I didn't want to cause a distraction, I said nothing until a more opportune moment afterwards. Keegan must have had his reservations before the Germany game, and I sympathized with his honesty when he said he wasn't up to the job, but having committed himself to carrying on he ought to have continued for a final match, not left the players in the lurch as he did.

His resignation was a poignant moment for English football. The failure of a coach who seemed to epitomize the spirit and enthusiasm we needed appeared to make the FA lose faith completely in English managers. The door closed on homegrown coaches taking the step up, and opened for a foreigner with seriously impressive credentials.

The Sven era was upon us.

I was never sure if Sven-Göran Eriksson was an international manager or international playboy. I know what he was best at. If his style of football had been as entertaining as his private life, England would have been world champions and he'd have been handed a twenty-year contract. The longer he spent in the job, the worse his status became as a football coach and the better it became as a Casanova.

His record still stands scrutiny against any of his predecessors', though. He reached three consecutive quarter-finals in major championships and boasted an impressive record in five years of qualification, losing only once. Nobody can deny he got results. His England side also claimed two of the most prized scalps in our modern history, defeating Argentina in the World Cup group stages and securing a 5–1 win against Germany in Munich. There are those who say he underachieved with the best squad England has had since 1966. I'm inclined to think he led England to its rightful level but fell short of adding the extra ingredient needed to upset the odds. Sven did a good job rather than an extraordinary one.

He arrived with a terrific reputation. His success at Lazio didn't especially convince me because he received considerable financial backing from Sergio Cragnotti. But his achievements with Benfica, Sampdoria and especially an unfashionable club like Gothenburg suggested this was a man who knew what he was doing. The Swedes won the UEFA Cup under him, Benfica reached the European Cup Final in 1990, and Sampdoria regularly won and challenged for honours.

Originally, we had this image of a rather dull, methodical, ultra-professional Swede who'd bring some stability to the job and demand everyone's respect. This didn't quite match the reality. No sooner had Sven arrived than we realized our preconceptions were ill-founded. We were given an early clue about his colourful lifestyle. Before one of his early World Cup qualifiers, a story broke about girls finding their way into the team hotel to provide some of the players with pre-match 'entertainment'. Eriksson summoned us for what we expected to be a stern warning. Instead, we received some fatherly advice.

'There's no need to have girls in the team hotel,' Sven told us. 'If you see someone you like, just get her phone number and arrange to go to her house after the game. Then we will have no problems.'

There was chuckling around the room, which was sparkling thanks to the twinkle in Eriksson's eye. We weren't exactly sure how serious he was. Looking back, I think he was being genuine. He was giving us his best tips.

Under his management, I was either doing the hokey-cokey or playing musical chairs. I was in and out of the team, usually in a different position from one game to the next, and could never establish myself as first choice. I accepted this. When everyone was fit, I never expected to start. There were more established players in all the roles I filled. Disappointments came if players were injured, particularly before big games. That's when you want to sense you've got the manager's trust. I never did.

I appreciated he had managerial talent. His CV speaks for itself. He undoubtedly brought something new to the dressing room, I just struggled to see what it was. He was an introverted character who rarely displayed emotion or revealed his innermost thoughts. If we won, lost or drew, his reaction was identical. This is the trend in many modern coaches. They're careful with their choice of words, using the language of politicians rather than football managers. My preference is to know where I stand. I don't like guessing games. I crave knowing if the manager thought I played well. I'm thirsty for some of their experience or knowledge so I can learn from them. I want to understand the reasons behind every tactical change or selection they've made. There was none of this with Sven. I'd leave training sessions and games none the wiser about why I'd played, been left out or been used as a sub. Some players love this approach. They just want to go into work, get told what to do, play the game, go home and forget about it. That's not me. I relive every kick, watch reruns of the match and try to analyse what went right or wrong. Under Houllier and Benitez, I had managers willing to go through the ninety minutes with me and explain where I could improve. Eriksson was the opposite. I wanted to become an England regular under him, but there was no sense of guidance or advice about what more I needed to do to achieve this ambition. I was always a peripheral figure, although I managed to play my part in his finest hour.

The 5–1 win in Germany in September 2001 should have been the platform for a sustained period of success for England. I was especially proud of the Anfield influence on the result. Mo, Steven Gerrard, Nick Barmby, Emile Heskey and I (as a sub) all played in the match. The goals were scored by Liverpool players. Eriksson can consider himself unlucky with injuries prior to the 2002 World Cup, which meant this performance was never repeated. Stevie pulled out because he needed a groin operation, while Mo and David Beckham weren't 100 per cent fit. I struggled with a knee injury all season and needed an operation. I faced a stark choice by May. If I'd gone to the World Cup, it would have delayed surgery and seen me miss the start of the 2002–03 season. The club came first. Eriksson told me I'd be in his squad, but there was no way I'd risk missing pre-season training with Liverpool, especially as I was always wary of new players impressing the manager. Besides, I knew I'd spend most of the tournament on the bench. The longer this was the reality, the less content I became to be a mere deputy.

Disillusionment began to shadow me around the time of Euro 2004. By then I was fully established as one of the country's top defenders. When England had problems at centre-half, I was confident enough to presume I should be in the side. In the warm-up games before we headed to Portugal, I replaced John Terry and played well. I was led to believe I'd be in the team for our opening game with France. As the fixture approached, there was a sudden backing in the newspapers for Ledley King. All the vibes I was getting from journalists I knew indicated King would play. The final training sessions before kick-off confirmed I was going to be overlooked.

My head spun with mystification. It wasn't the fact King was picked that upset me, but the process that put him in the side. I'll always believe that Eriksson changed his mind under pressure from the media. One essential question bugged me: if I wasn't his initial choice to face France, why did I play in the warm-up games ahead of King? Eriksson told me he preferred King's pace against France's Thierry Henry. I didn't buy that. My response was to ask if the manager had realized Henry was a bit nippy only when he got to Portugal. The draw had been made months earlier. We knew we'd be facing Henry when we played the warm-up fixtures. If this was Eriksson's plan, why wasn't King playing centre-back earlier? What kind of preparation was this for a young defender, pitched into such an important game?

It turned out King had a blinder, fully justifying his selection. There's no reason why he shouldn't have been picked. He's a great defender. But this was one of several occasions when indecision surrounded Eriksson's selections. His reign was particularly tainted by his inability to mould Steven Gerrard and Frank Lampard into a well-balanced midfield partnership. Eriksson's solution was to call his midfielders and captain for a meeting and ask their opinions on resolving the problem. He wanted a volunteer for the holding role in midfield. Neither Stevie nor Frank wanted the job. Both are at their best when free to get forward. David Beckham offered his services. Eriksson agreed, so arguably the best crosser of the ball in the world was switched to an unfamiliar defensive midfield role. The experiment lasted a couple of games, against Wales and Northern Ireland, and inevitably failed.

I was stunned when I heard how this decision was reached. Who was being paid to manage this team? Eriksson needed to be stronger. He needed to have the courage of his convictions, but there were times I wondered what his opinion was. Perhaps he didn't know himself.

The Gerrard–Lampard debate lasted for years; it should have been nipped in the bud. The obvious solution was for the manager to order Stevie to play the holding role to make the partnership work. If the balance still wasn't right, one would have to sit on the bench. Obviously, I'd say there's no way that could be Stevie. The difference between the two is this: Frank Lampard became a world-class player, Steven Gerrard was born one.

Eriksson gave the impression he relied too much on the guidance of others. In particular, his close relationship with Beckham became detrimental. Beckham was world class. Put aside all the hype and celebrity and judge him on his footballing talent and he's up there with Luis Figo as the finest right midfielder of his generation. At his peak, it's no wonder he had so much power.

Unfortunately, there are times when every player needs to be dropped or subbed for the good of the team, and you need a manager wise enough to see it, and firm enough to act appropriately. By the time of the World Cup in 2006 Beckham was in a more vulnerable position, but Eriksson stuck by him. There were occasions when he should have been subbed or started on the bench, coming on later in the game so he had more time and space to have an influence.

Eriksson's decisions were increasingly unpredictable and criticized. The holding midfielder experiment placed me back in the middle during a few warm-up games. I did as well as I could given my six-year absence from the position, but the idea was soon abandoned. To this day I have no idea why I played there or what more I could have done to impress the manager in the role. Then we were all dumbfounded when Arsenal's Theo Walcott was included in the World Cup squad for Germany ahead of Jermaine Defoe and Darren Bent. At seventeen he was nowhere near ready. Not only was it bad for the squad, it was unfair on the player. He's got to live up to his reputation as a wonderkid now. The profession is hard enough without that kind of unnecessary pressure.

England undoubtedly underperformed throughout that World Cup. I can't recall a game where we played to our potential, but a quarter-final place was no disgrace. We played our best football down to ten men against Portugal, when the preoccupation with tactics, systems and formations had to be abandoned and we showed old-fashioned English qualities of grit and determination. I don't believe the manager was a failure, as was suggested. I'd have preferred different players in the squad, but even if we'd played to our maximum I doubt we'd have gone much further given the injuries we had. The squad wasn't as good as the players, media and supporters made out before the tournament. The usual English disease of over-hype and over-expectation tripped us up again.

Everyone looked for a scapegoat. Eriksson took the blame, but for a while the investigation even focused on me. Eriksson's assistant, Tord Grip, highlighted my penalty miss as a chief factor in our demise. When asked why I was one of those involved in the shoot-out against the Portuguese, he explained, 'He took one really well for Liverpool in the Champions League Final.'

I've watched our penalty shoot-out win in Istanbul a thousand times since 2005. I've relived the magical moment of victory more times than this. To this day I still can't recall taking a penalty, and neither can the millions of others around the world who watched the game. I'm not imagining it, then. I definitely didn't take a penalty in the Champions League Final in 2005. The only people who seem to think I was one of Liverpool's takers that night are Grip and the journalist who wrote the story. It's frightening to think England's assistant manager could be so ill-informed.

Having said that, I'd fancied my chances against Portugal that night and readily agreed when asked to take one because my record in training was superb. I was screwed, because I buried my first attempt only to be ordered to retake it for shooting too early. I should have blasted the second, but I picked my spot and missed.

The text messages of consolation I received on the coach heading back to the hotel included one from Kenny Dalglish.

'I wud rather miss for England than LFC,' I wrote back.

'Don't worry, u will never be asked,' Kenny replied, cheekily.

'I can't remember u ever taking one,' I continued the argument. 'Didn't u have the bottle?'

It took Kenny another twenty-four hours to think up a reply to that one.

'I took 1 in a pre-season once and missed,' he belatedly admitted.

Regardless of the penalty, I never played well in that World Cup, partially because I was shattered. I played more games than anyone in Europe that season. Officially, there were sixty-eight in all, because of Liverpool's three rounds of Champions League qualifiers, the Super Cup Final and our involvement in the World Club Championship in Japan. Including pre-season games I was over the seventy mark.

My versatility had become a disadvantage. In my early twenties, moving from midfield or central defence to full-back wasn't a problem. After four years during which all my games for Liverpool were at centre-half, the switch back to right-back was uncomfortable because at that stage of the season I no longer had the legs for the role, and the mid-afternoon summer heat was exhausting. I knew Sven wouldn't pick me at centre-half, so when he named the team and I wasn't picked at all it started to feel like a relief. In fact I was starting to realize that if I wasn't in the squad exclusively as a centre-half, I'd rather not be there.

When I was subbed during our second game, against Trinidad and Tobago, my friends and family started to get upset on my behalf. 'Fuck off Eriksson, you shithouse,' was my dad's response to the decision. If he'd known he was sitting next to Sven's son at the time he might have been more restrained.

In the final game against Portugal, I thought my chance to play in the middle would finally come when John Terry picked up an early injury. Eriksson turned towards the bench and gave the call.

'Sol, get ready.'

The seeds of imminent international retirement were planted.

For my family, it was going to take more than the minor inconvenience of England's mediocre performances to stop the entertainment at that World Cup. The motto of the Gallacher family from the TV show *Shameless* might as well have been amended and daubed in graffiti on the hotel walls of Baden-Baden during the 2006 World Cup: 'The Carraghers understand one of the most vital necessities in life. They know how to throw a party.'

In their honour, English journalists dubbed the temporary home of the players' families 'The House of Scouse'. My guests were the only England fans who were smiling whatever the results. It's a wonder I ever concentrated on my football as I was taking phone calls from the FA following the latest 'incident' involving the WAGs and the FAFs, which is what my 'crew' called themselves. Friends and family. I don't know what friends and girlfriends would have been called.

I was still emptying my suitcase prior to the tournament when the first call from the FA arrived.

'Jamie, I'm afraid there's been a problem in one of the rooms booked under your name. It appears someone was keeping awake all the residents by singing anti-German songs.'

Four weeks later I was packing my bags and wondering how I'd missed my pen when the final bulletin was handed to me.

'Jamie, I'm afraid there's been another problem in one of the rooms booked under your name. Someone has thrown a bucket of water out of the window directly on the heads of some journalists who were sitting below.'

By now, I had only one response.

'Thank fuck this World Cup is over.'

The families, especially mine, had all the fun. While England's players laboured their way past Trinidad and Tobago and

Ecuador, I often felt I was in the wrong hotel. I'd head down there as much as possible, usually armed with the latest discarded training strips which I'd swiped from the team's base. Our kit men would dump all our used gear in a room on my floor, so I'd pop in every morning with a few carrier bags and fill them up. The FA staff must have been bemused by the sight of all the families walking around town with official England training tops on, some of them with the initials JC, DB, MO and SGE.

The WAGs were hilarious. Their unofficial queen, Posh Spice, adopted my dad as her bodyguard. What a pair they made. My dad first met Victoria Beckham in Portugal in 2004. He admitted being struck by blind panic as she walked towards him in the hotel lobby. He was on his way to the laundry room and got so flustered as Posh approached, he dropped all his dirty washing. He found himself on all fours desperately trying to retrieve his smelly underpants as Posh strutted past in her designer outfit and high heels. By the time of the 2006 World Cup Posh had enlisted his help to protect her from journalists. When she needed someone to give the paparazzi a threatening scowl, she'd find him in the bar.

Neville Neville, Gary and Phil's dad, was my dad's drinking partner. In fact, it was he who introduced Posh's dad to mine.

'This is Mr Adams,' said Neville.

My dad started talking about the Arsenal team of the late eighties and early nineties until it was pointed out it wasn't Tony's dad.

'I thought he looked a bit young,' my dad said.

Some of the girlfriends lapped up the publicity. I know a few of them were tipping off the photographers about where they'd be eating or drinking of an evening. I'm glad to say my Nicola has never sought the limelight like that.

'Are you going shopping again?' the paparazzi would ask her as she left the hotel.

'No, I'm taking my kids to McDonald's for their tea,' she'd shout back.

Even that would make *Granada Reports*, the local TV news show.

Everyone wanted a night out with the Carraghers, and there were many funny exchanges, as my family had to do little to confirm predictable Scouse stereotypes. When my brother Paul was discussing the hotel set-up with Paul Robinson's mum, he was hit by one.

'It's an amazing place,' Paul said to her. 'The way we've got security guards on every floor is brilliant.'

Robinson's mum gave Paul a cheeky grin and joked, 'I thought you'd be used to that, coming from Liverpool.'

There was a suggestion the presence of our families was a distraction. It's a daft theory. If having your wife and children near you before and after a big game can make you lose focus, I'd like to know why so many of us have performed so well for our clubs in Europe over many years. I slept in my own house the night before some of the biggest home games I've played with Liverpool, and it didn't seem to do any harm. As excuses go for our poor performances, blaming it on the fact we could see our wives and girlfriends in between games has to be one of the lamest.

Apart from the WAGs and FAFs, a few JAGs (journalists and gobshites) shared the hotel. Although many players distrust the press, it made a refreshing change. Apart from a few minor altercations it was a success to mix the families with the journalists. A lot of clubs and countries would consider this a huge no-no, but if you put a barrier between players and reporters it creates unnecessary tension and gives certain writers the freedom to go

overboard. Reporters will take a more sensible, less sensational-
ist attitude in their writing if they know they've got to have
breakfast with the wife or parents of a player the next day.
Criticism of the England team is part of the job, it's the personal
stuff that's avoidable, and 90 per cent of the journalists covering
the national team didn't overstep the mark, even though the
team's performances weren't very good. At a World Cup, it's also
important for everyone to be able to differentiate between those
who are reporting solely on the football and those who are there
for other purposes, like the paparazzi or showbiz reporters. Most
of the families appreciated the chance to get things off their
chest, and even left Germany respecting reporters they thought
they'd hate.

My dad had an issue with Matt Lawton from the *Daily Mail*.
Lawton had referred to one of my poor early England performances in order to criticize me in one of his articles. 'Why are you
still going on about a game that was four months ago? Don't be
putting shit in the paper about my lad,' my dad warned him,
though not so politely. By the time of the World Cup they were
able to shake hands and resolve their differences.

Most reporters I know are passionate supporters who want
the best for their team, but at times they can go a bit too far, particularly with England. I've had few problems with the media
throughout my career. The only gripe I have is the 'marks out of
ten' syndrome. It's utterly pointless, annoying, and can definitely
impact on a player's confidence. I've heard players seem less concerned about the manager's opinion and more worried about
what mark they've been given in a Sunday paper. If all sports edi-
tors could grant me one wish, it would be to get rid of this stupid
marking system.

Disturbingly for us, the biggest story of the 2006 World Cup was almost the journey home on the plane, which nearly didn't land. Players from Liverpool and United took a connecting flight to Manchester from Heathrow, but the stormy conditions were atrocious. As the plane dipped from side to side there was a moment when all of us genuinely feared we weren't going to make it. On the plus side, the plane was rerouted to Liverpool John Lennon Airport. I tried to remain calm to reassure my children James and Mia, but most of the women and children were screaming.

'Try and keep quiet,' I shouted. 'The kids are getting terrified.'

There was someone screeching in terror towards the back of the plane. I'd never heard howling like it before. Even my two-year-old daughter had never created such a noise.

'Whose child is that?' I asked Nicola.

When I looked myself, I noticed it wasn't an infant. Head in his hands, ducked into the safety position, was an inconsolable England and Manchester United superstar. It was Wayne Rooney.

Thoughts of international retirement grew as soon as I returned to Liverpool. Only two things stopped me there and then.

First, Steve McClaren's appointment excited me more than others. I figured an Englishman might recognize and trust my qualities more than another 'outsider'. If I'd felt I'd have to prove myself again, I wouldn't have bothered. I'd enjoyed working with McClaren when he was assistant manager. His training sessions were similar to those of Taylor with the Under-21s, full of fresh ideas.

I admit I had some doubts about his step up, though. There are times when promoting from within works, but so soon after the Eriksson era, with everyone, including the players, fancying a change, the timing was tough for McClaren. He had to handle a lot of the baggage from the World Cup. You always felt his toughest task was earning the respect a new England manager deserves. His early results and performances made it doubly difficult. There was no honeymoon period for him, but I was initially optimistic about my future under his leadership.

I also delayed quitting because I felt my form was as good as ever heading into 2006–07. John Terry is one of the best central defenders in the world, but over the previous two years I thought he was the only English centre-half who'd played better than me. I was confident I could challenge Rio Ferdinand for the second central defensive spot. Sol Campbell had been left out of McClaren's first squad, so I'd pushed ahead of him in the queue. A potential vacancy was there. All I needed was a chance. If I was given one big game alongside Terry, I was sure we'd be so formidable as a pairing the manager would have to keep me in. The opportunity never arrived. McClaren called up Jonathan Woodgate, and then he selected Ledley King ahead of me when Ferdinand was absent in what became my final international involvement, in Estonia in June 2007. Five days earlier I'd been sent back to full-back on my Wembley debut against Brazil. That Brazil game sealed the deal for me, but I wasn't prepared to cause a stir ahead of an important qualifying game. McClaren was oblivious to how upset I was, but when I was overlooked again for King I couldn't wait any longer.

All this came at the climax of a season when I felt my game was better than ever. I'd won man of the match against Barcelona, the most destructive attacking force in the world. McClaren had been at Anfield on the night we kept out Ronaldinho, Messi and Eto'o in the Champions League. Still I couldn't play centre-back for my country.

Enough was enough. I called McClaren shortly after the

Estonia trip and told him I wouldn't be available for England the following season. He was shocked, and pleaded with me to delay my decision. 'I promise you'll play the full ninety minutes against Germany at centre-half,' McClaren said, referring to the forthcoming friendly. 'In my mind, you are third-choice centre-back.'

I was taken aback by how surprised he was, but I'd rehearsed my responses.

'If I'm really third choice,' I said, 'why didn't I play in the middle against Brazil and Estonia?'

There was no comeback to that.

His vow to pick me next time didn't make me feel better. I wouldn't be in the team on merit, but because I'd forced the manager into a corner. That wouldn't have been right or fair on the other defenders. If I'd played badly in the next game, I wouldn't have been able to look McClaren in the eye.

McClaren even asked John Terry to call me and get me to think again. Terry had told the manager he thought I should partner him in the notorious fixture in Estonia, and he told me as much.

The only concession I agreed was not to announce my intentions, but it was leaked to the press so I had no choice but to confirm the story. Stupidly, I left a get-out clause saying I'd return 'in an emergency', but all this did was make me anxious about Terry and Ferdinand picking up injuries – which they both did. There was no way I was going to reverse my decision, no matter what.

I confirmed this to McClaren during one final meeting.

'The door is always open for you, Jamie,' he said.

I walked behind him and closed it.

I doubt the England fans would have had me back anyway, given their reaction.

Bootle Boys: With the lads on holiday in Cyprus in the late 90s – Gary and Steven Seagreaves, Pritch, my cousin Jamie, Kev, Sean and my brother Paul.

Holding the baby: My son James's birth in 2002 changed my life.

Proud parents: I made sure I was by Nicola's side for the birth of Mia in 2004.

In at the deep end: Becoming a father made football the second most important part of my life.

The perfect match: Nicola and I tied the knot in 2005.

Married bliss: Me and Nicola on honeymoon in Dubai.

The two nans: We couldn't live without them.

Granddad Carra: Dad and James on holiday in Tenerife in 2006.

Cute Carras: James and Mia attend St Mary's College in Crosby.

Angels...

Angels with dirty faces: James and Mia show they've already got the famous Carragher fighting spirit.

With dirty faces!!!!!

The Gallaghers know how to throw a party: Backstage with Oasis brothers Liam and Noel in Leeds, 2006, with (*front row*) my brother John, Dad, Mick Laffey and Uncle Pete.

The team of Carraghers: On holiday at Eurodisney in 2006.

Family fun: Playing with James and Mia at Eurodisney in 2006. The mythical Everton tattoo must be on my other arm!

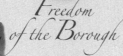

Freedom of the Borough

At an Extraordinary Meeting of the Sefton Metropolitan Borough Council held on the thirtieth day of June Two thousand and five IT WAS RESOLVED THAT in exercise of the powers conferred by Section 249 of the Local Government Act 1972, and having regard to the magnificent achievement of James Carragher as a member of the European Champions League 2005 winning team of Liverpool Football Club and the fact that he was born and educated in Bootle and still lives within the Borough of Sefton, the Council do agree to confer upon

JAMES CARRAGHER
THE HONORARY FREEDOM
OF THE BOROUGH

in recognition of his outstanding achievements and the inspiration and example that he provides for Sefton young people particularly.
IN WITNESS whereof the Common Seal of the Council was hereunto affixed on the 23th day of January 2006.

Mayor

Graham Haywood
Chief Executive

Bootle Primary Team, 1988

Above. Dancing Queen: Mia enjoys her ballet dancing and drama classes.

Left: Freedom of Sefton scroll.

Below: Scooby and Scrappy: James and Mia in fancy dress before their school Christmas party in 2007.

My world: Nicola, James and Mia.

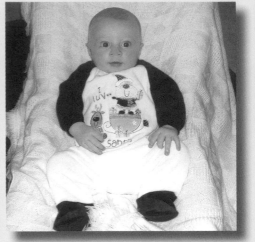

Baby John: My brother John's boy, the latest addition to the Carragher clan.

Below: Following in my boot steps: James was mascot for my 500th Liverpool game against Luton Town in January 2008.

As I drove away from Melwood during pre-season, I switched on TalkSport and heard a discussion about my decision. The presenter, Adrian Durham, accused me of being a bottler. I was raging. If the intention was to provoke a response, it worked. I felt compelled to defend myself, so I called Durham on air to confront him. I wasn't thinking about the publicity for the radio station, which they predictably milked for all it was worth, more about my own pride. I'd never imagined the news would provoke such hostility. I considered myself a fringe player, so why the fuss? I have no issue with anyone claiming King or Woodgate are better centre-halves, I just didn't agree with it. I'd reached the point where competing for the right to be number three centre back wasn't on my agenda. I was ready to step up and play alongside Terry. My record for Liverpool, and my dependability when it came to injuries, entitled me to feel I was worth a look.

The contradiction in all this is, when everyone was fit, McClaren was right. If I'd been England manager, I'd have picked Terry and Ferdinand as first-choice centre-backs. Ferdinand didn't deserve to be dropped as the balance was better with an out-and-out defender like Terry alongside him. Though it was hard to admit at the time when I was fired by an ambition, even a conviction, to claim that England centre-half berth as my own, the fact was I was too similar to Terry. He's a better version of me. This was the reality I had to come to terms with if I remained with England, but I didn't want or need to. As things stood, there was no point in my continuing as a player who'd never be first choice. I wasn't taking a decision out of anger or bitterness, but through common sense. I weighed up the pros and cons of staying with England and realized there was more to be gained in the long term by focusing exclusively on Liverpool.

There were some regrets. I'd long admired Terry Venables as a coach and wished I could have worked with him longer. I also welcomed many of the changes McClaren introduced in his backroom team. Sports psychologists are often maligned, and some can come across as quacks, but Bill Beswick was an excellent addition to the England set-up. I'm a player who embraces rather than resists change, and any innovation that can add a small percentage to a player's performance is welcome. There are some who aren't mentally tough enough at the highest level, and Beswick can only help. The only concern I had was this: McClaren became too dependent on Beswick's words of wisdom. There were times I was listening to team-talks uncertain if McClaren was presenting a prepared speech Beswick had written for him.

I recognized the inspiring stories and language Beswick used because I'd enjoyed my own appointments with him. He was particularly useful to me at the start of the 2006–07 season when I suffered a dip in form. 'I'm obsessed with football,' I told him. He advised me to learn how to switch off and develop more interests outside the game. Whether it helped or not, I played some of my best football a few months later. It certainly didn't do me any harm.

Not even an appointment with Beswick would change my mind about England, though, although McClaren's demise and the appointment of Fabio Capello led to a fresh attempt to bring me back into the international fold.

I would have loved to work with Capello. He's my idea of a proper football manager, so whenever the lads come back from an England get-together now, I'm always quizzing them about what he's like and how he compares to others they've worked with. All the reports I've had so far have been what I'd expect. He's very impressive.

I could have discovered this for myself had I responded to the calls from his staff to make a comeback. Briefly, I considered meeting for a chat, but it was more through politeness. At the end of January 2008 Liverpool had a match against West Ham in London, and I arranged to talk to Capello's right-hand man Franco Baldini. As the meeting approached I had second thoughts and cancelled. I didn't want to waste anyone's time.

There was a second phone call to my agent from the England camp at the end of the season.

'We've noticed Jamie is playing right-back for Liverpool again. Would he like to consider this position for England?'

Again, there was a courteous reply thanking the manager for his interest, but I wouldn't be changing my mind.

I've every confidence Capello will do a brilliant job for England, but I don't agree with the FA appointing him. To me, the England manager and all his backroom staff should be English. It's not a patriotic statement I'm making, but a practical one. We're supposed to be competing against other countries, not stealing their expertise. It's meant to be our best against their best, and for me that not only means players, but the manager and his coaches. If our best isn't good enough, tough. We should be doing more to ensure we improve. Head-hunting managers from abroad is an acceptance of defeat. Capello was the best candidate for the job, but it doesn't mean he was the right choice.

From now on I can make such comments as an observer rather than a participant in international football. I reached the end of my tether. Unless you're an established first-team starter, international football is a young man's game. I'd rather add two more years to my Liverpool career than jeopardize this for England. As I approached the age of thirty I lost my interest in being the dependable reserve. A career at the highest level is too short to waste your energy, especially when the trips away become more gruelling than exciting. I wasn't making a choice between playing for or turning my back on my country, I was picking between staying at home during international weeks with my wife and children or heading off to Estonia, Russia, even London to sit in a hotel for days and maybe, just maybe, get on the pitch for a few minutes if required. Those long, dreary afternoons in hotels were purgatory for me. I needed to escape. It would have been tolerable had I known I was going to get a game at the end of the week, but there was little prospect of more than a substitute appearance unless Ferdinand, Terry, Woodgate and King were all injured or suspended.

If I loved playing for my country as much as my club, perhaps the thought of retirement would never have occurred to me. That it did tells everyone I made the right call. I wasn't giving up my football career or my ambitions. Only England.

8

Rafa

Rafa Benitez introduced himself, apologized for his English, shook hands and invited the observations of the three most senior players at Anfield. If he was hoping for the first vote of confidence of his reign, he was disappointed.

'I'm not sure you appreciate how bad we are,' was the blunt response.

Welcome to Liverpool, Rafa.

I'd like to say it was me who fearlessly looked the new Liverpool manager in the eye and delivered this frank warning during our opening exchanges. It was Steven Gerrard who hit him with the home truth as if he was launching into one of his most ferocious ball-winning tackles.

The meeting was being held in the England team's hotel in Portugal where Stevie, Michael Owen and I were about to kick off the 2004 European Championship. Rafa was walking into a blizzard of uncertainty at Anfield, but none of us was convinced he recognized the seriousness of the situation on that blistering day when the temperatures in the hotel room matched those on Lisbon's burning pitches.

As a football club, we were at a crossroads that summer. Chelsea were closing in on Stevie's signature, and after Gérard Houllier's sorry final season we were anxious to hear the new man's plan to make us competitive again. If Liverpool got this appointment wrong, instead of regaining our place alongside the elite forces of Europe we were in danger of drifting further into the pack. For me, shaking hands with Benitez and hearing his strategy was the most important event of the tournament. For others, it would determine if they played another game for the club. The identity of those he was going to buy and sell would influence our mental well-being for the rest of the summer, and we were all hoping to hear revelations about members of Benitez's all-conquering Valencia side coming from the Mestalla with him. Aimar, Vicente, Baraja and Ayala had become household names on Merseyside, even more so since word of Benitez's arrival had leaked. Every Liverpool fan was eager for at least one to follow his former manager.

Rafa's initial observations said a lot about what was to come. Sammy Lee's decision to accept a full-time job with England meant that for the first time since Bill Shankly's arrival in 1959 there would be no ex-Liverpool players on the senior coaching staff. Rafa told us he was bringing his own men in, including his long-time assistant manager Pako Ayesteran.

'Pako is the best fitness coach in Europe,' he announced.

Then Rafa asked each of us what we thought of the team.

'There's not enough pace in it,' I told him, repeating a familiar complaint throughout the Houllier era. 'It's the one area we're lacking more than any other. In the Premiership, you've got to have the legs to survive.'

I listened attentively as Rafa explained his ideas. He sketched out a team, leaving a couple of gaps to be filled when the players he was targeting were signed. He had me down as a right-back, had no right-winger, and said he also wanted to buy a centre-half. The right midfielder turned out to be Luis Garcia, whom he bought from Barcelona. He agreed about the pace, but Djibril Cisse was arriving from Auxerre in a deal sealed by Houllier. Then he turned to Stevie.

'I've watched your games on video,' he said. 'Your problem is you run around too much.'

I stared at Stevie and could see the deflation. This was the player who'd just carried us into the Champions League. In the final games of the previous season Stevie had been inspirational, playing in the middle but popping up on the left and right for our cause in a desperate bid to compensate for our overall inadequacies. Without him taking that responsibility we'd never have been in the Champions League for 2004–05, and might never have been able to tempt a manager of Benitez's repute to the club. It was no wonder Stevie had done so much running in 2003–04, and now we had to be careful he didn't do a runner.

I felt sorry for him, but there was also truth in Rafa's observation. Anyone watching videos of our season from a strictly neutral perspective would have agreed the skipper was doing far too much for a central midfielder. I and everyone else connected to Liverpool knew it was out of necessity, but Rafa was hinting that Gerrard had unbalanced the side. They were both right.

It was then that Stevie responded by reminding Benitez he'd inherited a poor squad. 'If you think there's not a lot of work to be done here, you'd better think again,' was the subtext of the not-so-subtle message.

Michael was also feeling somewhat underwhelmed by the experience of meeting Benitez. The immediate impression was of a manager who believed he could transform Liverpool into contenders with a few minor alterations, but we didn't have the same faith in the squad Houllier had left behind. Messages about fine-tuning and evolution were no good. It was a revolution we wanted, and needed.

I can't say we left the hotel room feeling rejuvenated by the thought a bright new era was upon us. Our first opportunity to find meaningful answers had left us asking one another more questions. I was thrilled to meet the new manager, and thankful he'd made the effort to come to Portugal. It suggested he saw all of us as key to his plans, and I was optimistic we'd appointed the right man for the job. But I also knew there were unresolved issues and was worried Rafa wasn't fully aware how fed up Michael and Stevie were. They were hoping for a sense of purpose to clear their minds.

What followed were more weeks of stress, at the end of which two of my closest friends at the club would go, though the one I thought most likely to leave remained.

A month earlier there had been a different mood when the same players were in conversation with Rick Parry, enthusiastically greeting news of an exciting appointment. We'd all craved a new manager and a fresh start, regardless of our personal affection for Houllier. In the days following Gérard's departure, Rick visited Stevie at home, and I was invited along as the club gauged our thoughts on the identity of the next manager. Various candidates were being touted on a daily basis, and Rick admitted he'd sounded out a few of those being mentioned in the papers. He informed us the two up-and-coming British managers Alan Curbishley, then at Charlton, and Gordon Strachan, who'd done well at Southampton, had been interviewed. The Scot had impressed Rick most. Rick also told us neither was the club's first choice.

'How would you feel about a continental manager?' Rick asked. 'The chairman is concerned you might not want another foreigner.'

Jose Mourinho was the name on everyone's lips as he'd recently won the Champions League with Porto. 'I like his arrogance,' Rick said of him. 'He's a winner.' Mourinho shared an agent with Bruno Cheyrou, who informed us he was a supporter. He even had the club crest on his mobile phone.

If Liverpool were determined to look abroad, there were two names I'd been considering. Javier Irureta had led Deportivo La Coruña to the La Liga title in 2000, despite having moderate resources. I liked his team's style of football. The other manager who excited me was Benitez. Valencia had broken the monopoly of Barcelona and Real Madrid, and Rafa's sides had outclassed Liverpool in the Champions League and in a couple of pre-season friendlies. We'd come off the pitch on each occasion having scarcely touched the ball, and few other sides except Arsenal had impressed me with their technical expertise.

So when Rick suddenly began talking about Benitez in glowing terms, my eyes lit up. It became obvious the other candidates were red herrings and they'd already decided who they wanted. Benitez had spent time at David Moores' Spanish villa where Rick and the chairman were suitably convinced of his credentials during the course of a five-hour meeting. They'd been tracking him since Valencia had demolished us in Europe, and Rafa wanted to come. This was a done deal.

'He already knows a lot about Liverpool,' Rick explained. 'When he was talking about the squad he was asking me how Stephen Warnock was getting on.'

At that time Warnock was a reserve who'd been on loan at

Coventry. It seemed Rafa had already done his homework in readiness for a move to Merseyside.

'Stephen Warnock?' I said, feeling relieved at the new man's knowledge. 'In that case he must know who I am.'

I began my own research into the new boss, trawling any old magazines that referred to Valencia. 'They call him God over there,' I read. 'Not the fans, but the players. Rafa thinks he knows everything.' That stuck in my mind.

Benitez's appointment became the worst-kept secret in Liverpool's history. They stopped taking bets in the city's book-makers before the club finally confirmed the news to an unsurprised world a week before Euro 2004.

The fans took to the choice instantly, recalling as we all did the stylish way the Spanish champions had performed in our previous encounters. His team handsomely beat Marseille in the 2004 UEFA Cup Final, the side that had knocked us out of the competition. The viewing figures for that game on Merseyside must have hit a peak as anticipation grew.

Benitez's track record in Spain suggested he was perfect. He'd taken on the rich Spanish clubs by turning a team with potential into champions and European winners. Without the finances to compete in the transfer market, Benitez was now expected to upset Chelsea, Manchester United and Arsenal like he had Real Madrid and Barcelona. We wanted Liverpool to become the new Valencia, and Benitez was confident he could repeat his La Liga success without splashing millions.

That was the criterion on which he was given the job.

Liverpool's financial problems were well documented. The club was pursuing a new stadium, and no manager was going to come to Anfield expecting to make a series of record signings. He would have to be adept at getting the best out of what he had.

To outsiders we appeared to be a promising squad that wasn't fulfilling its potential. With improved coaching, decent players would become good ones and the world-class ones would sustain a title challenge.

Unfortunately, whatever the brochure looked like when Rick and the chairman convinced Benitez to accept the Liverpool position, he must have thought the landscape less glamorous once he arrived. The economic muscle of Chelsea was now even greater than Real Madrid or Barca, while Manchester United had built a formidable side over twenty years under Ferguson, and Arsenal had just gone a season unbeaten. Winning the Premier League with Liverpool was not comparable to winning the title with Valencia. Benitez may initially have believed he could repeat his trick by reorganizing our existing squad and adding a few new faces, but it wasn't long before he was singing a different tune. What should have been a summer honeymoon, raising expectations and building a vibrant squad, descended into a messy introduction.

The first crisis involved the skipper.

I knew Stevie was seriously considering his future when we met Rafa in Portugal, and nothing had been said or done to erase those nagging doubts. The rumours about Chelsea had begun when Claudio Ranieri was still the manager. Tentative moves to tempt Stevie to London were made in the summer of 2003. Roman Abramovich's takeover had led to constant speculation about £30 million bids. By the time of Euro 2004, tabloid gossip had proved a reality. Stevie was away from home hearing different voices every day (some undoubtedly with a cockney accent), many of them telling him his career would progress more at Stamford Bridge. All the indications pointed to another prolonged period of rebuilding at Anfield. Liverpool were at a junction, and so too was Stevie's career.

The decision he had to make was this: could he afford to be patient and follow the signposts telling him to wait a couple more years for a realistic title and Champions League challenge, or should he follow the course towards Mourinho's promise of instant success as part of the most expensive squad in the world?

Stevie's mind was being tugged in the direction of Stamford Bridge, but on the few occasions I had a chance to speak to him in the England hotel I urged him not to succumb to the temptation. I wasn't as close to Stevie then as I am now so I never felt in a position to pry too much into his state of mind, or persistently tell him what he should do. All I could do was appeal to the Liverpool fan in him to give Benitez at least one chance. I wanted his heart to rule his head. If there were no signs of improvement within a year, there was still time for him to move on. The summer of 2004 wasn't the right time for him to walk out of Anfield. But I never imposed my view or put pressure on him because, ultimately, he had to make the decision for himself. By the end of the tournament, like every Liverpool fan, I was resigned to his departure.

It was a depressing thought, losing our best player to Chelsea. It was crucial Benitez built a side around the captain rather than being forced to use funds from his sale to bring in replacements who could never be as good. I spent hours trying to think who we could sign and how the team could be restructured in his absence. It was a nightmare. We'd have needed three or four class players to compensate for his loss, and it would have sent out the wrong message to the football world. No matter how much we'd have received, people would have begun to see Liverpool as a club whose local stars could be lured away.

It's true no one is bigger than any football club, but in the context of our position, Stevie was far more than just another player.

He was a symbol of the club, a Liverpool lad who'd come through the ranks whom the fans saw as living their dream. Had he gone, it would have been the first time in our history a Liverpool captain had taken the decision to join one of our rivals. We'd have struggled to come to terms with that.

A day after our return to England I received a phone call from Michael Owen informing me a press conference had been called at Anfield to announce Stevie was staying. I switched on Sky as bemused as everyone else by the U-turn. The opportunity to discuss the situation with his family and friends had brought sanity to the proceedings. Whatever was said, it seemed a weight had been lifted from Stevie's mind on his return to Liverpool.

It felt like we'd made a new signing.

'U av made the right decision,' I texted the skipper.

Regardless of how our season went, I knew he had. The supporters would never have forgiven Stevie for leaving Liverpool then. Whether this was a permanent or temporary calming of the waters would become increasingly apparent as the season progressed. With Gerrard committed for at least one more year, the fans felt a catastrophe had been averted.

Rafa took a more pragmatic view and was prepared to accept whatever circumstances were thrust upon him. While many at Anfield were in a state of panic at the prospect of losing our best player, Benitez showed himself to be a manager who'd take everything in his stride. 'Whether Gerrard stays or goes, we'll move on,' was his message. His reaction to Stevie staying was no different to that when he thought he was going.

Once the crisis was resolved, there was no respite. The storm clouds were arriving from another direction once pre-season training got underway. My relief at Steven's decision to stay was undermined when Michael told me he was leaving.

This revelation arrived during our summer tour to America, where we played a couple of games in New York. There may already have been doubts in Michael's mind over how highly Benitez rated him, as the different styles of the new manager and Houllier were instantly apparent. In what turned out to be his last match for the club, Michael played the first half of a 5–0 win against Celtic, scoring a goal and creating another. As he was getting changed having been subbed, any hope of a word of con-gratulation was short-lived. He was tapped on the shoulder and told, 'You have to learn how to turn more quickly when you have the ball with your back to goal.'

I glanced at Michael, saw the look of astonishment on his face, and started laughing. First Stevie ran around too much, now Michael wasn't turning sharply enough. I'd not heard a manager speak to Michael like that for years. This was a player who was used to compliments, but it was going to take more than a decent half in a friendly to impress the new manager.

'This is what it's going to be like from now on,' I told Michael. 'This fella isn't going to be telling anyone how great he thinks we are.'

There was no suggestion Michael was going anywhere at that stage, but within forty-eight hours of his first brush with the new boss he was wrestling with the same dilemma Stevie had faced. I was sharing a room with Michael when he received the call that led to his departure from Liverpool.

'Real Madrid want me,' he told me. 'I fancy it.'

Benitez maintains the deal had been planned before he arrived, but that isn't true. It was a bombshell when the call came. I could see that in Michael's reaction to the news.

My advice to Michael was not to go. I saw Ronaldo and Raúl as the star players and no prospect of Michael breaking that up, no matter how good he was. At the Bernabeu, the coach doesn't pick the team, the club's politicians do.

'It was the same when I broke into the Liverpool side,' Mo argued. 'I had to get past Robbie Fowler and Stan Collymore.'

The difference, I maintained, was we didn't have a club president insisting Robbie and Collymore start every game.

Michael couldn't be persuaded. His self-belief is greater than any player I've known. He was sure he'd force himself into the side. On the basis of his goals ratio in Spain, he was right. He did earn a run in the team. Unfortunately for him, I was right too. The overall number of games he actually started proved form wasn't the criterion for selection.

I was disappointed Michael left because he was my best mate. To see someone I'd risen through the ranks with move on saddened me on a personal as much as professional level. It was a sign of how far we were drifting. There was once a time when our star players were untouchable. No one would bother trying to sign them because they'd have no chance of luring them away. As our run without title or Champions League success continued, so our reputation was being eroded. Our two best players could have left within weeks of each other. It had nothing to do with the new manager, it was more a consequence of years of moderate success catching up with us. It was a depressing, disturbing time.

Our fans were less forgiving of Michael's decision than I. They thought he'd confirmed lingering suspicions on The Kop he wasn't really 'one of them'. I saw Michael's situation as different to Stevie's. Stevie would have years to decide his future. I knew Chelsea and the European giants wouldn't give up on signing him. In comparison, this wasn't just Michael's first opportunity to join Real Madrid, it was probably his last.

Many ignore the context in which he made up his mind. We were facing more years of transition as Benitez implemented new ideas and he wasn't sure how highly thought of he was by the boss. From the moment he made his debut at seventeen, Michael made no secret of a long-term ambition to play abroad. He'd endured a lot of niggling injuries, his final year under Houllier had been a struggle, and Euro 2004 wasn't great by his standards. Wayne Rooney had burst on to the scene and become the England striker most linked with big-money moves. Michael feared the window of opportunity to seek a fresh challenge was closing. Given his contract situation at Anfield, it was now or never. He only had a year left at Liverpool, so he had to sign on for another four years and effectively stay for life, or break his ties.

I knew he was unsure about the direction of the club and was keeping his options open amid interest from others during Houllier's last season. It was understandable given our limited title chances, but fans will never accept that a Liverpool player may want to leave for professional reasons. They cling on to the far-fetched notion that their favourite players wouldn't even think of playing anywhere else. They became wary of Michael's and Stevie's refusal to say outright they'd stay, even though both were right to be careful not to make promises they may not have been able to keep.

The timing didn't help either: Michael signed for Madrid the day before our opening Premier League match with Tottenham.

'If Real Madrid came in for me, it would even turn my head,' I told the press on the eve of the match, trying to defend my mate's decision. I was helping a friend. I've never had any ambition to play abroad. I love home too much.

As a mate I wished Mo well, but the circumstances left us

struggling in attack for the rest of the season. The £8 million fee, which reflected the limited time left on Michael's deal, was nowhere near what it should have been for a player of his class. We were also given Antonio Nunez in part exchange. He suffered a knee ligament injury on his first day's training and wasn't up to scratch even when he was fit. Rafa had reacted to Michael's decision the same way as to the captain's – no fuss, just a matter-of-fact response to changing circumstances – but from his and Liverpool's perspective, this was a lousy piece of business.

While Michael was criticized in some quarters for taking a decision that was right for him, another friend was earning even less sympathy for suffering from the ruthlessness of football.

Danny Murphy had been one of our most effective players during the final years of Houllier's reign, but on the day we returned from America he was pulled to one side by Benitez and told he could leave. Charlton made a £2.5 million bid which was instantly accepted. Danny was devastated, and the speed with which the transfer went through shocked me. I thought it was a mistake to allow Danny to go, and the way our League season progressed proved it.

These deals, within twenty-four hours of each other, exposed the hypocrisy of some of the criticism Michael received. When a player has the power to decide his own future and opts to leave, he's accused of disloyalty, but all of us are vulnerable at any given time to the possibility of a manager calling you in and revealing you're up for sale. Outside the dressing room there was precious little compassion around for Danny when he was shown the door, even though he was Liverpool through and through. Michael benefited from his circumstances, Danny suffered because of his. That's the business we're in.

Those early deals weakened the squad rather than strengthened it, although some of the recruits were beyond Benitez's control. Liverpool made a strange decision to press ahead with Cisse's move from Auxerre. He was a Houllier signing and Benitez didn't want him. It was too late to scrap it, and there was a belief Cisse would be so good, any manager would be happy to have him. The reports I'd heard described Cisse as a cross between Emile Heskey and Michael Owen. He was supposed to be a strong, physical target man who scored goals. He was neither one nor the other. Djibril was exactly the same as Milan Baros: inconsistent, likely to impress in one game but disappoint in the next.

Even had Michael stayed, the choice of striking options would have been limited. Michael wouldn't have formed a partnership with Cisse. It was evident even before Mo left that we were in trouble in terms of the balance of our squad. Rafa would have loved to bring Heskey back because he'd been left without a target man – a problem he'd have to wait twelve months to remedy. The fans had been happy to see Emile go at the end of the previous season, but now we were crying out for a replacement.

Of Benitez's early signings, only Xabi Alonso immediately impressed me. He was a world-class midfielder whose passing added guile alongside Gerrard, which we'd been lacking. Elsewhere, Garcia sometimes couldn't cope with the demands of English football. His contribution would sum up Benitez's first season: fantastic in Europe, but infuriatingly inconsistent in the League.

Luis and I had a love-hate relationship on the park, just like he had with the fans. I'd always be shouting at him for losing the ball with one of his backheels or flicks, but then he'd volley one in from thirty yards (as he did against Juventus) and it was like all the indiscretions of the previous eight months could be forgiven. When I think of him now, I remember a player who contributed as much as any to winning my Champions League medal.

Josemi, Benitez's first signing, worried me. After swiftly deciding to persist with me as a centre-half, Rafa bought the right-back instead.

'He's like Carra,' Benitez told Stevie when Josemi arrived.

I took a look at him in training.

'Fuck me, how bad does Benitez think I am?' I asked.

Josemi made a decent start and some of our fans were saying they thought he looked the part.

'Give it time,' I told them.

Josemi was one of several signings from La Liga who struggled. When thirty-four-year-old Mauricio Pellegrino arrived on a free transfer from Valencia, an Argentinian defensive legend had joined the club. Sadly, the Pellegrino who was an outstanding member of Benitez's all-conquering Valencia side was coming to the end of his career. There was no doubting his knowledge of the game, however, and his experience was seen as a useful asset. Off the pitch he was a great character, which is why Benitez has now given him a job on his coaching staff for the 2008–09 season.

The greatest disappointment was Fernando Morientes, who arrived from Real Madrid with a superb reputation but showed only glimpses of his natural talent. The speed and physical nature of English football didn't suit him. He possessed the technical skill, but he was a yard off the pace.

In Benitez's defence, he wasted no time waiting for these players to bed in. Once he saw how they were struggling, he'd offload them. At the end of the first season, Nunez, Pellegrino and Josemi were all on their way out, and Morientes' days were numbered too. I liked that about Benitez. When he made a mistake, he wasn't scared to rectify it. Too often under Houllier we'd persevere with players far beyond their point of no return.

As when Houllier arrived, we spent the initial weeks weighing the manager up. There's no one more interested in sussing someone new out than me. I'd already looked into his background, reading an unofficial Rafa biography that had been speedily released, and once the season began I picked up more about Benitez from his mannerisms, his team-talks and his approach to training. You establish pretty quickly what makes a manager tick, and it's always fascinated me to note the differences in style of the most renowned coaches.

Just as Houllier's approach had been a breath of fresh air after Evans left, having Benitez on board triggered another wave of excitement. It's not that Rafa was better than Gérard, as fans and journalists lazily wanted to suggest during his honeymoon period, it's just that he was different. Like anything in life, when you've been used to a predictable routine, to hearing the same speeches for five years, a fresh perspective adds a spark. You go into training with a spring in your step. As someone who's been in one team my whole career, I suppose a change of management is the closest I've got to understanding how it feels to join a new club.

The most immediate contrast was on the training pitch. Rafa takes all the training sessions, adopting a far more hands-on approach than Gérard, who delegated many of the responsibilities to his staff. Much has also been made of Houllier enjoying a more personal relationship with players than Rafa. That's true, but again I don't see that as a positive or negative. You can argue either way about the merits of maintaining a purely professional association between player and manager. Gérard's interest in our lives off the pitch was welcomed by many of us, but we were young men then and he undoubtedly took it upon himself to be a father figure. There was never a question who was the boss under Houllier, but there were times when he was happy to relax in our company and show a more sociable side to his character. He'd ask about your wife and children, and take an active interest if he heard someone in the family was unwell, arranging for a bouquet of flowers to be delivered. I suspect that's rare in a manager, but we'd become used to it. I've never spoken to Rafa about anything other than football. The line between manager and player is far more clearly defined. It has been suggested Benitez sees players essentially as chess pieces to be shoved around to fit his tactical plans. That's taking it to the extreme, but from the outset he seemed to see everyone in the same way, regardless of their transfer value or status in the fans' eyes. Some players prefer a distance between the manager's office and dressing room, others liked Houllier's style.

I felt I got closer than most, if not all, of the players to Benitez when he first joined. I was able to get on with him instantly because he shared a distinctive feature with Houllier: his devotion to the game. Once again, the twang was different, but when we spoke about football, the language was the same. The ability to talk for hours about nothing other than players, tactics and opponents appealed to him and to me.

Houllier had always been keen on using videos to make me watch and learn from mistakes; Benitez took this further. He handed me DVDs of Arrigo Sacchi's legendary AC Milan side of the 1980s and was especially eager for me to analyse Franco Baresi's movements and organization of the defence. Benitez's defensive wisdom impressed me most. It was a step up from what

I'd enjoyed before. Houllier guided me towards becoming a top-class Premier League player, but Benitez has been the greatest overall influence on Jamie Carragher the defender. He's brought the best out of me, transformed me into a centre-half of European pedigree. I've played the finest football of my career under Rafa. Every training session has included advice on how I can improve my game.

Rafa is more of a defensive than an attacking coach, so naturally it's the defenders who've benefited most under his leadership. He made it instantly obvious how much he liked my aggressive style on the pitch, although he misinterpreted how far I was prepared to extend my fighting spirit off it. Rafa told me early on he wanted me to inject some of my toughness into my team-mates, but other than my usual shouting routines I didn't see how it could be done. Such a characteristic comes from within. After a disappointing defeat away at Birmingham, the manager pulled me in after training and offered some advice with a story from his Valencia days.

'When members of the squad didn't show the right attitude in the match, the Argentinian players would start a fight in the showers with the team-mates who weren't doing their job,' Rafa told me.

I looked at the manager to make sure it wasn't a joke and could see a glint in his eye. 'He's dropping me a hint here,' I thought.

'I don't think that's me,' I said, politely informing Rafa that verbal rather than physical tormenting of underperforming colleagues was more my scene.

Uninterested though I was by Rafa's advice on this occasion, it was comforting to know he trusted me enough to give me his blessing to confront some of the players he didn't like. There were plenty of occasions I felt like taking a swing at some of them, but it's a line I wouldn't cross.

Despite his reputation for being cold towards his squad, I was also reading plenty of praise about my performances from the boss. It's never bothered me whether a manager publicly applauds me. If it happens, great, but the pat on the back is secondary to the name on the teamsheet. Unlike Houllier, Benitez quickly developed a reputation for rarely handing out individual congratulations in the press. I know he thought it was an English trend to get managers to talk up their players. Our papers love writing about star players and sticking glowing headlines alongside pretty pictures. Over the years Rafa has come to understand that, but initially he was reluctant to talk about anything but the team. So when he did speak glowingly about you, it tended to mean more. You felt honoured to be an exception to his rule. I picked up the *Echo* one night and saw a headline in which Benitez compared me to Roberto Ayala, the great Argentine defender he'd managed at Valencia. I knew I wasn't in Ayala's class. More to the point, I knew Benitez didn't think I was as good as Ayala. But to know he'd said it certainly boosted my confidence.

Benitez repeated the trick during another press conference before a League game with Chelsea, but this time there was a sting in the tail. 'I've just told the media you're a better player than John Terry,' Rafa told me. Then he started laughing as he made a tell-tale signal, putting his hand to his nose and pulling it away to imitate Pinocchio.

I waited a few months and got him back. Before our Champions League semi-final with Chelsea, I was handed the press conference duties.

'What did they ask you?' Rafa quizzed me.

'I told them you're a better manager than Mourinho,' I said, and then repeated his Pinocchio mime.

He took the joke. He was enduring a tough debut season, but there was no questioning he could rely on me as one of his most loyal lieutenants.

The transitional period was difficult, and a couple of minor changes that were given publicity at the time were reversed as quickly as they were implemented. Much was made of Benitez splitting up an English 'clique' in the dressing room, insisting we rotated room-mates when we travelled away. Usually we'd stick with the same player, who tended to be our best mate at the club. I was unhappy at how this story was presented. The suggestion was we all sat on separate tables in the canteen because the English wouldn't mix with the foreigners. There was never a division imposed by the English lads. Any problems on that score were caused by the French players Houllier had left behind. Our 'gang', so to speak, was cosmopolitan, including the more established members of Houllier's squad. It was made up of the survivors of the 2001 side, really. Me, Stevie, Michael, Danny, Ginger (John Arne Riise), Sami and Didi all got on fine. When the Spanish lads arrived, they immediately fitted in. Xabi and Luis had no problem socializing with us, so to claim we had to be brought into line was mischievous. The only ones who were arrogant and aloof were the French, and many of them hadn't earned our respect through their playing ability either. Benitez would resolve this issue by moving them on, anyway.

The rotating room-mate plan came under pressure when all the players got together to complain. You need to feel comfortable before the night of a match; you can't be paired with someone who upsets your routine. Some players like sitting up playing video games for hours, others chill out reading a book or watching a film, some spend hours on the phone. You need to ensure the right characters are matched with each other. It's OK during pre-season when you're trying to get to know a new player, but not every week.

The occasion when I was rooming with Josemi turned into one of my most uncomfortable nights on the road. I like to have a chat about the game or read the papers and a book, and I usually go to bed about eleven p.m. to get a good night's sleep ahead of the match. Josemi stayed up late, returning to the room about midnight and then ringing his mates in Spain. He was talking in Spanish on the phone until about one a.m. I was left huffing and puffing, wondering when I was going to get some peace and quiet. I couldn't relax.

The pairings also gave away the team. You could work out who the strikers were from who was rooming together, as Rafa thought a good relationship off the pitch helped form partnerships on it.

When the flaws in the arrangement were pointed out, Rafa abandoned the idea. After that I always roomed with Stevie.

Hotel arrangements were the least of Rafa's worries that season as our form raised early questions about his and our prospects. People seem to forget exactly how bad we were in the League in 2004–05 because the Champions League masked our deficiencies. We'd lose to Crystal Palace, who were relegated, but then get a fantastic result against Chelsea in the European Cup semi-final four days later. There was no logic to it. Rafa's first derby was particularly traumatic. He played Salif Diao and Josemi, and left Xabi on the bench. We lost 1–0, handing serious momentum to Everton, who now justifiably believed they could finish the season above us.

The question of rotation – this time on the pitch – became a recurring issue as Benitez would happily change five or six players from one game to the next. I was lucky to avoid being part of the revolving team policy as he saw me as too important at the back, but his faith in the system has never wavered. The seemingly endless debate about its pros and cons is now part of the Anfield furniture. Houllier had also made changes from game to game, but usually two or three, never to this extent. But when a manager has won two La Liga titles adopting this approach, you can forget about saying he's wrong. The plus side is it keeps players fresh until the end of the season, which was demonstrated in successive years as we coped with extra time and penalty shoot-outs in our last matches to win cups. The question that will remain unanswered until we win the League is this: how much do the early-season changes impact on our chances of winning the title?

What I will say is I've never liked it, and I don't believe there's a footballer at any level, English or foreign, who ever will. The philosophy contradicts everything you learn while growing up to become a footballer. Certain principles are set in stone at an early age which breed a will to win. They include fighting for your shirt, playing for your place and doing everything once you're in the team to stay there. When I made my debut for my schoolboy side aged seven, I instinctively knew if I performed well I'd be playing a week later. The more I impressed, the more I'd cement my position as a first-team regular. It used to be the eternal football truth: play well enough to make yourself undroppable. In the modern game, managers don't use the word 'dropped' any more. You get 'rested' or 'rotated'. As players, we don't see it that way. I feel the same about my place in the side now as I did when I was at school. If I'm not in the side, it hurts. I feel left out, and I'm desperate to get back in to make sure it never happens again.

I feel sorry for strikers and midfielders, who've suffered far more than defenders since the shadow of rotation infiltrated our game. I've played alongside players who've scored hat-tricks and been left out of the next fixture. It doesn't matter how much the boss tries to explain it's for their own good, protecting their muscles for later in the season, players will always want to play and they will get demoralized if they're sitting on the bench.

The key problem with mass rotation, as employed at Liverpool, is it undermines the team ethic. Selfishness creeps into the ranks because you become more aware of how vulnerable you are to being left out, no matter how well or badly you play. I can well imagine there are players who come off the pitch after a defeat pleased with their own performance because it might be enough to keep them in. You don't get that with a steady line-up, where the result comes before any individual.

I believe you need a structure within the squad so the best eleven earn their places on merit and know they've got to keep their standards high to stay in the side. Such are the demands at a club like ours, where you can play over fifty games a season, I'd say you need a spine of at least eight players who start week in week out, with the rest fighting for a shirt. That's how United and Chelsea have operated. If anyone dips, they're out.

When we lost to Burnley in the third round of the FA Cup in January 2005, the mild discontent with Benitez's methods turned into hysteria. I was due to play in the tie at Turf Moor when it was first scheduled, but it was postponed due to a waterlogged pitch just as we were about to get changed. A week later, Rafa decided to leave me on Merseyside ahead of our away game with Southampton. It's a decision he later told journalists he regretted.

Whatever the rights and wrongs of his team selection, which packed the side with Academy youngsters, there was still enough quality to beat Burnley. Big Sami, Djimi Traore and Igor Biscan were in the side that lost 1–0, but the flak was flying at the manager as he tried to explain his tinkering. I was watching at home, exchanging texts with Steven Gerrard about the horror that was unfolding as Djimi backheeled the winning own-goal.

The merits of Rafa's argument were then undermined by an equally poor performance at Southampton, when the rested players returned. Peter Crouch, still a Southampton player, terrorized us. I dared not watch that night's *Match of the Day*. Actually, the more the season went on, the more I dreaded hearing its theme tune. Alan Hansen, obviously distressed at our form, said the club was in danger of becoming a 'relic'. I had to ask people what the word meant, but I could tell from the tone of his voice it wasn't a compliment. The motto had been Liverpool Football Club exists to win trophies. In that troublesome week, it seemed we'd redefined it to Liverpool Football Club exists to ensure they finish in the top four. As if I didn't already appreciate how serious our slump was, hearing the anguish in Hansen's voice brought it home. He was right. We were in danger of becoming a relic. Our glory days were in the past and everything pointed to an average season where we'd be lucky to qualify for the UEFA Cup. If that happened, Stevie would leave and we'd have no hope of attracting the calibre of players we needed to close the widening gap to the top.

I felt sorry for Rafa because every new manager needs time and he was struggling to come to terms with the peculiar demands of the English game. He'd underestimated the scale of the rebuilding job, but he needed to see the side's weaknesses fully exposed week in, week out before he accepted what we knew when we'd met him in Lisbon.

Midway through the season he was under no illusions how far behind we were, and how much he'd misjudged the capacity of some of his own buys to cope with the Premier League. We were also suffering from injuries. Cisse broke his leg at Blackburn early in the season, Baros returned from international duty with a nagging strain, and Xabi was out with ankle ligament damage. For much of the season the inexperienced Neil Mellor was our only fit forward.

During my meetings with Rafa I got a sense of him planning ahead, recognizing the need to bring in players more suited to our physical, fast-paced style. 'Managers have no power at this stage of the season,' he told me. 'I can't do anything until the summer. You can't drop or threaten to sell players now, so we'll have to wait and try our best with what we've got.' He was privately critical of our squad, which was reassuring in some respects, although he was just as negative about the Valencia side he'd left, which I'd thought was so good. In fact, you'd be hard pressed to get Rafa to say anything positive about any player or team he's worked with.

With regard to that 2004–05 Liverpool side, plenty were agreeing with Benitez's downbeat conclusions. The flak was flying again, but much of it was aimed at him. Every decision was being questioned, from the rotation policy and the position of Gerrard to the zonal marking he introduced. Every goal conceded from a set-piece triggered another debate about the validity of the system. It's impossible for any side to go through a season without conceding from a corner or free-kick, but overall I believe we've conceded fewer since Rafa introduced zonal marking. It may seem like more only because if you lose a goal with zonal marking, the system always gets the blame; if you do so with man-to-man, an individual gets the blame. As a defender, the only thing that matters to me is this: either way, the ball is in the back of the net.

Now, even minor details were being overblown as part of a wider critical look at the club. Some of it couldn't be ignored. Our League form was atrocious, and the only relief when we played our final home match to Aston Villa was the European final we had to look forward to. We'd dropped a place to fifth, but worse still it was Everton who'd taken our Champions League qualifying spot. The state of the League table horrified me. Everton deserved credit and merited their position, but we'd consistently underperformed.

Fortunately for us, the so-called power shift in Merseyside football lasted no longer than ten days. The League Cup and Champions League offered salvation. Without our sometimes staggering progress in those competitions, I dread to think where the club might be today. As others have written, we really were teetering 'on the brink'.

We'd ridden our luck on our way to Cardiff. Not until the semi-final did Rafa use any of the 'big guns', as it was a tournament he was prepared to sacrifice in pursuit of fourth spot. By the time we faced Chelsea in the first of our epic cup battles in 2005, priorities were being reassessed. Everything was geared towards stopping Jose Mourinho claiming his first trophy in English football.

The personal duel between Benitez and Mourinho was still in its early days, and despite our obviously higher profile world-wide and richer history, to some extent it seemed a mismatch. Mourinho had the luxury of instantly building a formidable side; Benitez felt he hadn't even started his reconstruction of Liverpool yet. In the summer of 2004, either could have ended up at Anfield or Stamford Bridge, and the fans who so loathed Rafa and Jose in Liverpool or west London would have been praising them. Rafa was always able to claim he'd taken on the tougher job as he didn't have the finances to build a side like Mourinho. He tried to belittle Mourinho's achievements by saying Roman Abramovich was really 'the special one' at the club. That was harsh – having so much money brings a different type of pressure: spending it properly and creating a winning team is not a formality – but it was a clever comment that went down well on Merseyside.

Mourinho liked to criticize our style of football, suggesting we were defensive and cautious. We were what we were because we had to be. They had better players than us, so our manager always organized us to nullify Chelsea and try to nick a win. The League Cup Final on 27 February was almost our first success. We led for seventy-eight minutes and were looking comfortable when Stevie scored a freakish own-goal and we lost in extra time. Mourinho celebrated the equalizer by taunting our fans, putting his finger to his mouth in a 'shh' gesture because, unsurprisingly, the travelling Kop had been so vocal when we were ahead.

I'm not sure if he knew what he'd let himself in for. I suspect he'd have wished to reconsider his actions two Champions League semi-finals later when he saw the venomous response to him at Anfield.

I enjoyed an altercation of my own with Mourinho during the game when he accused Luis Garcia of taking a dive and began complaining to the referee. You have to bear in mind I'd watched the Porto side Mourinho had led to European success. I can say without hesitation I'd never seen a more cynical diving team in my career than the one that beat Celtic in the UEFA Cup Final of 2003. I ran over to the touchline, and shouted, 'Don't you fucking start about diving – your Porto side was the fucking worst!' Mourinho was having none of it. We spent the next thirty seconds telling each other to 'fuck off' in as many different forms as we could manage.

Our fans loved it. So did his.

To his credit, he hunted me down after the game and asked, almost apologetically, 'You do know why I was complaining, don't you?' He was just fighting for his team, as I was for mine.

'Fair enough,' I said. The game was over now.

We shook hands and that was it, although that fiery introduction would continue into our next meetings.

I took Mourinho's comments in the press for what they were: deliberate attempts to take the pressure off his players and pile it on to himself. As long as he wasn't having a pop at Liverpool it was amusing. I wouldn't miss any of his interviews, they were so entertaining. Our fans didn't like him because of what happened in Cardiff, his ongoing war of words with Rafa, and the fact Chelsea were openly pursuing our captain, but he was a pantomime villain in the grand scheme of things, and we used the hostility of The Kop to our advantage when it mattered.

Many have tried to present Rafa and Mourinho as different characters, but I don't see it that way. The pair arrived in England as the two most respected coaches in Europe, breaking the monotony of the annual Wenger v. Ferguson conflict which had dominated our game. For all the barbed comments that flew between them, there was mutual respect. Mourinho was more brash and brazen in his arrogance, prepared to announce his special status to the world, but Rafa is just as certain of his own ability, even if he's more subtle in how he expresses it. All the top managers have big egos, motivated by an unwavering belief in their own ability. They all think they're doing as well as possible in their jobs and that they'd do better in someone else's. Few of them talk positively about their rivals, pointing only to their weaknesses. Benitez and Mourinho are cut from the same cloth.

I've never seen any evidence of Rafa's certainty in his own talent being shaken. He attributed our poor League form in his first season to the circumstances he'd inherited. In his mind, there was nothing more he could have done. His plans for the following season, allied to our progress in Europe, proved how good he really was. If he hadn't already been given the nickname 'God' by the Valencia players, and had it confirmed by our dressing room, he'd have been given it by the Liverpool fans.

The events in Turkey in the glorious summer of 2005 would have seen to that.

9

Istanbul

It was a little after midnight on a sizzling May evening when Steven Gerrard was handed Liverpool's first European Cup for twenty-one years. I was standing to his left, poised to pounce on to his shoulders as the UEFA official presented the most precious piece of silver in club football. Red confetti and ticker tape began to shower across the podium, but as I prepared to start my celebratory jig I felt a twinge rush through my legs. While the rest of the players danced, I fell out of sight.

The muscle cramps that had flared up during extra time against AC Milan had made an unwelcome and untimely return. As vice-captain, the first images beamed across the world ought to have placed me alongside my skipper as he lifted this cup of life-changing beauty. Instead, somewhat poignantly given how my career has progressed, I was hidden in the background while the spotlight shone on others.

It didn't matter. A bout of cramp wasn't going to diminish my sense of satisfaction. It healed soon enough once I got my hands on that trophy. The agony eased by the ecstasy of victory summed up the previous three hours. I'd plummeted to the deepest pit of misery, only to instantly recover to ascend the highest of peaks. It seemed appropriate to have a lingering reminder of the torment I'd been through to reach the summit.

There's yet to be a top-class sportsman who hasn't come face to face with the impostors of triumph and disaster. What's rare is sharing a date with the most extreme of these emotions on the same mind-blowing night. That's the best way to describe the events in the Ataturk Stadium, Istanbul, on 25 May 2005. None of us would have chosen such a way to win a final. No footballer fancies a sneak preview of the most humiliating defeat in sporting history. But having staged a comeback that will echo in eternity, none of us would want it any other way.

Istanbul – such epic nights can be recognized simply by naming the venue – is the greatest event in the history of Liverpool Football Club.

Fans across the generations can argue this for decades to come, but the evidence is too compelling. From the manner in which we reached the final through to the circumstances of our victory, nothing can compare. In contrast to Liverpool's previous four European Cup-winning teams, we were an imperfect side that not only punched above its weight, it floored the previously undisputed champions. And not only that, we did so having been on the verge of being knocked out several times before we'd even reached the last rounds. We would have welcomed our bid for glory being stopped by the referee on compassionate grounds at one stage.

This was an unparalleled football revival. Three–nil down at half-time to one of the most technically and tactically sound teams ever to have played, we looked dead and buried. Never have Liverpool's combined strengths as a football club been so necessary and so visible. No club other than Liverpool could have won the competition in such a fashion, bringing so many of the positive elements of our tradition together.

Because our fans played such a pivotal role at crucial times during our run to Istanbul, and during the game itself, this was the ultimate collective victory. Our pride at being a club that values the unique bond between players and supporters came to the fore when it was needed most. Even the mighty AC Milan, with all its superior skill and a three-goal advantage, couldn't survive.

We weren't the best team in Europe. We were nowhere near it. Player for player, if you compared us to those sides that didn't reach the final you would never have believed we'd be there. But on that particular night we were brave, the most passionate on and off the pitch, the team with the severest will to win.

I'd fantasized about winning the Champions League – there were even times during Gérard Houllier's reign I thought it might be possible – but when I was asked about our chances before we played our qualifying match against AK Graz of Austria in August 2004, I politely told journalists to think of a more serious question. The fixture was overshadowed by Michael Owen's imminent transfer to Real Madrid. Our star striker was on the way out, and the new manager had inherited a side much of which he didn't rate. I didn't think we were much good either. As an opening scene to what would become the greatest drama of our careers, this was a first draft badly in need of a rewrite. Fortunately, we could rely on a central performance from the captain, who would dazzle as the production progressed. Steven Gerrard set the tone for his tournament by scoring twice in Austria, but we were made to sweat at Anfield in the return, losing 1–0 to the minnows.

This was not the form of future champions, and our erratic

work in the group offered no clue as to how much we'd improve the following spring. Olympiakos, Monaco and Deportivo La Coruña made for a tricky rather than intimidating trio in the early phase of the competition, but by the time we played the Greeks in the final match of the first stage, elimination was on the horizon. The pre-match talk wasn't focusing on how we'd fare if we secured the two-goal win we needed, but the repercussions of our probable failure.

Stevie had been asked to UEFA's press conference on the eve of the game and was hit, predictably, with an onslaught of questions about his future. Our struggles in the League made a top-four finish increasingly unlikely, so he was more forthright than had been imagined. 'I don't want to wake up on the morning after the match and be out of the Champions League,' he said. 'If we don't qualify for next season, I'll have to consider my future.' He could have straight-batted his responses, and I'm sure if he is ever again faced with the same situation he will do so, but the truth probably looked a lot worse in print than it sounded out loud.

The repercussions were felt for the rest of the tournament. From the moment we kicked off against Olympiakos, it seemed winning was as much about keeping Stevie at Anfield as lifting the trophy. There were times I privately began to resent this. I'd be asked the same question after every game, win or lose: 'What do you think this means for Gerrard's future?' Even if Stevie wasn't in the side and we played well and won, everyone wanted to talk about the implications of the result for his state of mind. 'There's more than one player at this football club, you know!' I felt like shouting. That is no criticism of my captain, but of the preoccupation with him by the media and even some of our own fans.

Despite all this, it could be argued his pre-Olympiakos comments actually helped us win the competition, because there was no shortage of inspiration from his boots in the months that followed, starting on 8 December against the Greeks. Stevie's twenty-five-yard piledriver in the eighty-sixth minute completed a stirring fightback: 1–0 down to Olympiakos at half-time, we'd needed to win 3–1 to qualify on goal difference.

The Kop said the evening revived memories of the famous encounter with St Etienne in 1977, when Liverpool won by the same scoreline in virtually identical circumstances. 'You can't really compare this to that,' I'd say to supporters. 'Not unless we go on to win the competition like the 1977 team.'

I'd have been mad to presume we would. Realistically, I still believed qualifying from the group stage was little more than an extension of our mini adventure into Europe rather than a statement of intent.

The teams of the 1970s and 1980s entered the competition expecting to win, but clearly it was a different Liverpool Football Club that returned to the European Cup after the Heysel ban. I hoped we could excel, but the experience of facing the greatest players of my generation as well as the crucial financial rewards to ensure we remained competitive at home had become a more sensible priority. Match previews seemed to focus less on the games and more on how much reaching the next round was worth to the club. Winning the tournament was a wish more than a demand of our fans, unlike the early eighties when failure sent shockwaves across the continent.

During our sixteen-year spell outside the tournament, Liverpool fans and ex-players couldn't stop themselves saying how much easier it was to win under the new format. 'It's the get beat and have another go league now,' supporters would say, especially to Manchester United fans as they struggled in Europe year after year before finally winning it again in 1999. When we were participating, we felt differently. Allowing four teams from each major country to take part certainly made it easier to qualify. As for winning it . . . it's harder now than it was during Liverpool's heyday.

Earning the right to enter was the toughest part for Bob Paisley's and Joe Fagan's men. Under the old rules, we'd still be trying to enter. The European Champions Cup was exactly that, first place only was the criterion for participation, and many believe it was better for it. But once in it, it's no wonder the dominant Liverpool side performed so consistently. The strongest nations had only one entry each rather than four. I'm not demeaning their success. They were the best team in Europe, and probably lost out a couple of times because of the instant knockout format in the early stages as much as they benefited from it. Unlike today, one bad night in October was all you needed to miss out twenty years ago. Had it been a league then, who's to say there wouldn't be six European Cups engraved on Anfield's Paisley Gates instead of three?

But in today's competition, once you get to the last sixteen, it's impossible to win without meeting two, three or even four of Europe's strongest teams, back to back. It's possible to have to play all four of Italy's top clubs, or those from Spain, before you reach the semi-final. Every season the same names are there: Barcelona, Manchester United, Real Madrid, Arsenal, Chelsea, Inter Milan . . . The fact we'd even joined this list was to our credit. Beating them was going to take a monumental leap in class, and I didn't feel we had the players to do it.

Being paired with Bayer Leverkusen in the first knockout round of 2005 offered a chance of further progress, although we paid the price longer term for what was, on paper at least, an attractive draw. The Germans' star striker was Dimitar Berbatov. Benitez had revealed to me earlier in the season he hoped to sign Berbatov during the January 2005 transfer window; he and Fernando Morientes were the two candidates he was considering. Unfortunately, once we'd been paired against Bayer there was no prospect of them selling us their best player ahead of our meeting. That gave the club no choice but to pursue Morientes, and we never had another chance to sign the Bulgarian, who's since gone on to treble his value at Spurs.

In fairness, few of us could have foreseen that over the course of those two legs. He was anonymous as we battered Leverkusen 6–2 on aggregate, avenging our defeat in the quarter-finals three years earlier. What was most significant was the manner of our success home and away. With Gerrard unavailable for the home tie, Igor Biscan played central midfield and belatedly produced his best performance for the club. To go any further in the competition our best players needed to play to their maximum, and our limited ones had to show quality beyond that which I'd seen before, and in some cases more than I thought they were capable of.

My lack of belief in our ability to win the Champions League wasn't just based on a lack of strength in depth. I didn't believe our best starting eleven was anywhere near good enough at the time either. We defied our own expectations as much as those across the rest of Europe. Thrillingly, many of the fringe players, some of whom knew they had no future at Liverpool beyond the end of that season, found form at exactly the same time. It was as if the Champions League anthem were transforming certain average players into world-beaters.

Juventus's arrival at Anfield for the first leg of the quarter-final summed it up. Scott Carson, just nineteen, was thrust in for his European debut with French forward Anthony Le Tallec, who had barely played under Benitez. I didn't believe Le Tallec would start another senior match under his management, but in our 2–1 first leg win he was exceptional. The Kop played their part by creating a feverish atmosphere and we took advantage of the Italians' failure to come to terms with the hostile environment to lead 2–0 within twenty minutes. That blistering opening effectively won us the tie. Juventus had possession for the remaining seventy minutes of that night, and the entirety of the second leg, but they only scored once. Liverpool home advantage really could be worth a goal start. In that case, it was the equivalent of a two-goal lead.

After that home win but before the trip to Italy, I felt proud we'd given ourselves a fighting chance, but I still thought of us as outsiders. My lack of confidence was fully exposed during a conversation with my captain. Stevie told me he'd felt his hamstring in training and asked me what I thought he should do. I had no doubts.

'We can't afford to lose you for the rest of the League season,' I told him. 'Don't risk it against Juventus. We only need to lose 1–0 and we're out, and if you get injured, that's it for us this season. We won't catch Everton.'

My long-term fear was Stevie was a bad injury away from leaving Liverpool. Keeping him fit enough to finish fourth was my priority, not risking him in a competition where the prospect of winning was such a long shot.

He didn't travel to Italy, but with Xabi Alonso back from injury Rafa out-thought Fabio Capello tactically. We played a 3–5–2 formation, nullifying the threat of Pavel Nedved by packing midfield. Juve hardly had a sniff of goal. It was a tactic we'd successfully use again later in the competition, although in far more dramatic and desperate circumstances.

When the game was over and I recognized what we'd achieved, it dawned on me for the first time we were genuine contenders to win the competition. If a side including Traore, Biscan, Le Tallec, Nunez and a rookie keeper could defeat the Italian champions, with players of the class of Buffon, Cannavaro, Nedved, Thuram and Ibrahimovich, anything was possible.

The excitement among the fans was building and transmitting itself into the bodies and minds of the players. They also had a new anthem to accompany our European tours. 'Ring of Fire' by Johnny Cash was already a favourite among a small group of supporters. Paul Cook, who used to play for Tranmere, Mick Laffey, Gary McGowan and my dad said they'd been using the tune as their theme song on the road for years. They used to meet at The Fantail pub in Kirkby before our away games, and as their coach made its way along England's motorways and A roads they'd put their 'Live from San Quentin' tape on and sing the der-der-der-der-der, der, der, ders. I'd first become aware of this against Middlesbrough in 2003 when I was invited on board. I was recovering from my broken leg and couldn't stand sitting at home listening to our Saturday matches on the radio, so I joined the minibus regulars on their trip to the north-east and sat in the away stand. The 'Ring of Fire' chant was soon heard inside the ground, and it slowly began to spread across the whole of our fanbase. My ears were pricked at a League match at Fulham early in the 2004–05 season when it was as loud as I'd known it, but it seemed to take on a life of its own as we progressed in Europe. By the time we met Chelsea in the semi-final, the words of the song had caught the imagination of all the fans. If we could get them back to Anfield on equal terms, never mind a ring of fire, they were going to face a towering inferno of passion.

Everything it was possible for a club to do wrong ahead of a semi-final, Chelsea did in 2005. Every cocky interview they gave, every idle boast, worked in our favour, and every neutral in the world wanted us to win. Even a few Manchester United fans must have been tempted to back us over Jose Mourinho's side.

This wasn't a typical European semi-final, it was a battle fuelled by the growing hostility that had been festering between the clubs. In all my years at Anfield I've never known our supporters want to win any fixture more. Not even countless meetings with Everton or Manchester United have triggered such a tidal wave of ill will towards an adversary.

The Carling Cup Final had added to the mutual disrespect in the stands, but to our supporters Chelsea as a football club characterized everything they despised. They seemed even more brash and arrogant than they were in the 1990s as the darling of Tory fans like David Mellor. Some of their officials and fans created a fresh definition for the word 'smug' every time they were interviewed. Chelsea behaved like they had a divine right to be instantly considered one of Europe's greatest clubs, just because they were wealthy. Every time they spoke about being seen on the same level as Liverpool, Real Madrid or Manchester United, you couldn't stop yourself thinking if it wasn't for Roman Abramovich's billions most of them wouldn't even be at Stamford Bridge, let alone claiming Chelsea were one of the biggest clubs in the world. Their approach seemed as much about belittling everyone else as promoting themselves. They represented the opposite of all I believed in. Unlike Liverpool, they didn't have the emotional bonds to go with their economic might. They had plenty of what we wanted – money – but The Kop possessed something they couldn't buy, and which can only be bred over the generations: passion.

Our supporters and manager focused on the financial aspect of Chelsea's success as an easy way to undermine their achievements, but the point for me wasn't that the Londoners were minted, it was the way they handled their good fortune. When Abramovich took over, they acted like lottery winners, rubbing the rest of the football world's noses in it. They began openly to tap up players, and, prior to Mourinho's appointment, even thought the England manager was there for the taking. Having a billionaire owner didn't make them better than everyone else, only wealthier, but there seemed little desire to behave with dignity, humility and integrity. Football's rule book, it seemed, could be rewritten by those with the largest cheques.

That said, I found some of the remarks about Chelsea 'buying their success' hypocritical. I felt no resentment towards Abramovich for spending heavily to make them a superpower. Every Liverpool fan was hoping for a similar tycoon to come to Anfield and plough the same level of cash into us. Had he joined us and pumped so much money into the team, he'd only have had to wear a red scarf in the directors' box and said a few kind words and we'd have loved him.

You could argue Abramovich has been good for English football. Not only did he raise the stakes by taking Chelsea to a new level, forcing everyone else to get their act together, he's probably invested as much in other Premier League clubs as his rival chairmen. Manchester City wouldn't have received £20 million for Shaun Wright-Phillips and West Ham wouldn't have earned the millions they have from sales had Chelsea not been prepared to pay over the odds. On the other hand, the level of spending now has reached ridiculous levels, piling the pressure on other clubs to take financial risks. The knock-on impact of trying to compete with Abramovich led to the Liverpool takeover, and we've all seen how detrimental it can be if you sell to the wrong foreign owner. Still, for the rest of us to complain about their spending is sour grapes. And anyway, as I know to my cost at Anfield, having money is no guarantee of success. The skill is spending it on the right players.

It wasn't Abramovich who sparked the hatred between Liverpool and Chelsea that season, it was the historical and philosophical differences between the clubs, aided and abetted by the conduct of their players and the war of words between our managers. We relished being seen at odds with them – the working-class fighters taking on the middle-class toffs. We were going to squeeze out of our pores every last drop of sweat to stop them. And if any of us even felt a tingle of weakness, our fans were going to burst their lungs urging us to go beyond what many of us thought possible. The will to win is as important as the ability to do so. Chelsea had the class in their squad, but they couldn't beat our desire. In simple terms, our fans wanted it more than theirs.

We also knew how little they fancied our chances. Their biggest mistake was underestimating us. They presumed their superior strength in depth, and overall quality, would make victory inevitable. While we were battling to that 0–0 draw in Turin, I later heard many of the Chelsea lads had gone out for a drink in west London to watch the game on TV. Mourinho's side had come through against Bayern Munich a night earlier, and we already knew which direction the draw was taking us. Flying high in the League and having already beaten us three times during the season, naturally the Chelsea players hoped we'd be in the semi. Juventus looked a more formidable opponent. Our weaknesses had already been exposed domestically. I was informed that when the final whistle blew in the Stadio Delle Alpi it was the cue for celebrations in west London. Then, in the weeks before the semi-final, all we heard about was the inevitability of a dream final between AC Milan and Chelsea. Nothing our rivals said or did erased our suspicions that they thought they were as good as through.

Perhaps that explained their low-key approach to the first leg on 27 April, when, having anticipated a cauldron of noise at Stamford Bridge, I walked out wondering if this really was one of the biggest games of our careers. There was nothing to distinguish it from a routine Premiership game. It was as if the importance of the occasion hadn't registered with Chelsea fans. As I lined up and heard our away section in full voice, there was only one conclusion. This game meant far more to Liverpool than to Chelsea. I'm not talking about their players; I know how hungry their squad and manager were to get to the final. Had their fans shown the same intensity, maybe we'd have found it tougher to cope in the first game. But nothing exposed the difference between the values of the two clubs than the contrasting atmospheres at Stamford Bridge and Anfield.

The first game was dull, memorable solely as the only occasion I've seen Benitez lose his rag in the dressing room. He laid into a couple of players at half-time, accusing them of not working hard enough. We rarely threatened a goal, but we defended superbly. The only blemish was a late booking for Xabi Alonso, courtesy of Eidur Gudjohnsen's dive. 'I knew you were a yellow card away from being suspended,' the Icelandic striker admitted after the game. Such was our lack of resources, losing Xabi seemed a potentially crippling blow. The Kop wasted no time using the manner of his suspension to point the finger at Chelsea's 'cynical bastards'. Didier Drogba and Arjen Robben had already secured their reputation in this respect that season, so Gudjohnsen joined their rogues gallery.

A 0–0 draw was all we were playing for, so it was a job expertly executed. 'I'm sure 99 per cent of Liverpool fans think they're now through,' said Mourinho, using his mind games to try to shift the pressure on to us. It was a useless strategy, and Phil Thompson, a pundit for Sky on the night of the first leg, delivered the perfect, instant riposte on our behalf, ensuring we needn't bother rising to Jose's bait. 'Jose is wrong,' said Thommo. 'A hundred per cent of Liverpool fans think they're now through.' Was Thommo guilty of Chelsea style arrogance? No, there was a difference. He was reminding Mourinho he was right to be extremely worried about what the fans had in store for him a week later. Nothing Jose and his players had experienced previously in football would prepare them for this.

In fact, nothing I had experienced compared to the evening of 3 May 2005.

There are three Anfield nights which, above all others, are worthy of a permanent shrine in the club museum: the first leg against Inter Milan in 1965, when Bill Shankly's side beat the Italian champions 3–1 in the last four of the European Cup; St Etienne in 1977, when Liverpool needed to score two second-half goals to reach the semi-final of a competition they'd go on to win for the first time; and Chelsea in 2005. Some seasoned Anfield observers claimed we topped this illustrious list.

We hadn't waited just the week that separated the two legs for a fixture of this magnitude. The club had gone through two decades of frustration to get here. We'd done everything we could to help whip up the fans in the days before the return leg, but there wasn't any need. Every interview we did we just dusted down the annual tributes to the 'twelfth man' of The Kop, but it was more a case of predicting they'd make a contribution than asking them to do so. The supporters required no rallying cry.

For every motivational quote we provided, Chelsea's players and manager tended to go one further. Stories began to appear about hospitality packages already being offered to their fans for the final. Then we heard they'd booked a club in Liverpool for a private party to celebrate after the match. I'm not sure if that's true, but the owner of the club was quoted in the *Liverpool Echo*, so it had the desired effect of making us more determined. Chelsea certainly messed around with our preparations with their arrangements on Merseyside. Prior to every home European game we would stay overnight in the same hotel. I'm not superstitious, but when you get into a familiar routine as a player, even a minor disruption can play on your mind and fester. I was livid to discover Chelsea had booked into our usual accommodation. Did they do so deliberately? I suspect so, but most of my anger was aimed at the hotel for allowing them to get in first and stay when they should have known we'd want to be there.

'Do you want us to win this trophy or what?' I'd have asked them.

By the day of the game, the intense sense of anticipation had swept across the city and was encircling the perimeter of our very own 'Ring of Fire' – the Anfield stadium. Even during the warm-up the volume of noise was several decibels higher than most League games. The Kop was full early, there were more banners and scarves than I could remember, and a full repertoire of songs escorted us through our preparations. It was like seeing a multi-coloured dreamcoat of bedspreads daubed with graffiti.

'This is going to be a special night,' I thought.

As Thommo had warned, the fans really had turned up believing we were going to win. Now we felt it too, and the Chelsea players couldn't avoid being affected by the surge of absolute conviction coming from the stands. They'd later admit they'd never known an atmosphere like it. Despite the hype beforehand about Anfield's terrifying sounds, playing in those conditions was tough for them.

Just as Juventus had needed half an hour to come to terms with the hostility, conceding two goals in the process, so Chelsea succumbed to our immediate momentum. Luis Garcia scored what became known as 'The Phantom Goal': his tame shot dawdled before deciding to cross the goal-line, sucked in by the inhalations of twelve thousand Kopites. Nobody has ever been able to prove the goal should have stood. Crucially, nobody has ever been able to disprove it either.

Plenty tried, of course. In the days following the game I was starting to think the nation's scientists had been ordered to find conclusive evidence it didn't go in. Sky TV repeated it every minute of every hour, using as many gadgets as they could to expose the scandal of the linesman's decision. What Chelsea sympathizers neglected to emphasize was the referees' explanation of what would have happened had the goal not stood. Chelsea keeper Petr Cech would have been sent off for clattering Milan Baros in the build-up to the strike, we'd have had a penalty, and Chelsea would have had to play virtually an entire game with ten men and a reserve goalie. Given the option, I might have preferred it at the time.

There was no injustice in our victory. Chelsea had 180 minutes plus six minutes' injury time to score a single goal. They failed. Only Gudjohnsen's last kick of the match, when he volleyed across the face of The Kop goal, threatened to break our resolve. The 'Ring of Fire' chant set The Kop ablaze during those final stressful seconds, as supporters manically waved their scarves above their heads, pleading for the final whistle.

The emotion was overwhelming at the end. As I leapt for joy, I felt I'd completed my best 180 minutes in a Liverpool shirt.

It's easy to accuse Liverpool of being over-romantic when it comes to their football, but this was one of many occasions when the self-congratulation was fully warranted. As one of the banners that night claimed, we had genuinely shown there are some things money can't buy. In an increasingly cynical football world, our victory seemed to send out a message that the game was as unpredictable as ever, and all the better for it.

It was the first time Liverpool had been such overwhelming underdogs in Europe, and we used this to our advantage. Usually, semi-final wins are meaningless unless you follow it with a trophy. There was no danger of this victory ever being dismissed, no matter what happened in Istanbul. This was special in its own right. The thrill that night was as much stopping Chelsea as reaching the final itself.

As I'd suspected, every impartial viewer was supporting Liverpool. Among the first calls Stevie and I received after the game were from Thierry Henry and Patrick Vieira. Arsenal hated Chelsea as much as our fans, and they were genuinely pleased on our behalf. 'You deserved it,' they told us. It was a nice touch, and one of the reasons why there's always been so much mutual respect between Liverpool and Arsenal players during my time at Anfield.

Once we'd finished celebrating on the pitch, we couldn't get away from the ground and into town any quicker. We headed to the city centre still in our tracksuits to join the supporters for a drink on this historic night.

As I poured another beer down my throat, the conversation gradually shifted from what we'd just achieved to what might still be accomplished. We'd secured an unforeseen success, and now our sights were fixed on a miraculous one. 'It's meant to be,' the supporters told us. The more obsessed fans even listed a series of bizarre coincidences to prove conclusively that winning was our destiny. Trivial, increasingly ridiculous news events were used as a means of explaining why we'd come so far.

When Liverpool won the European Cup for the first time, in 1977, the date of the final was 25 May, the same as the 2005 final.

In every year we won it, we'd played in traditional red and our opponents in all-white, the same as the 2005 final.

In 1981, Liverpool won the European Cup in the summer of Prince Charles and Lady Di's royal wedding. In 2005, Charles married for the second time. (So did Ken and Deirdre Barlow, we were informed as the imagination of the fans went into overdrive.)

A Wales grand slam victory in 1981 and 2005 was also an indicator of Liverpool European success. Even the death of Pope John Paul II couldn't escape the superstitions. He took office in 1978 while Liverpool were beating Bruges at Wembley, but passed away just before we headed to the 2005 final.

'Everything points to a Liverpool victory,' the Scouse psychics insisted.

Fate, we'd soon realize, hadn't finished having some fun with us yet.

*

I've never allowed myself to be intimidated by an opponent. Reputations count for nothing, and I wouldn't fear any side. But when I looked through the AC Milan line-up in the weeks prior to the final it was impossible not to feel concerned about what they'd do to us if they played to their potential.

I couldn't see a weakness. Cafu and Paolo Maldini ranked not only as the two greatest full-backs of their generation, but arguably the finest in the last century at any level. Alessandro Nesta was established as Italy's most accomplished centre-half, while his defensive partner Jaap Stam was already a Champions League winner with Manchester United. In midfield, Andrea Pirlo and Gennaro Gattuso would be the inspiration for Italy's World Cup win a year later. Clarence Seedorf is one of the legends of the game. He was aiming to win his third European Cup with his third different club – a feat he later achieved against us in 2007. Then there was Kaká, on the verge of establishing himself as the best player in the world. And if that wasn't enough, the pre-Chelsea Andriy Shevchenko was recognized as the world's most lethal striker, and Argentina's Hernan Crespo had already commanded fees in excess of £70 million. He was one of the most expensive footballers on the planet. The pace, movement and intelligence of this duo were mesmerizing.

I knew I was playing the real deal here. This was a side at its peak; professional, talented and ruthless. Our only chance, or so we thought, was to frustrate them for as long as possible and hope to steal a 1–0 win, or get to a penalty shoot-out. I had some ideas about how we could achieve this and thought I could guess Benitez's tactics based on our success against Juventus. Milan had more flair than Juve, but in my experience all Italian sides tend to play the same way.

Juve used Nedved floating between midfield and the forward

line and Kaká played a similar role for Milan. In fact, Kaká's position was easier to cater for tactically because he tended to stick to a central zone behind the two forwards. Nedved was more likely to drift to wider areas of the pitch, which could drag your holding midfielder – in our case Didi Hamann – out of position.

There was no question in my mind Didi was the man to nullify Kaká's threat. It had never occurred to me, or him, he wouldn't start the final. Consistently the man for the big occasion, he was one of those in the dressing room who could be trusted to deliver. Such certainty was shaken three days before kick-off when Benitez confided to Stevie he was going to pick Harry Kewell.

'I can understand that,' I remarked when informed of this secret bulletin. 'Cafu piles forward so there may be space for Harry on the left.'

Stevie shook his head, alerting me to the fact I'd misunderstood. 'Harry is playing as a striker,' he said, his voice almost quivering with disbelief.

This snippet allowed us to work out the rest of the line-up. Our success against Chelsea was based on Stevie playing behind a lone striker, protected by Alonso and Hamann. If Gerrard was now returning to a more orthodox central midfield role, either Alonso or Hamann were out.

I realized Didi was going to be on the bench and spent the next forty-eight hours trying to avoid the subject of the team while I was with him. He was one of my best mates, but there are some things you can't say on the eve of a match. I wasn't supposed to know the team until just before kick-off, but part of me wanted to speak out and tell the boss he'd got it wrong.

Even as Benitez announced his line-up in the changing room

an hour before kick-off, it didn't instantly register with Didi. 'I heard him name the back four and then Stevie in midfield, and my first thought was, "I can't believe he's not playing Xabi,"' Didi informed me later.

The risk was taken. Milan expected a rigid, defensive Liverpool. Instead, we were going for it.

Despite our misgivings about the tactics, there was no sign of negativity as we headed to the tunnel. I could see players such as Gerrard, Alonso, Hyypia and Baros were ready to give the performances of their careers. Then I glanced at Djimi Traore. There was a look of nervousness on his face. I turned my head away, knowing I had to focus on my own state of mind rather than worry too much about his.

Djimi's first touch, straight from kick-off, was edgy, immediately giving away possession. His second contribution within thirty seconds was to concede a free-kick in a dangerous position to the left of our box. A minute had passed, and Pirlo's free-kick allowed Maldini to score.

The horror began to unfold. There's a suggestion Milan came out of the traps and battered us throughout a one-sided first half, but we played better football than many think. In terms of possession we were enjoying ourselves, and at 1–0 I wasn't as dispirited as might have been expected. Our problems were purely tactical. Italian sides excel on the counter-attack, and we continually fell into their trap. We tried to be ambitious, but the speed with which they hit us on the break was devastating. The second and third goals, which arrived shortly before half-time, were Italian works of art, crisp, incisive passing moves that would have ripped any defence apart. We didn't do much wrong, but the quality of Shevchenko and Crespo made us look ridiculous.

When the third went in, I'd never felt so helpless on a football pitch.

People ask what was going through my mind in those moments before half-time. As I walked towards the dressing room, I was suffering from a depressing combination of despondency and humiliation. I couldn't bear to lift my head up and glimpse the faces in the crowd, or the banners and red jerseys scattered around the Ataturk. I looked towards the floor and saw nothing but endless dejection. My dreams had turned to dust. I wasn't thinking about the game any more. My thoughts were with my family and friends. I was so sorry. Daft, seemingly trivial ideas scattered themselves across my mind, such as 'What will everyone at home be saying about this?' The thought of going home a laughing stock disturbed me. Never mind The Chaucer after the United defeat in 1999, it would have felt like the whole city, the whole country, even the whole world was taking the mickey out of us. There was a sense of shame to go with my sorrow. The Liverpool fans had taken over the stadium and there was nothing we could do to make amends.

I almost began to regret reaching the final. All defeating Juve and Chelsea had achieved, it seemed, was to allow AC Milan to outclass us and possibly secure the greatest ever margin of victory in a European Cup Final. They'd beaten Barcelona and Steaua Bucharest 4–0 in the 1994 and 1989 finals, and now I feared we'd create history for the wrong reasons, at the receiving end of a record defeat, by five or six. Keeping it at 3–0 and at the very least restoring some respectability was all that mattered to me now.

Nothing was said by the players as we returned to the dressing room. A mythical fifteen minutes in the Liverpool legend was upon us, but it didn't feel that way. The trickiest test in such circumstances is ensuring you don't give up. It would have been easy for us to accept our ambitions were in tatters, that nine months of toil were going to end in catastrophe. Mentally we were all over the place, but I knew it wasn't in my nature to accept this fate. No matter how bad it was, we were going to have to face up to our responsibilities.

Fortunately, there was at least one sane head in the room prepared to restore our battered spirits. In that Ataturk dressing room Rafa Benitez cemented his place in Anfield folklore.

My admiration for his handling of the situation is unlimited. Rafa's conduct rarely changed, regardless of the circumstances. His calm demeanour was never required more than now. Privately, he must have felt the same as us. He too couldn't have failed to think about his family, or what the people of Spain would be making of his side's battering. Here he was, still struggling with his English, trying to instruct us to achieve the impossible.

'Good luck,' I thought to myself.

He showed few signs of emotion as he explained his changes, but the speed with which he made a series of tactical switches showed how sharp he still was. First, he told Traore to get into the shower. That was the polite code for telling a player he's being subbed. Djibril Cisse was told he'd be coming on to play on the right side and was already getting kitted out.

As Djimi removed his shirt, an argument was brewing between Steve Finnan and our physio Dave Galley. Finnan had damaged a groin and Dave told Rafa he thought he should be subbed. Finn was distraught and pleaded to stay on. Rafa wouldn't budge. 'We've only two subs left because we've already lost Kewell with an injury,' he explained. 'I can't afford to make two now, and if you stay on I've lost my last sub.' Traore was told to put his kit back on. Then, as if struck by a moment of clarity, Benitez made an abrupt decision. 'Hamann will replace Finnan and we'll play 3–5–2,' he explained, displaying an assured conviction in his voice which, temporarily at least, gave me confidence. 'Pirlo is running the game from midfield, so I want Luis and Stevie to play around him and outnumber them in the middle so he can't pass the ball.'

The swiftness of this decision confirmed to me he may have considered this formation earlier. The same set-up had worked in Turin, although that had been a purely defensive strategy. 'OK,' part of me was thinking, 'forty-five minutes too late, but we got there in the end.' Given the circumstances, it was still a brave move.

With both Cisse and Hamann now preparing to come on, there was only one problem.

'Rafa, I think we've twelve players out there now.'

Djibril would have to wait a while longer for his introduction.

When we emerged from our desolate dressing room, I wasn't encouraged by the look of steely determination on the face of Maldini as he led his side back out. There were claims after the match of premature celebrations in the Milan camp at half-time. I was upset on their behalf by that pack of lies. Traore gave an interview after the game suggesting the Italians were cocky at 3–0, but I think he was naive in his answers and it was twirled into a fairy story by the newspapers. It simply didn't happen. Milan were far too professional for that. There was no way their captain, with all his experience, was going to allow anyone in his dressing room to take victory for granted. Nothing I saw suggested Milan were already popping champagne. I have too much respect for them even to suggest it. Even if they did, privately, believe they had both hands on the cup, who could blame them? As I headed back into the arena I was sure Milan were going to win, so were the forty thousand Scousers in Istanbul, so why shouldn't they have believed it?

I could hear 'You'll Never Walk Alone' in the distance, and as I exited the tunnel it grew louder. It wasn't the usual version of our anthem though. There are different moments when The Kop summons Gerry Marsden's classic. Before every home game it's a deafening rallying cry, as if to inspire us to perform and frighten our opponents into submission. If we're winning in the closing stages of a huge match, it will be sung again, this time in celebration. But there are other occasions the words of the song have greater meaning, and at half-time in Istanbul the fans were singing it in sympathy more than belief. There was a slow, sad sound to it, almost as if it was being sung as a hymn. The fans were certainly praying on our behalf. To me, it was the supporters' way of saying, 'We're still proud of what you've done, we're still with you, so don't let your heads drop.' There was probably a hint of a warning in there too, as the walk back to my position felt like a guilt trip: 'Don't let us down any more than you already have.' Our coach Alex Miller's final instructions at half-time were for us to 'score a goal for those fans'. That was the mindset we had. Get one and pride might be restored.

Just as the first half is mischievously remembered as Milan taking us apart from first minute to last, the start of the second is seen as our attack versus their defence. It wasn't like that. Milan looked more like grabbing a fourth before we scored our first. Jerzy Dudek had to make a few more saves before we entered the Twilight Zone.

Then it began.

A John Arne Riise cross.

A terrific Gerrard header.

At 3–1, we had hope.

A ray of light appeared amid the previously unrelenting grey clouds. I saw Stevie run towards our fans and urge more noise. Dejection was replaced by passion again.

Vladimir Smicer almost instantly cut the deficit to 3–2. Now we added the ammunition of belief to our mission impossible.

Two features stand out about Vladi's goal. The first was my screaming at him not to waste possession with an ambitious twenty-five-yard shot. His strike record wasn't impressive, so as he pulled the trigger I was ready to give him an earful for his deluded self-confidence. The second point relates to Kaká. As our attack developed, I noticed the Brazilian stop to fix one of his shin pads. Having watched the goal a million times or more since, I'm convinced had Kaká tracked back he'd have been in a position to cut out the pass to Smicer in the build-up to the goal. At 3–1, perhaps it didn't seem so important. A split second later, I've no doubt Kaká wished he'd waited before making his running repairs. I've lost count of the number of times I've heard managers emphasizing the 'small details' that can change the course of a game. There's no finer example than that.

When Dida was beaten, I not only felt we were back in the game, our momentum was such an equalizer was inevitable. I looked towards both benches and the contrast with twenty minutes earlier was extreme. Our coaching staff and substitutes were going berserk. The Liverpool fans were screaming their approval. AC Milan's manager, Carlo Ancelotti, looked stunned. His backroom team and reserves sat motionless, slumped in their seats, showing the same frozen expressions we'd experienced when Crespo chipped in the third before half-time.

Milan restarted the game. We regained possession. This time I found myself with time and space on the ball. I spotted Milan Baros and played a precise pass. Usually I'd hang back, this time I kept rampaging forward, creating space for the attackers. Baros's clever pass sent Stevie into the box and Gattuso tripped him as he was about to shoot. Two thirds of the stadium erupted in demand of a penalty. No referee was going to argue.

While my team-mates celebrated, my first reaction was to call for Gattuso's sending-off. He'd fouled Gerrard on the edge of the six-yard box and denied a clear goalscoring opportunity. In normal circumstances a dismissal would have been inevitable. My pleas left me open to allegations of unsporting behaviour. Players who try to get their fellow professionals sent off are frowned upon. I had nothing against Gattuso. My quarrel was with the injustice of Milan still having eleven men on the pitch. There's a difference between trying to get a player sent off and pointing out a mistake has been made if an opponent hasn't been given the correct punishment. Gattuso's survival meant, although we equalized, Milan were able to recover from their slump.

After arguing with the referee, my next row before Xabi Alonso's pen was with Luis Garcia. I must have looked like a man possessed, lashing out at everyone. Benitez always decided who'd take penalties before the game, and Xabi had been given the nod. For whatever reason, Luis grabbed the ball and was ready to assume responsibility.

'Fuck off Luis, this is Xabi's,' I said.

I was saving him from himself. Had he taken it and missed, Benitez – and the rest of us – would never have forgiven him.

Not that Xabi fared better, but before we had time to curse Dida's save from the spot-kick the rebound had been slammed in and we were chasing the goalscorer to the corner flag.

Milan had been hit with a six-minute tornado. As swiftly as we'd lost control of our destiny, we'd regained it.

The Italians managed to recover their composure after our torrential pressure, but their three-goal advantage had been washed away. Psychologically, we had the upper hand, but football has a peculiar way of forcing you to reassess your aims depending on how much you have to lose. We felt fearless at the start of the second half because, emotionally, we were already beaten. The pre-match nerves had gone, substituted by the feeling 'Fuck it, let's just go for it and if we go down, we go down fighting'. At 3–3, the earlier anxieties returned. Now it was time for us to put our foot back on the ball, ease ourselves back into a more orthodox pattern and stop piling forward.

I recognized we had something astonishing on our hands now, and we didn't want to let it slip again.

Logically, we should have continued to push on in the carefree manner that had led to three goals, but that was too risky for the remaining half an hour. We chose to consolidate our newly discovered sense of equality, conserve what energy we had for the looming prospect of extra-time and wait for another chance to come without forcing the issue.

In truth, I barely remember any clear opportunities in normal time after Xabi's equalizer. The final whistle was a Godsend when it arrived. We were tiring, Milan had fully recovered from their trauma, and the sooner the penalty shoot-out started the better so far as I was concerned.

Those additional thirty minutes were the most tense, strenuous and, ultimately, rewarding I've ever spent on a football pitch. At the end of my career, if there's one period of play I believe I'll be remembered for, it was this. We were under constant pressure. During the second period of extra time I stretched to intercept a cross and my leg cramped. Anyone who has suffered cramp will know how painful it is. Even breaking my leg didn't hurt as much. It was brief and it was instantly treatable, but I knew my body was weakening as Milan finished strongly.

Thirty seconds after the physio sent me back on to the pitch an identical pass was sent into our box and I had no choice but to stretch the same leg to make a decisive tackle on Shevchenko. As I did so, it seemed the whole world was wincing on my behalf, appreciating the physical torment I was enduring. I hadn't thought twice about throwing my body in the way. Whatever grief it was going to cause me for a few seconds was nothing compared to how I'd've felt had I hesitated and watched him score.

Courage, character, grit, willpower and raw strength – these are the virtues people have instilled into me since I was seven years old. I'd come a long way from the snotty-nosed kid who wanted to come off the pitch early because it was raining. I bet if there's one moment my dad rewinds on the DVD, it's that one. As I deflected away another goalbound Milan shot, I know he must have been prouder than he'd ever been. The strikers can have their winning goals, the goalkeepers their career-defining saves. A series of lunging tackles on the Milan strike force will be my fondest personal memories of a life in football.

We were hanging on now, assisted by the fact that Djimi Traore had overcome earlier anxieties to give the performance of his life, and also the manager's capacity to think on his feet. Milan's remaining ace was the Brazilian wing-back Serginho, who instantly found gaps on our right flank, where Smicer was playing an increasingly defensive role which was beyond his capabilities. Gerrard was moved into his third position of the game, shifting to right-back to cut off the supply. It's a tactical switch often overlooked, but in the context of the evening it was as important as many others made that night.

Regardless of our own input, we'd still need a final contribution from the fella upstairs to survive for penalties. Shevchenko headed from six yards only to be denied by a Dudek save which created one of the most enduring images of the evening. The improbable became real. A reflex movement of his wrist prevented a certain winning goal. Maradona spoke about the 'Hand of God' in the 1986 World Cup. As a Pole, Jerzy claimed it was the 'Hand of the Pope' providing divine intervention. Our keeper would dedicate his success to the recently departed John Paul II.

'That was the moment we knew we'd win the cup,' many fans commented later. I didn't There was still more work to be done before I'd accept someone up above was wearing a red scarf. One way or another, penalties were going to provide a fittingly theatrical conclusion to the season.

Dudek is one of football's nice guys. That's fine when you want to go for a pint, but when you're looking for that extra edge which is the difference between winning the European Cup and going home devastated, it's time to offer some guidance on the finer arts of craftiness. Prior to the shoot-out I headed straight for Jerzy and told him to do everything possible to unsettle the Milan penalty takers. Put them off, distract them, mess with their heads. I didn't care what Jerzy did, I just wanted him to make it even more difficult to score.

'Remember Bruce Grobbelaar in the Rome shoot-out in 1984,' I was saying to my keeper.

Grobbelaar famously wobbled his legs on the goal-line as if he could barely stand up due to nerves. As the Roma penalty takers stepped forward, his antics seemed to have an impact as they blazed a couple of kicks over the bar and Liverpool won. He became known as 'spaghetti legs' afterwards. Also, my knowledge of the history of football, recalling how such matches had been won in the past, helped us in this situation. Years spent memorizing the contents of *Shoot* served their purpose, and my competitiveness kept my mind racing about what more could be done to influence the result. If Jerzy could make just one gesture to put off one Milan player, that could win us the Champions League. My conscience was clear. Winning was the only thing.

While I choreographed Dudek, Benitez was selecting the penalty takers.

'Do you want to take one?' he asked me.

'Definitely,' I replied.

He ignored me. Cisse, Hamann, Riise, Smicer and Gerrard were selected. Even Xabi, who'd been allocated the job in normal time, was overlooked. Benitez also refused to allow Luis Garcia a spot-kick. He was clever with his choices. If he sensed the slightest physical or mental weakness in a player, he wouldn't let him take one. Leaving Gerrard until penalty five was an astute move too. The consequences of winning or losing on his future were still apparent. Had he scored the winning pen, there's no way he'd have wanted that to be his last kick for Liverpool. Had he missed and we'd lost, he would have felt exactly the same way.

Milan's penalty takers duly faced Jerzy's strange dancing. He kept imitating a starfish, moving across his line. Did it upset the Italians? We'll never know. If it made a slight difference, that was enough to justify it. By the time Smicer stepped up to take our fourth pen, Serginho and Pirlo had already missed, while Cisse and Hamann had given us the advantage. We were two pens from winning the European Cup when Vladi struck the sweetest of spot-kicks to Dida's left. This was his last kick for the club, and the emotion showed. He kissed the badge and celebrated.

I thought he was too premature, but we knew how close we

were now. If Andriy Shevchenko missed, it was over. Even if he scored, Steven Gerrard would have the chance to finish them off.

Shevchenko stepped up and hit one of the tamest pens you'd ever wish to see. Dudek saved.

What followed was bedlam. Nothing will ever beat the feeling of securing that victory. It was the most pure sense of euphoria imaginable. I ran as fast as I could towards the crowd, not thinking about my direction, or which stand to head for. Incredibly, as I got close enough to see the blissful faces of the fans, the first people I spotted were my brother Paul and cousin Jamie. In a crowd of eighty thousand I picked out two of those closest to me. There's a photograph that seized the moment: I stand hands aloft and my family is clearly in the background.

The snap of Stevie and me kissing either side of the cup is my favourite. Once we had hold of it, we never wanted to let go. We didn't need to. As five-time winners, tradition declared Liverpool got to keep the trophy. Stevie slept with it that night. I simply wanted to fill it with as much alcohol as possible and take swigs from it.

But I was also careful not to milk the moment of victory. There's nothing I hate more than seeing the cup winners rub their opponents' noses in it, so part of me felt for the Milan players. Many of them were experienced enough to take the defeat with the dignity I expected. Most already had winners medals, which doesn't lessen the pain but certainly offers some perspective when you're going through the grieving process. No sooner had some of their players been handed losers medals than they dumped them. Our young reserves were delighted, snatching them up before leaving the stadium as precious souvenirs.

The party shifted from the pitch to the dressing room. There was none of the quiet reflection of the treble season there. The music played, cloudbursts of champagne drenched our shirts, and every VIP in Istanbul wanted to get in to congratulate us. One such guest I ushered in myself. Gérard Houllier and his brother Serge appeared, the former boss beaming with pride at our success. Houllier was later criticized for turning up as he did, but I wanted him there to share the evening. 'Eight or nine of this side were your signings,' I told him, pointing to Dudek, Riise, Smicer, Finnan, Hyypia, Baros, Cisse, Traore and Hamann. He still felt like 'the boss' to me and Stevie. He'd repeat this to journalists later, and be attacked for doing so, but it was true. It was my way of thanking him for his influence on my career. I was indebted to him, and although his time at the club had ended badly, a year on it was only natural I should remind him how grateful I still was for guiding me through some tough times.

Liverpool prides itself on being a family club, where every contributor to our glory, past and present, is recognized. I didn't just want Houllier partying with us, I'd have liked Roy Evans and Ronnie Moran in there too. If Kenny Dalglish had turned up, as he did when the celebrations moved to Liverpool, better still. And had they been alive, Bob Paisley, Joe Fagan and Bill Shankly could have filled a glass and toasted victory with us. That's what this club means to its former players and managers, so for Houllier to be criticized for acknowledging his impact on the likes of me and Stevie was unfair.

Not everyone shared my opinion. I know Benitez thought it was strange the ex-boss was there, but I didn't see why it should worry him. There was no way the new manager wasn't going to get the credit for our extraordinary win. John Arne Riise wasn't too impressed by Houllier's arrival either. He'd made some critical remarks about the old regime during the course of the season, and Houllier tended to remember such details. Riise had just emerged from the shower when Houllier spotted him.

'Do me a favour, John. Stop criticizing me in the press, will you?'

I wish a photographer had snapped Riise's face. There he was, enjoying the pinnacle of his career, and he's getting a dressing down from his old manager. Priceless.

'I'm going to become manager of Lyon this summer,' Houllier informed me. 'Hopefully we'll meet in next year's tournament.'

I hoped so too. An emotional return to Anfield would allow The Kop to give him a proper thank you. Perhaps so soon into Benitez's reign, with memories of Houllier's departure still vivid, it wouldn't have been so heartfelt; but if it happened now, I'm sure the healing hands of time would ensure Gérard received the applause he deserves.

Stage three of the party was in our team hotel.

'Where's the real Special One?' asked chairman David Moores as he concluded a brief speech eulogizing Benitez's tactical skills.

Prime Minister Tony Blair sent us a message telling us we'd done the country proud.

I was too busy to eat or drink. I spent most of the evening blagging as many of my mates into the hotel as possible. 'Yes, they're all with me' was my catchphrase for the evening as every Red in Bootle verified their credentials. One of those who didn't make it was a lad we call 'Cracker', who ended up sacrificing three days of partying for a few minutes on the pitch with the team. He'd run on to the turf pretending he was one of the coaching staff, and posed for photographs with the team and the cup. He got arrested and had to spend the next two nights in a Turkish prison cell, missing the hotel party and the homecoming.

Cracker wasn't the only friend of mine feeling blue in the

aftermath of our success. Switching my mobile phone on gave me an opportunity to relive the fluctuating emotions of the match. At half-time I'd been bombarded with texts from the Evertonians. To say they were taking the piss is putting it mildly. It was a glimpse of what would have been in store for me had the second half followed the same pattern as the first.

As I scrolled down the phone, the messages became less frequent, and their tone changed. 'JAMMY BASTARDS' was the last one, courtesy of James 'Seddo' Sedden, a bitter Blue I've been friends with since my schooldays, whose hatred of Liverpool has never wavered despite my switch in allegiance. Seddo had called a bookmaker at half-time to check the odds of victory. He was given a price and laughed. 'What, mate? You're actually giving them a chance?' He now says he wishes he'd put a quid on us just so he could have made a couple of grand to ease his grief.

Another tale I heard was of the Evertonian who needed to get up for work at four a.m. the following morning, so he went to bed at half-time, safe in the knowledge we were beaten. He was awoken at midnight by fireworks going off. 'What the fuck's going on here?' he said, drawing back the curtains. He turned the telly on, saw us running around with the cup and thought he'd died and gone to hell.

Throughout our Turkish celebrations, my thoughts were on getting home and seeing the reaction in Liverpool. I recalled my anti-climactic feelings after our treble win, when the peculiarities of the fixture schedule denied what I'd call a traditional celebration. The scenes in town in 2001 were humbling, but I knew this would be on a far grander scale. Merseyside police warned us the city would be brought to a standstill by our homecoming. I expected around a hundred thousand people to be lining the streets as our open-top bus made its way from the airport.

It's estimated over half a million turned out for us. It seemed every Liverpudlian on Merseyside wanted to catch a glimpse of the trophy. There were even some Evertonians along the route (they're not all as bitter as Seddo). As the bus crawled past each city landmark I'd receive another text message. 'Wait until u get 2 Anfield' one would say, forewarning us of more gridlock ahead. At Anfield, we were brought to a virtual standstill, swamped by fans. My phone went again. 'Town is unbelievable' it read.

We were on the coach about four hours in total, and by the time we reached St George's Hall, our final stop in the city centre, I'd never seen such scenes. There's a famous photograph of Bill Shankly in 1974, lifting his arms to calm the thousands of fans below who'd turned out to celebrate our FA Cup win. 'Chairman Mao has never seen such a show of red power,' he said. This was even greater. It seemed people would put their lives in their hands to see us, climbing up lamp-posts or on to the roofs of multi-storey buildings. You found yourself frantically moving your head from one side of the bus to the next to make sure you didn't miss any of the banners or homemade European Cups people were waving.

The most spine-tingling sight of all was the look on the faces of the fans. If there were half a million people there, every single one of them was wearing the broadest of smiles. You can't under-estimate the feelgood factor such a win brings to a community. Those simple expressions of joy explain why football matters so much. Whatever troubles any of us had were put to one side to share this one intoxicatingly pleasurable experience. Nothing quite brings a group of people together like winning an impor-tant football match, and even though the Evertonians may disagree, it's the whole city that reaps the reward. Because of our efforts, the name of Liverpool was seen to represent something good, positive and noble.

'It will never get any better than this,' I said to Steven Gerrard. 'No matter what we do or what we win in the future, this is always going to be the highlight for us.'

Some players rate winning the World Cup as a greater achievement, and I'll never know how it feels to compare, but as a proud Liverpudlian I know it couldn't eclipse this. I was playing for my club, my city and my people. That always meant more to me. Had I been playing for anyone else in that European Cup Final I'm sure I'd have been just as elated, but something would have been missing. I wouldn't have been sharing the euphoria with those closest to me. My family and friends would have been pleased for me, but they wouldn't have been as integral a part of it as they were in 2005. Winning with England in a World Cup Final just couldn't have given me the same sensation.

To win the Champions League with Liverpool, especially in the circumstances we did it, was as close to perfection as any homegrown player could get. That's why I wouldn't swap being a Champions League winner with Liverpool for being a World Cup winner. From a purely football point of view, the standards and demands of Champions League football are also greater than those at a World Cup. All the best managers and players compete in the Champions League; that's not the case at a World Cup. International teams aren't as strong as club sides. No matter what the country, 90 per cent of top players tend to play consistently better for their clubs than their nations. There are some world-class players who've never even played in a World Cup.

The gulf in class between Liverpool and the AC Milan side we beat was so tough to bridge, when I watch the DVD for the millionth time I'll still be astounded we won. I still feel gutted at half-time; I want to run to the rebound when Xabi misses the first penalty; I need to remove my heart from my mouth as Jerzy makes the double save from Shevchenko. As Dudek makes the decisive stop in the shoot-out, I want to be back in the centre circle, preparing to run triumphantly to the supporters again. I've always analysed my matches, and none will ever fascinate me more than this one. Whenever I've three hours to kill, it'll always find its way back on to my screen.

It's impossible not to consider the importance of this win in the context of our recent history leading into 2005. When we'd walked past the European Cup as it was on parade before kick-off, we could have felt intimidated by the reflections glittering from it. If we'd indulged ourselves more than a passing glance, we might have seen images of Bob Paisley or Joe Fagan smiling back, reminding us of a glorious past we were being urged to live up to. We'd only recently re-established our credentials as a European superpower. Prior to Houllier's UEFA Cup win, the club's membership of the elite was due to a rich inheritance rather than grand modern achievements. Endless tales of Rome 1977 and 1984, Wembley 1978 and Paris 1981 diverted attention from the fact that at the turn of the millennium, on and off the pitch, Liverpool were a club needing to be dragged kicking and screaming into the twenty-first century.

It was exactly twenty years since Liverpool's last European Cup Final appearance when Benitez led us to Istanbul. Our success not only revived our reputation, it helped remove any lingering stains from the previous two decades. The supporters had endured two tragedies that defined a generation; regular cup humiliations at the hands of lower-division clubs; a series of failed multi-million-pound signings; and false dawns under honest but ultimately flawed managers. Worst of all, the sight of Sir Alex Ferguson indulging in his yearly open-top bus tour of Manchester underlined how we'd replaced our north-west rivals as the club endlessly living off former glories. Houllier deserved credit for starting the process of rehabilitation by winning the cup treble in 2001, and now Benitez had fully restored the fans' sense of self-worth. United and Chelsea may have been swapping League titles, but Benitez had not only denied Ferguson and Mourinho the prize they craved most, he'd presented The Kop with more ammunition to mock United and Chelsea. Now they could sing about how we actually owned a European Cup.

Nowadays, should any of us feel inclined to head to our club museum to give that famous trophy a polish, the only reflections staring back will be our own. It's the faces of me and my team-mates that night in the Ataturk, regardless of their overall contribution during their period at Anfield, which I'll always see glinting off that silver cup. Collectively and individually, we gave everything to take possession of that prize. Steven Gerrard's performance especially took his status to another level. Before Istanbul he was world class. Afterwards, I considered him in the top four or five players in the world. He commanded the same status as Kaká and Ronaldinho now.

The winners medals weren't the last awards to be handed out after the final. UEFA host a gala evening to honour the year's top performers, from the goalkeeper through to the striker and manager. Naturally, Benitez was the coach of the year, but we had candidates all over the pitch. Gerrard beat Kaká, Ronaldinho and Lampard to midfielder of the year, and also rightly took the title as the 2005 MVP – most valuable player. I had high hopes in my category, despite the competition, and was encouraged to discover I'd been short-listed alongside Paolo Maldini and John

Terry. They're up there as defenders I admire most in the modern game. They're better players than me, and over the course of a career I'd never claim to meet their standards consistently. In 2005, however, during the Champions League run, no one could have performed any better than I did.

I was honoured to hear both Maldini and Italian legend Franco Baresi paying tribute to my efforts. Prior to that I'd never dared presume either of them had a clue who I was. I rate my two performances against Chelsea in the semi-final, and in the thirty minutes of extra time against Milan, as my finest. I was also under tremendous pressure to perform to my absolute maximum in each round. Juventus, Chelsea and AC Milan had the best strikers in the world in their line-up. Liverpool were playing one upfront, and with respect to Baros and Cisse, central defenders didn't have as much on their plate as I did facing Drogba, Del Piero and Shevchenko.

I was gutted to get the call informing me Terry had won UEFA defender of the year in 2005. Judged on the domestic season, I had no complaints. Based on Champions League performances alone, I was right to feel aggrieved.

The awards ceremony took place in Monaco on the eve of our Super Cup Final against the UEFA Cup winners, CSKA Moscow. As Terry was named the winner, and Stevie collected his personal award, I was in the team hotel, watching from afar. I was at the centre of events when my team won the Champions League, but back on the fringe when it came to UEFA acknowledging my contribution. Hidden from view again, I could feel an annoying twinge in my heart. I knew I should be standing next to my captain. While others were in the spotlight, I was elsewhere nursing my private agony.

It was like being back on the podium in Istanbul.

10

A Team of Carraghers

Recognition from UEFA's bigwigs may have been elusive, but a Champions League winners medal wasn't my only precious reward in 2005. In the eyes of The Kop, I'd become indispensable. My renewed sense of security was captured with a new entry in the catalogue of Anfield chants: 'We all dream of a team of Carraghers'. Bayer Leverkusen were our opponents in the quarterfinal of our European Cup-winning campaign when I first heard this ditty. It's sung to the tune of The Beatles' 'Yellow Submarine'.

It may sound like a small gesture, the supporters singling you out for attention and belting out your name, but I wasn't going to shrug this off as a trivial development. I loved it. Beyond medals, what every footballer craves is reassurance and appreciation. It's a short career, and the enduring fear is the prospect of having to pack your bags every couple of seasons and settle into new surroundings. Liverpool players, or any of those at a 'big four' club, usually have to expect this lifestyle more than most. It's a hazard of the profession, especially these days. Fans crave change if a team isn't competing for trophies, and new managers often swing the axe when they arrive. If a player has the crowd on his back, especially The Kop, his days are numbered. If he's a fans' favourite, a manager will have to work overtime to shift him should he want to.

Only a select few remain attached to the same side for the entirety of their playing career. By now, I'd not only survived the regular culls at Anfield under Houllier and Benitez, I was excelling. I was seen as one of the senior players whose opinions were valued by fans and board members alike. To see my approval ratings hit such a peak cemented my relationship with The Kop and my position at the club. This ranks alongside my proudest achievements.

I was now revelling in my position at centre-half, performing at the same levels of consistency I always felt I enjoyed, but in a role more suited to my natural strengths. My reputation was enhanced to a point where I was not only viewed by Liverpool fans with the same esteem as Steven Gerrard, in the eyes of many I'd become even more popular because of ongoing fears the skipper might leave for Chelsea. As supporters became increasingly disillusioned with other events at the club, they became more appreciative of me. They trusted me on and off the pitch. I'd see more youngsters around Anfield on a match day wearing 'Carragher 23' on their backs, and it was immensely pleasing to consider how far I'd come.

When I first heard the 'Team of Carraghers' chant I guessed it was my dad and his mates egging on a few of the lads around him. As the 'Ring of Fire' episode showed, my dad had infiltrated the travelling Liverpool fan club to the extent he had as much influence on the song choices as anyone. But this was more than a selective bunch from Marsh Lane. Pretty soon I was hearing thousands joining in. Now, when The Kop is at its most vibrant on a European night and I make a crucial tackle or interception, the whole stadium sings it.

It was a humbling and mind-blowing experience to be compared with some of the greatest defenders of Liverpool's past. I even read a newspaper column by Alan Hansen claiming I was a better defender than he was. Naturally, I didn't agree. I'd need a few of his League titles for the comparison to stand up, but for a player of his class to be so complimentary is incredibly rewarding.

While my performances were undoubtedly the main contributor to this image transformation, I recognize I also benefited from the circumstances created by others. It can be no coincidence my popularity soared after Stevie almost joined Chelsea for the first time and Michael moved to Real Madrid. Before the Chelsea saga, Stevie was perceived in the same way as me, but he flirted with someone else. Rightly or wrongly, he had to win the trust back of some fans. Once again, I benefited from supporters' natural tendency to make comparisons.

It wasn't simply my football ability the fans were yearning for, it was my personality and character. The Kop loved me for what I represented. I was now being valued as a symbol of what a Liverpool player should be. I read one article saying if Steven Gerrard was the heart of the club, I was its soul. I liked the sound of that.

Now they didn't want one of me, but another ten.

Some players are wary of ever stating outright they'll never leave a club, just in case they're tempted in the future. I, on the other hand, had no hesitation confirming I had every intention of playing out the remainder of my career at Liverpool. My team-mates could argue my situation was different to theirs. Firstly, I didn't have Real Madrid, Barcelona or Chelsea trying to sign me. My love of my city and my hopes for my family mean I wouldn't have moved even if they had. At the height of the Gerrard/Chelsea hype, Sky Sports' Geoff Shreeves asked me if I'd ever consider leaving for a 'bigger club'. I was bemused by the question. 'Where's bigger than Liverpool?' I asked. I was aware such a statement would be pounced upon, but I meant it. My medal collection compared favourably with most modern players'. The fans lapped this up. They began to wish all our players had the same attitude, so the notion of dreaming of a team of Carraghers was born.

For me, this 'team' was in existence already, but it's more of a squad. It comprises my family, my friends and all those who've dedicated themselves to supporting my career. There's my wife Nicola, and children James and Mia; my brothers Paul and John; my mum and dad; and the Bootle boys such as Tony Hall, Sully, Bucko, McGhee, Alfie, Uncle Peter, Fran Bentley, Joe and Tom Foley, and my cousin Jamie Keggin. These are people who've been with me from the start and who define Marsh Lane dependability and character in my eyes. I couldn't have wished for a more faithful and reliable set of friends and family, supporting and guiding me through a demanding career. They're the real reason why I've never wanted to leave Liverpool. I could never have left my squad behind. Yes, I'm fortunate the club has the stature it has, but it's my settled family life that ensured I could never have found fulfilment elsewhere. Once I'd established myself in the Liverpool team there was only one football club and one city I ever wanted to be attached to. In the modern era, I'm somewhat of a rarity. I'm a one-club man. I'm faithful to the red shirt, ultra protective of everything it represents, and for better or for worse I would never want to stray.

Liverpool are the second biggest love of my life nowadays,

though. The toughest challenge in recent years has been to find enough space in my heart to devote to the club and the game now that I've dedicated it to my family. My wife and children have achieved what I thought fifteen years ago to be impossible: they've ensured football is my second priority (although it's a very close second). Obviously your family always comes first, even when you're a youngster, but it takes time to fully appreciate that and act in a way that proves it. For too long I behaved as if everything played a supporting role to my professional ambition. Now I've come to understand my success as a footballer is geared towards providing the best for Nicola, James and Mia.

I couldn't have wished for a more perfect wife than Nicola. She's funny, feisty and clever (and she's looking over my shoulder as I'm writing this to make sure I get it spot on), and also my biggest companion and best friend. I knew this kind-hearted Liverpool girl during our schooldays, long before my football career kicked off.

She has no interest in football at all. I knew this before we got together because I was aware her family were Evertonians. I'm not sure if I could have been with someone who shared my love of the game. You can't spend all day at work discussing and playing football and then go through it all again when you get home to your wife. It would drive anyone insane. We have the same view of life, though, and share a similar sense of humour, and the fact we're both from Bootle means we're instinctively on the same wavelength in our attitude to success.

This part of my life story is the one I find most difficult to tell. I could talk for hours expressing my fondness for certain players or football teams, but doing the same thing about the woman you love? For someone from my background, public expressions of affection aren't the 'done thing'. I've never strolled around a park holding hands with my wife. We've never cuddled up to each other in a bar and started kissing in front of everyone. Nicola's not the type who'd want me making that kind of fuss in public anyway. To us, those sorts of things should be kept within the confines of your own home. We're an ideal partnership, really, although it's fair to say I'm not a hopeless romantic, just hopeless at being romantic.

The day I asked Nicola to marry me proved that.

It was 2002, our first Christmas Day together as a family in the house we'd built in Blundellsands, a more exclusive area of the luxurious suburb of Crosby. My son James had just been born, so I thought it was time to pop the question. Unfortunately, the question didn't quite pop out. I bought an engagement ring, got my mum to wrap it up and plonked it on top of all her other presents (two cookbooks and Ulrika Jonsson's autobiography).

Nicola looked at it, slightly uncertainly. 'Is that . . ?' She paused, then unwrapped the ring and tried it on.

It didn't fit. I hadn't checked her size.

Disguising my embarrassment, I confirmed her suspicions about the proposal, then tried to change the subject by asking her to go and make my breakfast.

A miffed Nicola decided she would only wear the ring after I'd proposed properly, which I did. She didn't get me down on one knee as I asked her to marry me, but at least she now felt comfortable telling family and friends about our engagement.

I was lucky to have known Nicola Hart since childhood. At St James', the primary school we both went to, Nicola and I shared a love of sports. She was the first and only girl to win the Sefton cross-country title two years running. I was three years older, but as she was also from Marsh Lane we saw each other around Bootle throughout our teenage years.

Nicola's brother John was well known around the area as a promising footballer. Sadly, he was struck with meningitis as a youngster and was unable to fulfil his dreams.

When Nicola turned eighteen, I had one of those moments when you realize how much you're attracted to someone. I spotted her queuing to get into Sullivans, a club in Bootle, so asked her to let me push in. It was a good excuse for me to get talking to her, and I kept my eye on her from then on, waiting for an opportunity to ask her on a proper date.

I was never one for chasing girls; I'd never had a proper girlfriend until then. Why chase the rest when you can wait for the best? That was my philosophy. And once I had my heart set on Nicola I knew that was it, although every lad has to go through a few nervous moments to make sure the target of his interest feels the same way.

John told me Nicola had been given her first mobile phone, which was a big thing at the time, so I pestered him to give me the number. I called, but there was no response. (She only had her mum and dad's number stored on the phone so didn't want to answer a strange number straight away.) Instead, she rang me back.

'Who's that?' she asked.

'It's James.'

'James who?'

'It's me, James Carra. I got your number off John.'

I was then faced with the uncomfortable task of explaining why I'd called.

Thankfully, Nicola gave me a chance. We went to an Italian restaurant, Antonelli's in Waterloo, Crosby, which was coincidentally owned by Michael Owen's relatives. I'd like to say the banter instantly flowed, but you know how it is. Nerves get the better of you when you're trying to impress on your first night out. You're careful what you say to make sure you don't make a fool of yourself. Eventually we started to share our experiences of growing up in Marsh Lane and had a laugh together.

Before we met I'd bought myself a flat in Crosby and was living the perfect young bachelor's existence. I'd go to my mum's round the corner for breakfast, pop in later on to give her my dirty washing, and be back for my tea. The flat was just a glorified bedroom at first. Nicola changed that, and helped me grow up.

I was happy for her to do the usual female trick of easing her way into the flat without me even noticing. We all know how women think. First they stay overnight, then you notice the toothbrush and extra towels in the bathroom. Before you've even considered the possibility you're living together, the wardrobe starts to have as many of your girlfriend's clothes as your own. I enjoyed the transition. There was no point where we decided 'this is it, we're going to spend the rest of our lives together'. It progressed comfortably and naturally, which is exactly why I knew I'd met the right person.

After a couple of years together we decided we wanted our own family. I'd reached a stage in my career when I wanted to settle down. Football would now have to share my affections, and there was an internal struggle before I faced my new responsibilities. My dedication to the game has been my professional inspiration and the key to my success, but it wasn't so long ago it was also my personal flaw.

I still think about football constantly. If we've a match approaching, my mind will drift towards what I need to do in the days leading to kick-off. After a game I rush home and tune in rather than switch off. The Sky Plus recording is instantly replayed, and I'm reassessing what went right or wrong. If I've played badly or made a mistake, I don't want to get out of bed the next morning. If Liverpool aren't playing, football will always find its way on to the television. Whenever there's a live game, be it in England, Spain, Italy or the African Nations Cup, I'll find myself drawn towards the TV. Instead of *Shoot* magazine, it's newspapers and football talk shows on TV and radio that grab my attention now. When there's no live action, Sky Sports News stays on permanently. The appearance of that yellow ticker bar to signal 'breaking news' means everything grinds to a halt so I can listen to what's going on.

This has been the Jamie Carragher routine for years. It's only in recent times I've come to recognize the need to come to terms with what can only be described as my addiction. Football elates you one week and sends you to the depths of despair the next. As a teenager, such mood swings can be tolerated by those around you. When you've a wife and children, you've a duty to control such emotions.

Many footballers find a release by taking an interest in other sports, but you won't see me with a golf club in my hand. A snooker cue, perhaps, or you might spot me ringside at the boxing, but I've never cared about any pastime other than football. Bill Beswick, the psychologist I worked with as part of the England set-up, spelt out the need for me to broaden my interests, add balance to my life and learn when not to prioritize football. Ultimately, maturity and the building of my own family has provided me with that much-needed escape from professional commitments.

The mistakes I made in the early years of my relationship are my biggest regrets. I look back with a sense of shame I didn't put key events in our lives above all else, and also with gratitude I was given the chance to learn from those errors. To my eternal embarrassment, the biggest of these came in 2002, when I missed the birth of James.

Liverpool were playing a Champions League group match in Basel, Switzerland. It was a decisive game we had to win to qualify for the knockout stages. The baby was two weeks overdue and Nicola's check-in was scheduled for ten a.m. on the Sunday, a day before we travelled, which left twenty-four hours for the baby to be born. I spent all day with Nicola and slept in the hospital overnight awaiting the birth of our boy.

After a tiring night, the baby had still not arrived by mid-morning. I had to delay leaving the hospital twice, first because the team was meant to assemble at Melwood and then to meet up with the players' coach at Anfield. I had a dilemma. Should I stay with Nicola or head to the airport to join the team? There were two signposts in front of me. I'm ashamed to say I chose professional responsibility ahead of family loyalty. I was thinking far too much about the game and not enough about the fact my life was about to change.

Part of me questioned the decision not to stay, but truthfully, there was no way I wasn't going to play in the match.

My mum was on holiday at the time, and Nicola is convinced if she'd been around she'd have made sure I remained. I think she's right. I probably would have been tied to the chair. Nicola's mum didn't feel it was her place to influence my decision. Others did, but it made no difference.

As I sat at the airport, I was given some words of advice by Danny Murphy.

'You should go back to the hospital, Carra,' he said.

Danny had a child of his own. He recognized how important my presence at the birth would be for Nicola, and could foresee how remorseful I'd be if I didn't act.

I wasn't listening.

Nicola had an emergency Caesarean, and at 3.08 p.m., just as I was arriving at the team hotel in Basel, James Lee Carragher was born, weighing in at nine pounds twelve ounces. The news triggered celebrations in Switzerland. Houllier led a toast on my behalf at the team dinner, but by now I was sensing the first tinges of regret. I was in the wrong country to appreciate the magnitude of the occasion. Nicola and I knew privately she was having a boy before she gave birth, and now I wished I'd been there to see him come into the world.

My dad and his mates hoisted a banner in the stadium in tribute to Baby James when the game kicked off the following evening.

'Why aren't I with Nicola and the baby?' I was thinking to myself. 'I haven't even seen my own son.'

While I was on the pitch, Nicola was sharing a ward with all the other new mothers. There was no special treatment because she was the girlfriend of a Liverpool footballer, and she wasn't using my name to get any extra attention. She watched as all their husbands and boyfriends turned up one by one. The only way she could see me was by staring at the television. When anyone asked where the father was, she'd tell them he was away. Her mum told her not to say that because it made it sound as though I was in prison.

Liverpool drew 3–3 in a game they had to win to stay in the Champions League. In normal circumstances our elimination would have been the focus of my attention for days.

But for the first time in my life I had concerns greater than football.

I returned to Liverpool, held my son, and realized how stupid I'd been.

Today, as in the six years since the birth, I still owe Nicola a massive apology. I badly let her down. My obsession with football affected my judgement. There was no way I should have got on that plane until James was born. It would never happen again, but like all the blunders I've made I put it down to my immaturity. I'll be eternally grateful to Nicola for putting up with this fault of mine, although I'm sure she'll admit I've changed for the better since.

Our second child, Mia, was born on 14 May 2004 in altogether different circumstances. She arrived the day before our final game of the season against Newcastle, Houllier's last as Liverpool manager, but there was no question of me being AWOL this time. If Mia had been born at five minutes past four on that Sunday afternoon when The Kop effectively waved goodbye to Houllier, I'd still have been in the hospital.

Nicola had a planned Caesarean this time, and I made sure I followed the perfect father manual to the letter of the law, wearing all the medical gear and holding Nicola's hand as all eight pounds four ounces of Mia Rose Carragher were delivered at 10.17 a.m. I was ecstatic to be the proud father of two beautiful children.

In 2005, it was time for Nicola to join James and Mia and become a Carragher. We wed at St Andrew's Church in the grounds of Western Hall in Shropshire and it was the biggest party the Carraghers and Harts could host, assisted by the double celebration of Champions League glory. That's what I tell Nicola anyway, because she has trouble recalling all the details. She had to go to bed early because the adrenalin and nerves of the day took their toll. She hadn't even had a drink because she was unwell, and still regrets missing out on the partying, which continued into the early hours.

The offers came in from *Hello* magazine for the photographs, but we weren't interested. 'I'd rather sell my photographs to *The Kop* magazine for a pound,' I joked at the time, but there was a serious side to my response. Three of my best friends – Michael Owen, Steven Gerrard and Danny Murphy – took the magazine route, and good luck to them. There's no right or wrong way of enjoying your perfect wedding day. But what's good for one couple isn't the same for all. In our case, we weren't bothered about the extra money or security operation required when you agree to exclusive wedding photographs. We were happy enough for our mates to take as many snaps as they wanted. I'd never judge others for doing what's right for themselves. I certainly don't consider us superior in any way because we've steered clear of the relentless pursuit of fame. It's just how we are, and we're comfortable with that. We're ambitious in our determination to enjoy the best in life for ourselves and our families, but not in terms of presenting ourselves as something we're not. The people here are happy for you if you achieve a level of success, but they don't like to see it go to your head.

I'm not going to shirk the issue. As footballers, we do have to be more careful because there are women who make it a career aim to marry a top Premier League player. I've seen them interviewed in magazines or on TV shows saying it's their mission in life.

'What do you want to be when you grow up?' they're asked.

'A WAG,' comes the reply.

They want the glitz, the glamour, the wealth and the chance to hang around with famous friends. I suspect the identity of the superstar they get hitched to is the least of their concerns. Half of them probably check which club a player plays for before deciding if he's famous enough to go on a date with.

Nicola is a million miles from those kinds of girls. Her parents, Pat and John, have brought up her, her brother John and her sisters Bernadette and Elizabeth the same way as my mum and dad brought up me and my brothers. She and I would have been together even if I'd never progressed beyond the Sunday League and we were still living off Marsh Lane.

We've always followed as 'normal' a routine as possible. We still live only a couple of miles from our old neighbourhood. I used to pick Nicola up from her work at Johnsons the cleaners at 3.30 p.m. every day, drive her to her mum and dad's for her tea, head to my mum's for my tea, and then pick her up to go round to my flat later in the evening. She was earning a living rather than relying on her footballer boyfriend, and only stopped work when the two children were born. She's gone back to work now, running her own business in Liverpool (Little Day Spa, Oxford Road, Crosby). We enjoy our wealth as much as anyone in a similarly privileged position, but we've made choices that are true to our backgrounds.

James is now at an age when he's realized his father has an unusual day job. He used to see me signing autographs and wonder what the fuss was about. Now he knows. He is the opposite of me as a child. He's Liverpool mad, although he prefers Torres and Gerrard to his dad. That's the fickleness of youth for you. I'm sure he'll want to follow me into football. I'd encourage him every step of his journey if that's the case. It's the best job in the world.

He enjoys his football training twice a week and practises his skills with me every night. He's even had his first taste of Liverpool coaching. James joined the other youngsters at our

Academy during the school holidays. He didn't tell anyone who his dad was. Only the coaches knew. At the end of the session they asked the kids if they knew any good Liverpool songs.

'I do,' James said. '"Team of Carraghers".'

My dad takes him to every home fixture, and I'm looking forward to the days when I'll be able to take him to all the matches, introducing him to the same football characters and fanatics I met at the same age. He's even been a mascot, when I made my 500th appearance against Luton in the FA Cup in January 2008. It was like Christmas all over again for James. 'How many sleeps before I'm a mascot, Dad?' he was asking me for weeks. It was just as well I didn't have a bad injury. He wouldn't have been able to sleep for months waiting for me to hit the landmark.

Mia takes after her mum. She's got the same nickname, Bette Davis, because of all her theatrics. We've discovered the first few minutes of the day will dictate Mia's mood for the next twelve hours, so it's important to tread carefully when waking her up. She's already attending LIPA – the Liverpool Institute for Performing Arts, also known as Paul McCartney's 'Fame' School. Nicola rehearses Mia's dance routines every night. While James has ambitions to perform at Anfield, Mia has already performed in the musical *Annie* and has her heart set on appearing in *High School Musical*. We know we've a little actress on our hands. 'I'm not going to nursery today,' she'll tell us, speaking like a four-year-old going on fifteen. She's an independent, feisty little girl. I sometimes feel like a United Nations negotiator trying to convince her to get out of bed, and even at four she won't allow anyone else to dress her. I find it hard to discipline her because I see her as my little angel.

Fatherhood has undoubtedly changed me. In fact, I'd say it's the ideal preparation for a future career in management, dealing with two very different characters and learning how to cope with their personalities. I'm a doting parent and I share the duties with Nicola, to whom I'm forever grateful for being so patient with me. My ambition for my children is that they grow up seeing Nicola and me as two of their best friends as much as their parents. That's the relationship I have with my own mum and dad.

Growing up, you hear people say how they'd die for their wife and kids, and you don't pay much attention. Once you're married and have children of your own, you feel exactly the same way. I'd do anything for my family, in the same way my parents put me and my brothers above all else. You understand and acknowledge the sacrifices made on your behalf when you have the same responsibilities thrust upon you.

When James first learned to speak, we were concerned because he developed a slight stutter. We took him to a specialist and the problem was resolved, but for weeks I couldn't sleep with worry. I'd lie awake wishing it was me rather than him. That's when I knew football was no longer my main obsession. My family is. In fact, I believe having Nicola, James and Mia in my life has made me an even better footballer. I left the naivety of youth behind me.

I've looked after myself far more since I became a family man. I take far more pleasure from a simple act like tucking my children into bed than going out on the ale with all the lads. It helps to have someone like Nicola who is an ideal mother. I have no worries when I'm away from home – the children are being looked after properly. If Liverpool are away on a pre-season tour, Nicola will prepare a photo album of the children for me to look at every night. When I return, James and Mia will have spent the day preparing a welcome home card.

The advice I received from Gérard Houllier was right. Any emerging player who wants to add five or six years on to his career at the highest level should find a girl and settle down. Your priorities start to shift, but it enhances rather than diminishes every aspect of your life.

I'm very fortunate to be in a position where I can support my family, but it's never been the case those closest to me have relied on or asked for my financial help. My brothers Paul and John still work full-time. Of course I've helped them out by ensuring they have good houses and a high standard of living, but no one has ever wanted my charity.

John is an electrician and Paul is a ceiling fitter. Like me, their surname has advantages and disadvantages. I often think how much harder it is for my family than it is for me. I chose a life of notoriety by pushing myself to be a famous footballer, but it's been thrust upon my brothers and parents by default. Whether they like it or not, my fortunes impact on them. If Liverpool win, they'll get the congratulations; if there's flak flying, they can find themselves a target. As soon as anyone hears who they're related to, they'll find themselves engaged in a conversation about the club for the next thirty minutes. If they're involved in any bother, or they achieve success in their own right, people will refer to them as Jamie Carragher's brother, or dad, or mum. It must be a bit like having all the hassle of being a footballer without getting all the rewards.

Given my success at Liverpool, though, I think the benefits have outmuscled any negative consequences of being related to me. I know John is one of those who's milked those benefits. He needed to be signed off work sick a few years ago, but when he gave his name and details to the doctor he saw in Bootle, instead of having a check-up he spent an hour discussing the situation at Anfield. The doctor ended the conversation asking how long John needed off.

'Don't you want to check if there's anything wrong with me first?' asked John.

I'm surprised he reminded him. His nickname among his colleagues is 'Gone' Carragher because he has a reputation as a bit of a skiver.

The flip side of the coin is the malicious rumours they've had to put up with over the years. I've not suffered too much, but there are plentiful examples of how things can get out of hand.

My brother Paul went for a haircut in Liverpool city centre just after I'd broken into the side. No sooner had he asked for a short back and sides than he was hearing a detailed conversation about a stranger's weekend of passion. Not knowing who Paul was, the barber had asked the lad alongside him what he'd been up to the last few days.

'Ah, mate, I had a great weekend,' he said. 'You know that Jamie Carragher? I was shagging his bird.'

Paul gave a knowing glance, and I spent the next few days wondering who the mystery woman was. I didn't have a girl-friend at the time. It's just as well. This may sound trivial, but it wouldn't have been had I been with someone. The Evertonians probably would have started singing songs about it. It shows you how quickly fairy stories are spread in Liverpool. No doubt everyone who had their hair chopped that day and for a few weeks later was hearing how my non-existent other half was put-ting it about.

Whatever characters me and my brothers are, it's fair to say we're often overshadowed by my dad. No matter what peak I've enjoyed on the pitch, Philly Carragher has ensured himself a comical supporting role off it. English journalists have become increasingly aware of my dad's shenanigans. You won't see him on the official trips to Liverpool games, or sitting with all the VIPs. He's still organizing coach trips from Marsh Lane for our away matches, and he'll take pride of place with the hardcore fans.

Many reporters fondly remember my reaction following an England friendly against Holland at Villa Park in 2005. I was asked what Sven-Göran Eriksson had said to me in the dressing room immediately after the game. 'Your dad's just been arrested,' was my response. As usual, he'd found himself in a scrape because he thought he was helping out one of his mates.

Whenever I have a match away from home, be it for England or Liverpool, the Marsh Lane routine remains intact. My dad arranges a minibus for twelve of his mates and I supply as many tickets as I can. On this occasion an extra body joined the trip, leaving the party a ticket short. My dad decided to give his away, reckoning he could get himself sorted for a ticket nearer kick-off by ringing me and getting more spares. When this failed, his last resort was to try to get into the ground by playing the 'I'm Jamie Carragher's dad' card. Since he'd been drinking, the police in Birmingham neither recognized, believed nor cared who he was. As my dad became more intent on getting in, a scuffle ensued. He spent the night in a cell, ended up in court and was cautioned, fined and banned from away matches for a while.

It's fair to say this wasn't his first brush with the law.

In 2000, while I was celebrating being named Liverpool captain for the first time, my dad was coming to terms with a twelve-month jail sentence for tax fraud. He fiddled the Inland Revenue with the help of one of their own employees to earn tax rebates. I felt no sense of shame – he's always cut corners, my dad – but it was strange having to fit visits to Walton or Kirkham jail around our treble season.

No matter what he'd done, I stood by him as proudly as I've always done. His influence on my career is there to see throughout every chapter of this book. He brought me up to be a winner, and he's been alongside me every step I've taken on the path to success as a footballer. If I was ever going through a tough time, the first person who'd stand up on my behalf is my dad, so it's the same the other way round. I've been taught family and friends are the most important things in your life. Whatever happens, you stand by them. This was a hard period for us, but we got through it.

I don't think my dad looks back at his stretch as a great hardship. His mates were kept together, and I suspect the regular supply of signed footballs and match tickets kept the screws on his side. The incident even earned him a new nickname. The people in Marsh Lane started calling him Ken Dodd.

I have to admit, having my dad trip up on the wrong side of the law wasn't entirely surprising as he grew up trying to outwit the police. When my mum had a brush with the law, I was a bit more concerned.

The demolition of the famous Moat House Hotel in Liverpool was to blame for this. On the final night it was open, my mum, my Auntie Mary and their mates decided to stay and join the party to wish it goodbye. There were six middle-aged women sharing a twin room and during the course of the night they noticed how furniture and paintings were being cleared away. They presumed it was all heading to the skip and, in all innocence, thought they'd be helping out the staff by taking some souvenirs of their own. Before checking out, then, a few of them decided the pictures in the bedroom could be packed away rather than go to waste before the bulldozers arrived. Unfortunately, as they stuffed their bags they were spotted by a cleaner and were met at reception by the police.

I'm pleased to say my mum wasn't one of those who'd filled her boots and bags, which was a big relief as she was asked to empty her belongings. The poor women left behind were put in a police car and lined up for mug shots at the nearest station. The thought still makes my mum crease up laughing. She can't get the image of her friends having their photos taken out of her mind. You can imagine that film *The Usual Suspects*, with fifty-five-year-old women from Bootle worried about where their handbags have gone as the policeman tells them to look right and left.

When asked why they'd taken the pictures, one of my mum's mates replied, 'Because I thought they'd look lovely in our hall.'

I'd have been far more upset had my mum ended up in the papers over such a minor incident. She's always kept out of the limelight and has made sure my success has had as little effect on her life as possible.

There are, of course, times when my status in the city has unavoidable consequences on my home life. When I was still living with my mum, my car was vandalized in the early hours of the morning, graffiti and paint thrown all over it. I could hear a commotion outside, and when I looked out of the window there was Paula Carragher, at three a.m., furiously cleaning it all off before any of the neighbours spotted it in the daylight.

There were other occasions when, in her innocence and naivety about the game, I almost got myself fined by the club. I'd jump out of bed every morning, eager to be one of the first at the training ground to show my enthusiasm, but on one particular day my alarm – otherwise known as my mum – didn't summon me for breakfast. It was a Bank Holiday Monday, and I was enjoying a lie-in of teenage proportions when I was woken up by some familiar voices. 'Is Jamie ready?' my mum was being asked. My youth team-mates Dave Clegg, Andy Harris and Dom Morley were making their routine stop at our house. As we all lived in the Crosby or Bootle areas of Merseyside and only one of us could drive, we'd share a car to training.

I could hear the conversation downstairs progressing with growing confusion.

'What are you doing here today?' my mum was asking the lads. 'Don't you know it's a bank holiday? There won't be any training today, will there?'

It doesn't bother me that my mum steers clear of the football. I know how proud she is of my achievements, and she knows they wouldn't have been possible without her. I don't need her cheering me at the stadium every week to see that. My mum's only ever been to Anfield twice, for the Youth Cup win in 1996 and the Champions League semi-final against Chelsea in April 2008. Her only other matches were the Carling Cup Final in 2002 and the Champions League Final in Athens in 2007.

Since I was a lad, she's seen football as male territory. Following her split from my dad, she was happy to take a back seat and allow him to take me to the matches and not intrude into this area. That's never changed. The rest of the family headed off to Dortmund, Istanbul and Cardiff, but she'd stay in Liverpool and watch on the television. Physically she wasn't part of the post-match celebrations, but spiritually and emotionally she was with us. I imagined her toasting those successes, quietly registering her approval.

Every television show, newspaper or magazine that has mentioned or featured me over the years, she's kept on tape or as a cutting. And no matter where I am in the world, or how I've played, I can always depend on the text message either congratulating me or commiserating with me. She won't go seeking any thanks for her role in making me the person I am, but deep down she'll know the way she brought me up was a job well done.

The Kop sings 'We all dream of a team of Carraghers' because the fans are showing their respect to me. When I hear it, I think it's the perfect tribute to my entire family.

11

Spanish Steps

I was speechless. Rarely, if ever, have I been left feeling in such a state of numb shock.

I stood in front of Rafa, listening attentively to what he had to say, assessing if the words coming from his mouth were a joke or some kind of test. It was the summer of 2005, I'd just played what I believed to be my finest games in a Liverpool shirt, and I'd performed a major role in winning our fifth European Cup. Now, I was hearing this.

He wanted to give me a new contract, but there would be no pay rise. I'd given my all to create history for Liverpool, and the best he could come up with was two extra years and a pat on the back. That was the deal.

Had I heard him right? Did he really say I wouldn't be rewarded for my efforts against Juventus, Chelsea and AC Milan?

I kept staring at him as he spoke, soaking up the news, sussing out if it was serious, desperately trying to think of the correct response but failing to do so. Usually I'd have my wits about me and be able to react with such strong arguments he'd be the one struggling to get a word in, but I wasn't prepared for this.

I'd gone into the manager's office on the first day of pre-season training believing we'd be talking football, or about new signings and our ambitions for the year ahead. But as Rafa made me a contract offer unlike any I'd ever received before, I was fighting off feelings of disbelief. I had no response because I was so taken aback by his remarks. A bit like our Champions League win, I hadn't seen this coming.

I should make it absolutely clear that money was only part of the issue. It was the manner of the offer which staggered me most. My previous four contracts had always been negotiated with the minimum of fuss. My agent, Struan Marshall, whom I've trusted since I was twenty-one, would meet Rick Parry, tell him what I was looking for and then ring me to advise me I'd been offered a good deal. I'd agree and sign. No bother, no delay, no speculation. I hardly got involved other than to put my signature on the contract. Unlike the long-drawn-out negotiations you often read about, I liked sorting it quickly, as did the club. I wanted to stay, I usually felt I was worth a reasonable rather than spectacular pay rise, the club would duly reward me, and that was that.

I was always baffled to read newspaper reports about players in 'talks' for a new deal. 'Talk' was the right word where I was concerned. One conversation, quick agreement, sign the contract. Get on with the football. Simple.

Rafa decided to take a different approach. He put me on the spot, reminding me of the club's ongoing financial problems, which meant they couldn't afford lucrative salary increases. The proposal he made was, in my view, disrespectful. I was offered a four-year contract (a two-year extension) on the same wage, the only 'rise' as such coming through bonuses if I played a certain number of games or won trophies. I liked the bonus aspect of it.

It was a new addition Rafa introduced as a way of preserving the players' motivation and keeping everyone on their toes if they weren't in the side. The other terms left me disheartened.

He believed he was looking after the best interests of the club by trying to juggle the figures to ensure he could afford new players. I could see it from his point of view. He'd inherited a squad where a lot of players were on excessive deals that far outweighed their contribution. Rafa was determined not to repeat those mistakes, but I didn't believe he'd put me in the same category as those he'd failed to offload because they were big earners. I wasn't expecting preferential treatment, but I thought he'd know I'd be more clued up about his intentions than he seemed to give me credit for. In the aftermath of Istanbul I was aware of my value. Now it felt an assumption had been made I'd never leave, so there was no need to offer me any significant reward for my efforts.

At first I thought it was cheeky, but then I concluded I was being badly treated, as though the manager wanted to ignore the usual protocol to save Liverpool money. I know the kind of figures I'm talking about are beyond what my mates or most working-class lads would sympathize with, but in any job up and down the country you judge yourself against those in your line of work. Harry Kewell had recently concluded a high-profile libel action against Gary Lineker following remarks in a newspaper column during which his salary was publicly revealed. There was a significant gap between his earnings and mine. I did not begrudge him being paid so much – 'Good luck to him,' I thought – but given my service and dedication to the club, it was staggering Rafa couldn't understand how hurt I would be by the deal he was suggesting.

I was now vice-captain at Liverpool. That didn't mean I

should be the second highest paid, but I was worth more than Rafa was talking in that meeting. To put it into perspective, Rafa was proposing I remain on the salary I'd been given when Houllier gave me a new contract two years earlier, while I was recovering from a broken leg. Surely I'd progressed into a more important player since then? Sometimes working your way through the ranks and pledging the best years of your career to one club can act against you, and this was an example of that. I've never wanted to leave Liverpool, but I was entitled to believe my salary should reflect the level of player I'd become.

Only in the hours that followed did I think of the questions I wished I'd asked in the meeting. 'Do you really think that's what I'm worth?' I should have screamed at Rafa. I wasn't looking to be put in the same bracket as Steven Gerrard, I just wanted the going rate for someone of my status. 'I'm not asking for the wages John Terry earns at Chelsea, but I'm as important to this team as he is to them,' I told myself, again wishing I'd made the point a few hours earlier. I knew players like Terry and Rio Ferdinand were on six-figure sums per week at their clubs. I was looking for around half that, which sounds astronomical to most people, but it reflected my reputation. They were at clubs that could afford to pay them so much. I knew we couldn't do the same at Liverpool, which is why, relatively speaking, my expectations weren't excessive.

The more I considered the incident, the more it festered and annoyed me. It wasn't even the terms of the offer that were irritating me in the end, but how they had been put to me, as though a deal could be sneaked through the back door without involving my agent. The first Rick knew about our discussion was when Struan, having realized how upset I was, called him to ask what was going on.

It was an unnecessary episode that showed how much Rafa enjoyed overseeing every detail of the club. With a more tactful approach it would have been resolved much quicker. I couldn't help but feel let down. I believed I'd become a confidant of the new manager during his first season. Now I sensed he saw me in the same way he saw every other player. Gérard Houllier or Roy Evans would have said to me, 'Get what you can, son, you deserve it.' If I was a manager and saw a player contribute as much as I had the previous season, this would have been my message too. The incident showed no matter how close you thought you were to Rafa, he'd always find a way to remind you who was the boss.

Once Struan and Rick met, the negotiations were concluded as swiftly as ever, but this time the usual PR claiming I'd agreed and signed within two minutes was wide of the mark. My experience was hidden from public view, partly because Rick, Rafa and Struan were involved in a far more explosive contract story.

I was always intending to commit myself to the club, but any hopes of Istanbul removing the mist that had been hovering over Steven Gerrard's future the previous season were short-lived. When the European Cup became a permanent resident of the club museum, Liverpool fans thought they could see nothing but golden skies again. We were champions of Europe – sounded great, that – we had an outstanding manager who'd proved he could outwit the best, and the threat of our skipper leaving appeared to have been erased when Shevchenko struck his penalty, Jerzy made the save and our players ran like maniacs in the direction of the fans. 'How can I leave after this?' was Stevie's immediate reaction to lifting the European Cup. All those lingering problems on and off the pitch could be put to rest now, we hoped. Well-documented financial problems appeared to be eased by the UEFA winnings, top players fancied a taste of the unique Anfield atmosphere which had been restored, and after questioning the direction of the club even Stevie was ready to banish the doubts and join the queue of those hoping to pen new deals.

Rafa had been trying to make the captain commit his future throughout the previous year, but Stevie was understandably biding his time while so many unanswered questions remained. Once he'd lifted the Champions League trophy, destiny had spoken and, briefly at least, he knew exactly what he wanted. The club should have shoved the contract straight in front of him on the plane home. He'd have signed it.

Instead, a potentially calamitous mistake was made after the homecoming: everyone went on holiday.

While we were enjoying our break and I was preparing for my wedding, Stevie was becoming increasingly unsettled by the delay sorting out his future. There had been an urgency for him to commit himself before the European Cup Final, but now we'd won it was presumed the panic was over. It wasn't.

After weeks of becoming frustrated at the lack of negotiations, the captain was confused when he returned to training to discover there was no offer on the table, which seemed strange since he had been asked to sign on three separate occasions a few months earlier. The conspiracy theories went into overdrive. He believed Rafa was now stalling because he was secretly planning to sell him and use the money to reinforce other areas. Reports in a Spanish paper linking Stevie with a move to Madrid made the skipper think there was a plan afoot to sell him to raise funds. When Chelsea made another bid, Rafa believed Stevie wanted to go. It was the mother of all misunderstandings.

I knew we were in trouble on the day of my wedding when I saw Struan, who also represented the captain, and Stevie heading to the corner of the room and talking frantically on their mobile phones. Now a transfer request was being prepared. That was a mistake born out of frustration. Unlike 2004, there seemed no way back. We had several training sessions without him. It was as if he'd gone already.

I couldn't understand why Stevie had thought of leaving a year earlier, and I was bemused at how the latest crisis had come about, but I'd sympathized with him during the course of the previous season. He was one of the best players in the world, and with two years left on his contract he knew the next move would determine the rest of his career. He had his choice of clubs, so if he felt Liverpool weren't going to be competitive, or, even worse, didn't want him, it was easy to see why he thought of moving on. Although we were progressing through the rounds in the Champions League, realistically we were still way off the pace in terms of fighting for the title and he had to be sure he was prepared to be part of the rebuilding job.

As the last remaining Academy players, I'd become a lot closer to Stevie over the previous twelve months, and I felt more confident about offering advice.

'If you go, don't go to Chelsea,' I told him. 'If you go there, it won't matter how many League titles you win, you'll never be able to come home and have the respect of the Liverpool fans. You've got to think beyond your career and consider the implications for the rest of your life. Go abroad instead and do what Ian Rush did. Then you can always come back.'

He could have taken out the Champions League brochure and picked a destination. Real Madrid, Barcelona, AC Milan and

Inter would have taken him. But it was the Premier League title he craved.

When the news broke of Chelsea's bid, I was as devastated as every Liverpool fan. The blame game went into full swing. For a while it was less about keeping Steven Gerrard at Liverpool and more about ensuring one side or the other was apportioned responsibility for his departure. Even poor Struan was getting stick, but all he'd ever done was present the options and respect our decisions. I've never been advised to do anything I didn't want to do, and Struan's never done anything on my behalf I haven't asked him to do. The same applies with Stevie. When Chelsea made their move, he was obliged to let Stevie know of their interest. I often think what an awkward situation Struan found himself in two years on the run, having to tell Chelsea the deal for Stevie was off. Thankfully, that's what he had to do after another epic night of soul-searching by the skipper. I'd say he had another change of heart, but deep down I think he always wanted to stay. He just needed to get his head around what had gone wrong and feel convinced the club wanted to keep him.

I was having breakfast in the Melwood canteen when Rick Parry popped up on Sky TV accompanied by the yellow breaking news ticker.

'Steven has decided to stay,' he said.

I spat out my cornflakes.

People said Stevie's heart ruled his head. I think that was more true in the summer of 2004 than 2005. There were far more valid footballing reasons for staying at Anfield now.

Stevie and I can examine our careers and recall the same highs and lows. Our medal collection is identical. We have every honour in European club football except one. He could have gone to Chelsea and completed the set with the Premier League, but the satisfaction of one title with Liverpool, no matter how long it took to get it, would eclipse three or four won at Stamford Bridge. Ultimately, he realized that. There was never going to be an instant fix at Anfield, but we still had plenty of years ahead to claim the trophy we craved most.

Stevie returned to the Melwood dressing room to be greeted by his relieved and elated team-mates, but some unfinished business remained. Rafa called a few senior players to his office to address the issue of the captaincy. 'Stevie should keep it,' I insisted, knowing I'd be next in line for the armband but uncomfortable at seeing my friend effectively punished for considering a move. I did impose a condition, however. 'We can't have this every season,' I said. 'That's got to be it now. He's got to stay for good. Stevie's the captain. We can't have another year like the last one where we're answering questions about his future every week.'

To my and the Liverpool fans' relief, Stevie agreed.

We signed our new four-year deals at the same time, posing for the happy, smiling photographs as if we didn't have a care in the world. The press made comparisons between Stevie's long-drawn-out affair and my instant, uncomplicated agreement. The fans did the same. 'You don't get any of that messing with Carra,' some of them said. 'He just signs and gets on with it.' I read such comments and nodded my head.

'Usually . . .'

With his vice-captain and skipper on board ('the two best signings of the summer' according to the club's press release), at least the manager could now turn his attention to new recruits.

Becoming European champions usually signals the climax of a manager's rebuilding process. In 2005 we'd done it back to front. Winning the Champions League couldn't disguise the lingering flaws in our squad. As Rafa contemplated the direction we should take, it was our League rather than European form which was the basis for his conclusions. If he'd underestimated the scale of the restructuring job in 2004, not even the European Cup could deflect his attention from our weaknesses in the summer of 2005. The manager struck me as a quick learner, which gave me confidence he'd bring in the right players, suitable for English football, and allocate whatever money he had wisely. He'd spent a season analysing the Premier League, recognizing before we could even think of winning the title that we had to make ourselves difficult to beat again. Those miserable afternoons at venues such as Goodison, St Andrew's and Selhurst Park had to end. We needed to be more consistent, to show the physical strength that had been so visible during Gérard Houllier's more successful period.

Managers like to talk about their ideas as working in stages, and although Benitez never spoke publicly about 'five-year plans', it was obvious things had to progress a step at a time. We finished thirty-seven points behind Chelsea in 2005. There could be no Istanbul-style miracle to turn that deficit around within one year. Rafa's first season was about getting us through the turmoil. Somehow we emerged with an inexplicable triumph. Year two was focused on strengthening the spine of the side, making us more competitive and giving us a platform on which to improve later. He achieved this, although my big regret was our failure to add a proven goalscorer to the ranks at the same time – or, more specifically, a proven goalscorer from Real Madrid.

If the conclusion of the second instalment of the Gerrard saga prompted a sense of déjà vu, there was more to come when Michael Owen's future dominated the headlines again. Rafa confided with me he was considering bringing Michael back, and I couldn't get on the phone quick enough to try to make it a reality. My mobile bill probably hit record levels over the next few days. There had been a suggestion Manchester United were ready to make a move, but I believed Mo was exactly the kind of player we still needed and I knew there was only one club in England he wanted to join. The problem was the price, and no matter how eager I was to have my room-mate home, I could understand Liverpool's reluctance to get involved in a bidding war with other clubs. On a matter of principle, you can't pay £16 million for a player you only sold for £8 million a year earlier.

Newcastle ruined our chances by making a ridiculous offer, which ended up messing with Michael's head.

He made no secret of his preference, announcing Liverpool were his first choice. At the Super Cup Final in Monaco, the Liverpool fans even started singing his name as a deal seemed to be edging closer. On the August Bank Holiday, the last day of the transfer window, I was on the phone to Michael every hour checking developments. He met Rick and Rafa before heading to the north-east for talks, but my confidence was draining as midnight approached.

Correctly, we weren't prepared to match Newcastle's bid. To get his number 10 shirt back Michael was going to have to call Madrid's bluff and insist he wouldn't go anywhere but Anfield. He was unable to take the risk. With his family desperate for him to come back to England, he was compelled to accept the only offer on the table rather than get stuck in Madrid any longer. No matter how much I tried to change his mind, or he willed Liverpool to make a firm bid, there was no solution.

We met up for an England get-together on the day he was unveiled at Newcastle. I still couldn't believe what he'd done. 'They're bottom of the League!' I said. 'I can't believe you've gone there.' But as I said, family rather than football reasons made his mind up. I'd never criticize him for making what he believed was the right decision for his wife and children, but he should be a Liverpool player today.

For some reason, our fans were less understanding. Michael returned to Anfield in Newcastle colours later that season and was the recipient of shameful abuse from a section of The Kop. I was disgusted on his behalf. As he stood in the penalty box at The Kop end the crowd began singing 'Where were you in Istanbul?' I could see the deflation in his eyes, and recognized how hurt he was after the game. He'd have been entitled to turn on all those supporters jumping on the bandwagon, a few of them who were no doubt singing his name in Monaco when they thought he was coming back, and ask, 'Where were you in Cardiff in 2001?' To see a player who'd played his heart out for us on the end of a reception so untypical of those that former Anfield heroes normally get was depressing. Over the years I've seen players who didn't contribute half as much as Michael, and in some cases were only here a season or two, being welcomed back to Liverpool as if they'd played five hundred games and won dozens of trophies. It made no sense to me for Michael to be targeted like this, and having spoken to many fans since, I think there is a certain level of shame at what happened on his return. I was happy it wasn't repeated on Michael's next visit to Anfield during 2007–08 – he missed the 2006–07 encounter with his cruciate injury – and I'm sure, given time, in future years The Kop will show their appreciation and give him the kind of reception usually accorded to ex-players.

Our loss opened the door for others. There would be an emotional return for another Anfield striking legend the following January. Robbie Fowler it was who made the improbable homecoming, signing for free from Manchester City. It was a move that delighted the players as much as the fans, even if it was only a brief cameo at Anfield for 'God'.

Michael's move to St James's Park also led to a reprieve for Djibril Cisse, who'd earned sympathy for the way he was treated during the pre-season. Cisse, who'd spent just twelve months at Anfield and had battled back bravely from an horrific broken leg, would have had to make way had Michael returned. Rafa was frantically trying to agree a deal for him or Milan Baros to raise funds for a bid for Mo. Football is a ruthless business, and the fans could see Rafa's cold streak in the way he left Cisse and Baros on the bench for our Champions League qualifiers: neither played a minute of the matches to avoid being cup-tied. Beneath the pity for the pair it was also impressive to see the manager deal with a delicate situation in such merciless style. Baros was sold to Lyon and Cisse was interesting Marseille, but the breakdown of talks with Michael meant he lived to fight another season.

Djibril would have to be content with back up status, though. For the 2005–06 campaign The Kop welcomed a new and unlikely striking hero from Southampton in a transfer that shocked us as much as the rest of football. Our defeat to the recently relegated Saints the previous year was one of our most miserable of the season, but the performance of Peter Crouch had made a huge impression on Rafa. He'd decided the side needed to be strengthened down the middle, with Crouch the focal point of his system. So, along with Pepe Reina, the Villarreal keeper he'd been pursuing for over a year, and Momo Sissoko, an athletic, ball-winning midfielder he'd managed at Valencia, Rafa bought Crouch, the giant target man he'd hoped Morientes would be.

For Benitez, it was all about finding pieces for his chessboard, and he's never made a more astute series of moves. Crouch wasn't regarded as a world-class striker, but for the tactics we played in Benitez's second season he was ideal. Since Heskey's departure we'd had no one who could make it stick upfront to allow our strongest players in midfield to get forward. Even in our most successful games in the Champions League we'd often had to rely exclusively on a rearguard action, keeping our shape for long periods of defence. We didn't have the physical presence upfront to give our opponents a problem or relieve the pressure on the back four. Crouchy undoubtedly changed that, surprising us all with his quality on the ball, while Sissoko added energy and aggression, and Reina instantly settled as our finest goalkeeper since Ray Clemence. Jerzy Dudek must have wondered what he'd done wrong after being the hero in Istanbul, but he was suffering the same way as the man he'd replaced, Sander Westerveld. The manager simply rated Reina higher, and he has since been proved right. With Petr Cech, Pepe has consistently been the best keeper in the Premier League.

There was a presumption Crouchy would need time to win over our fans, but a negative reaction from The Kop never arrived. Our fans are funny like that. If they see someone getting unfairly criticized, they're more likely to get behind him. If Crouchy had come in being hailed as the future of English football, they'd probably have been more suspicious. His underdog status, allied to the fact he played so well in his first games, made him instantly popular. All he needed to secure his newly found cult status was a goal.

He waited.

And waited, and waited . . .

Even this cemented his relationship with the fans. I've never seen a forward have so much bad luck over so many games as Crouchy after his debut. He had goals disallowed, he hit the post, he even missed a pen. His lack of goals became a running gag in the media, but his contribution to the team was already there to see as our League performances were a drastic improvement on the previous year. Even when he did break his duck after nineteen games – a deflected shot against Wigan – it seemed the TV crews were on a crusade to take it off him.

By then, I was ready to take on anyone on his behalf. He'd endeared himself to my friends not just because of his performances on the pitch, but with his efforts to blend in off it. One of Crouchy's first acts as a Liverpool player was to join me in The Solly on Marsh Lane on karaoke night. He sang 'Hey Jude' and brought the house down, earning a standing ovation. There were no worries about him not being a crowd favourite afterwards. The Bootle Kopites made sure of it.

While he was getting battered, he was temporarily the most popular player at the club, having his name sung as much as Fernando Torres now. Once his luck turned and the goals began to flow for club and country, Crouchy saw the other side of being a Liverpool footballer. He could do no wrong in the eyes of Rafa when he needed support, but once he'd become a star player for Liverpool and England, I saw how their relationship changed.

'I'm worried about you,' Rafa told Crouchy once after he returned from England duty, having scored a few goals, earned rave reviews and probably indulged in one robot dance too many.

I started laughing. 'Not as worried as you were when he went nineteen games without a goal,' I said, trying to ease the tension.

That's Rafa for you. It's his way always to be negative. I've never heard him tell a player how well he's doing. He's always picking holes and trying to make them improve.

Some journalists used to describe Houllier as a 'professor'. I see Benitez like one of those teachers you had who would often get on your nerves by being at you all the time, but when you looked back years later you realized how good he was and how much you learnt from him.

My other view of Rafa is as one of those fellas you see sat in the corner of every pub who's an expert on any subject. If you tell a story, he can always go one further. If you tell a joke, he'll say he's already heard it, or tell you how to deliver the punchline better. The trouble with those kinds of characters is they wind everyone up so much during the week, when it gets to Saturday night and everyone's had too much to drink it only needs one loose word and the know-it-all gets knocked out. I'd best tell Rafa to be careful where he drinks!

He certainly got it right with his 2005 signings. The impact of Crouch, Sissoko and Reina strengthening the heart of our line-up was self-evident. We earned eighty-two points in the League, which was our highest since the Premiership had been formed. The three key signings added an extra 30 per cent to the side, and we coasted to a Champions League spot. Stevie's performances were also at a peak. He scored twenty-three goals that season to win the PFA Player of the Year, and he won't mind me saying not all of them were from right midfield.

Overall, I rated that season much higher than 2004–05. We were strong, consistent, in tune with Rafa's methods and tougher to beat. In terms of my personal performances week in, week out, 2005–06 was my best season. Throughout my career there have been times it seemed there was too much responsibility on me or Stevie to pull the side through; the encouraging aspect of this year was the broader input of every player. We had six or seven contributing at the highest level rather than two or three in

The Merseybeat goes on: My dad, Tony Hall, Oggo and the rest of the Bootle Red Army fly the flag ahead of a Champions League clash in Kiev, 2001.

here we come: Bootle's finest prepare for the UEFA Cup Final in 2001, with a flag that eart swell with pride.

Apprenticeship served: Winning the FA Youth Cup with Michael Owen and David Thompson in
set us on course for the first team.

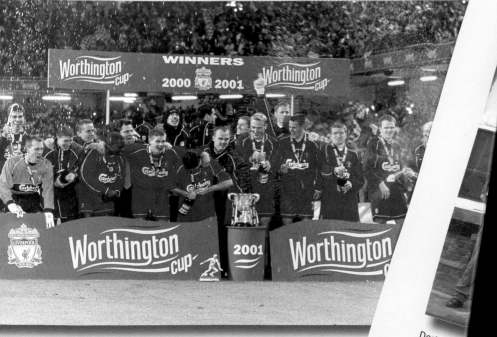

The first of many: My first senior trophy at Liverpool, after beating Birr
Cup Final, 2001.

Dortmund
made my h

The Glory Days return: The 2001 UEFA Cup was a thrilling climax to Houllier's historic treble.

World Cup woe: My substitute appearance against Portugal in Germany 2006 signalled the beginning of the end of my international career.

Turk that: Ecstasy in front of the fans at The Ataturk.

Fate lends a hand: I spotted my cousin Jamie in the Ataturk crowd, with my brother Paul nearby.

Above: The morning after the miracle: The victorious Champions League team of 2005 assembled at the team hotel, with some sore heads, for this snap.

Below: The Red Sea: Hundreds of thousands lined the streets of Liverpool to celebrate our Champions League win.

No one compares to you: Enjoying the post-Istanbul party with Nicola, 2005.

Champions of Europe: The post-match celebrations with my dad, John, Uncle Pete, Paul and Billy McGhee.

Leading from the front: I skippered the side to victory in the Super Cup Final 2005.

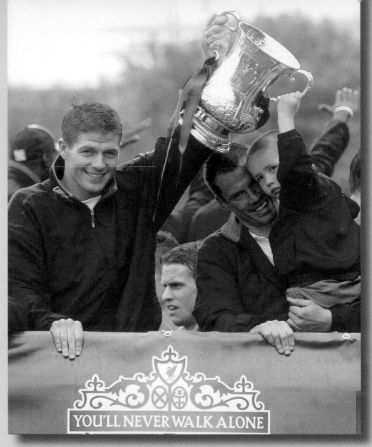

'The Gerrard Final': Another bus tour in 2006, this time with two treasures – my son James and the FA Cup.

Scouse pride: Stevie, Robbie and I celebrate the 2006 FA Cup win with chairman David Moores.

the campaigns before. That's why I rate it above the others, even if the trophy return wasn't as illustrious as 2000–01 or 2004–05. There was a real sense of progress across the pitch. We only finished a point behind Manchester United and nine points behind Chelsea, which was an exceptional turnaround within two years of Rafa's arrival. It felt as good as the 2001–02 side again, with just a few minor alterations needed to ensure we could finally challenge for the title.

There were disappointments, certainly. Our European campaign ended much earlier than it should have following defeat to a Benfica side that punished us for uncharacteristic mistakes. We were better than a year earlier, and Benfica were nowhere near as good as Juve, Chelsea or AC Milan, but we never played to our potential.

But in general, I'm not sure Rafa received as much credit as he was due for the astonishing upturn in our League form. He oversaw a transformation during unstable times, with Michael leaving, Stevie's future in the balance, a host of poor, overpaid players to shift out and expectations as great as ever. Because we have the name Liverpool, it's taken for granted we should be competing for top honours every season, but circumstances don't always permit that. Rafa had to cope with some of the toughest conditions any Liverpool manager has ever experienced on and off the park (which were about to get worse), but we still managed to win trophies and finish with a points tally which in some years would have been enough to take the title.

Throughout his period, it's often seemed as though there have been as many battles to win off the park as on it. It's staggering how many obstacles and distractions we've had to overcome. We even had to fight for the right to defend the European Cup, as

UEFA decided whether we or Everton should be England's fourth representative. The FA insisted Everton take their spot for finishing in the top four, and there were those making the astonishing claim we should be the first European champions in history not to compete for their own title. Much was made of the controversy, but I never doubted we'd both end up in the competition.

The compromise meant we played in three qualifying rounds against a series of part-timers. It was no great hardship, as the games were little more than glorified pre-season fixtures without the mass substitutions, but I'm sure they took their toll by the time we reached the World Cup in 2006, and had a roll-on effect at the beginning of the following season. Some of us effectively played a full twelve months, including a December trip to Japan for the World Club Championship.

Those days in Japan were traumatic on and off the pitch too. Many regarded the championship as a distraction, a Mickey Mouse tournament not to be taken seriously. Not me. It's the toughest domestic tournament in the world to qualify for, and the fact Liverpool hadn't won it made it an illustrious honour so far as I was concerned. We prepared for the tournament as well as for any Champions League game.

Prior to our final against São Paulo, Rafa's father died. We were desperate to win the trophy for him, and the sense of deflation when we lost was as great as any I'd felt. This was a rare chance to create history which might not come our way again. I don't know how Rafa coped with the strain of being so far from his family during such demanding circumstances. His professionalism and dedication to the team were exceptional. I know I wouldn't have been able to concentrate on football in such a situation.

Our form at that time was majestic. During our first game in Japan we broke the club record for consecutive clean sheets by a Liverpool side, although I was fuming with Rafa for forgetting the milestone in the closing stages against Costa Ricans Deportivo Saprissa. We were 3–0 up so Rafa decided to sub Sami Hyypia and give him a rest fifteen minutes from time. I was doing my nut, waving at Rafa not to change the back four. He was looking at me confused as to why I was so annoyed. Only after the game did he realize I was thinking about the record, which was eleven shut-outs, a game better even than Alan Hansen and Mark Lawrenson twenty years earlier. 'I completely forgot about that,' Rafa admitted, able to afford himself a smile that his substitution hadn't made any difference.

Defensive records tumbled throughout that season, and I hold those as dear as some of my winners medals. At one point we went 762 minutes without losing a League goal, and a further 573 minutes in Europe. No Liverpool side had ever done that. Strikers are able to measure themselves by their goals-per-game ratio; I do the same in terms of how many we've conceded. A clean sheet is a job done, so no matter what the score or how far we're ahead, there's no such thing as a 'meaningless' goal against us. You'll have seen me as annoyed conceding a goal in the last minute of a match we're winning 3–0 as if it was 1–1. That's how all defenders should be. My regret from that 2005–06 season was failing to beat the club record for most clean sheets in an entire season. We had thirty-two shut-outs in sixty-two games, just one behind the target.

I must pay tribute to my defensive partner, Sami Hyypia, for his part in this. There have been numerous overseas players in the Premiership who've been described as the best imports there have been, but pound for pound, none has eclipsed Sami. You don't get so many headlines when you're a defender, but for him to spend ten years at Liverpool playing to the standards he has puts him not only with the best foreigners we've seen, but with the greatest defenders ever to grace Anfield. When you talk about Alan Hansen, Mark Lawrenson, Phil Thompson, Emlyn Hughes, Tommy Smith and Ron Yeats, you won't be able to leave Sami's name out. He's up there with them. He's arguably the bargain buy in Anfield's history too. People talk about Shankly finding Kevin Keegan at Scunthorpe. Bringing in Sami for £2.5 million from Willem II, in modern terms, is at least the equal of that.

Sami and I were proud to return from Japan having secured some defensive records, and I was just as relieved to get back to England having narrowly escaped getting a criminal one following an impromptu brush with the law.

After a week away, and deflated by our 1–0 final defeat, we were determined to see more of Tokyo than the inside of our hotel room. Whatever the result of the final, we'd decided a night out was the least we deserved for our efforts. No sooner had the coach returned to the hotel than most of us sneaked away to meet up with my mates who'd made the journey to Japan. Rafa didn't give us permission, but he was relaxed enough to let it go, recognizing the hard work we'd put into the tournament.

Arsenal and Chelsea were playing that afternoon so we headed to a bar and settled down to enjoy the game, although it should be remembered a four p.m. kick-off in England was around eleven p.m. in Tokyo. By the time the game finished the drinks had been flowing for a few hours and we'd gone from drowning our sorrows at our loss and Chelsea's win to drunkenly singing

Kop songs with the fans who'd been growing in numbers as news of our presence spread. Every away supporter in Tokyo had now found the pub with the Liverpool squad, no doubt texted by all their mates as to where to head.

At which point things started to get messy. Most of the lads decided to return to the hotel, which was the cue for the supporters to jump on the taxis to stop them driving the players home and bringing their night out with the Liverpool squad to a premature end. This chaotic scene prompted the Japanese police to decide enough was enough.

The arrival of their local constabulary wasn't exactly met with a shudder of fear. They're not the most towering, physically intimidating race in the world, the Japanese, and this didn't go unnoticed. In fact, faced with the sight of a dozen or so short policemen, one of the supporters shouted out, 'Where's Snow White?' The response was a series of arrests of anyone within jumping distance of a cab, including me, Didi Hamann and my mate Mick Laffey. We were all too busy laughing at these little fellas shouting at us in Japanese to realize what was going on.

Then it suddenly dawned on us we'd be in severe bother if we were flung in a cell overnight because our flight home was first thing the following morning. It was apparent the police were serious about keeping hold of us, so there was only one option. We had to do a runner.

'I'll get a couple of lads to start some more bother to distract their attention, and you two do one as quick as you can,' Mick suggested.

We weren't handcuffed, so there'd be no problem getting away.

As we were led towards the police station, the operation was put into practice, and when the police pounced on the fans, I sprinted as fast as possible in the opposite direction, screaming at Didi to do the same. After going full pelt for ten minutes, I finally found an alley where I hid for the next half an hour, removing my Liverpool tracksuit top to ensure I wasn't spotted as I made my way through the deserted streets of Tokyo at four a.m. I finally felt safe enough to get a cab back to the hotel.

I immediately called Didi's room. He was sharing with Sami, who wasn't pleased to be woken up at such an unholy hour.

'Is Didi there?' I asked.

'No. He's not come back.'

I couldn't sleep and kept trying the room every hour. Sami grew increasingly agitated.

By breakfast there was still no sign of Didi, and I resigned myself to the possibility of us heading to the airport without him, and the likelihood of our trip ending in a drunken scandal. Just as I was thinking I'd have to explain the situation to Rafa, I looked out of the window and saw Didi get out of a taxi and head straight to the breakfast room, trying to disguise the fact he was still half-cut.

Where had he been for the last five hours?

'I didn't get away when you did a runner,' Didi explained. His pace was never his finest asset.

Mick had accepted all responsibility for the bother outside the pub by saying he'd started a fight with Didi, whom he insisted was an innocent bystander.

'Why would you, Liverpool supporter, start fight with him, Liverpool player?' asked the policeman.

Mick had scratched his head for a second, before confidently bluffing his way through an elaborate fairy story.

'Well, the thing is, my favourite Liverpool player of all time is Kevin Keegan,' explained Mick, not even pausing as the bullshit steamed from his mouth. 'In 2001, this fella alongside me scored the winning goal at Wembley which forced my hero to resign as England manager, and I've never forgiven him since. I've been waiting for my chance to get him back, so when I saw him tonight I had a go at him.'

There were tears streaming from our eyes as Didi told this story. Fair play to Mick, we all thought. Never has so much inspirational shite been spoken for such a needy cause.

Didi still spent the night in the cell, but fortunately was able to join us on the flight home without anyone hearing about the incident. Until now, Rafa didn't know about it, and the journalists who shared the eleven-hour flight home from Japan with us never got a sniff either. It was a lucky escape though.

Japan and the Champions League may have been disappointments, but the season ended in more triumph thanks to the FA Cup, as Rafa banished those memories of the Burnley defeat in the 'Gerrard Final'.

So much has been written about Steven Gerrard's contribution to Liverpool FC. It's been impossible to write this book without Stevie's impact overlapping mine, and I'm proud our careers have become so interconnected with each other. People look at us as the symbols of the side and I've felt privileged to be on the same pitch as him for so long. I'll look back in years to come and be thankful I was playing in the same era. He's one of those rare players who can turn a good team into European champions. Without him, our recent history wouldn't be so illustrious.

That's why I'm prepared to say, alongside Kenny Dalglish, he's the greatest footballer ever to wear a Liverpool shirt.

I know that statement will be questioned by others. I can hear the groans now from those who'll say Kenny is and always will be the number one, out there on his own and untouchable. I'm biased, I know that, but I'm persuaded by the context in which these legends played.

Kenny will always be the favourite at Anfield for his overall contribution as player, manager and ambassador for the club. But when it comes to just playing, even he might admit Stevie has matched his efforts. Kenny played alongside numerous world-class players and joined Liverpool when he was twenty-seven, when we were already European champions. He made us virtually unbeatable for a spell, but he was part of solid foundations. Steven Gerrard has shone under more trying circumstances. He's elevated dreadful seasons with a series of individual performances the likes of which I've never seen in the modern game. He's also made his mark on the biggest occasions when only he could have turned the game back in our favour, not only in the Champions League, but in the FA Cup Final. The list of season-defining games where his contribution is the most significant is in double figures. Most players can pick out one or two in a life-time, but it's virtually one a season with Stevie.

If there's one match to convince me more than any other of Stevie's right to be seen as Kenny's equal, it's that FA Cup Final against West Ham in 2006. We were poor that day in Cardiff, and had Stevie not thundered in the last-minute equalizer from twenty-five yards there'd have been no complaints about our defeat. He saved us again. He'd done it so often in the past, but to do it on such a stage, when no one else had anything left to give, separates good players from legends.

I had double cause to thank him as I could have felt responsible had we lost.

'I had a dream last night,' my mate Pritch had told me on the morning of the match. 'You're going to score today.'

With my record, I should have known as soon as I was told about this premonition it would be an own-goal. It's rarely mentioned now, but had we not shown that will to win it could have been the lowest point of my career. I gave West Ham their early lead, deflecting a Lionel Scaloni cross into our net. I was grateful it happened early enough in the match for us to cancel it out, although we did it the hard way again, going 2–0 down before we started playing. Even when we were a couple of goals behind, we believed we'd come back and win, which we eventually did on penalties. The captain saved us with two goals in the 3–3 draw, assisted by an inspired performance by Sissoko which is often ignored, and a Cisse goal as important as any on the day. It was like a re-run of Istanbul.

As a club, there's something in our DNA which makes us incapable of accepting defeat. Our rivals call it luck. I've heard Liverpool fans say the same about Manchester United, as no matter how poorly they've played, or how little time they have left in a game, somehow they regularly find a way back. It's not good fortune, it's part of the culture of both clubs. They've got it, and so have we. No matter what the occasion, you've got to sweat it out for the full ninety minutes (or in their case ninety-five!) to beat us. It happens too much to be coincidental. The shame from our perspective is our inability to apply this never-say-die cup spirit to every League game. United have done that over recent years.

The May homecoming bus ride was becoming a thrillingly annual journey, but after two trophies in two years and a vastly improved League performance we were occupying similar territory to 2002 and facing up to the same old question.

'When are we going to win the League?'

The comparisons between Rafa and Gérard at the same period

of their reign couldn't be ignored. Houllier had spent two full seasons assembling his side until we fully understood his philosophy. The same was now true of Rafa, who was adding new faces more gradually but had now fine-tuned the squad and seemed a lot wiser about the intricacies of the English game.

If 2005 was about adding muscle, the next stage was about finding players with the necessary skill, pace and style. These are always the toughest signings in football. Houllier stumbled at this point, now Rafa had to find the players who possessed what I call 'The X Factor'. We were still a methodical rather than extravagant side and would need more to make the most difficult step of all, from title wannabes to winners. Where Manchester United could call upon a Rooney or Ronaldo to create goals from nothing, and Chelsea had Drogba or Lampard regularly bailing them out, as an attacking force we still relied too much on Gerrard. Not for the first time in my Liverpool career, I found myself believing the next three or four signings would determine if we leapt forward or stumbled backwards.

I'm sad to say it was the latter. Craig Bellamy signed from Blackburn and added pace; Dirk Kuyt, a Dutch striker from Feyenoord, provided physical presence; Jermaine Pennant, from Birmingham, and Chilean winger Mark Gonzalez were described as solutions to our lack of speed and skill on the flanks. We didn't seem far off being a title-challenging team, but yet again, when the club needed to make sensational signings, taking us from being a good side to a world-class one, we weren't competing in the same transfer market as Chelsea and Manchester United. The squad was improved, but not enough. At the same time, world-class players such as Didi were coming to the end of their time. His departure to Manchester City was especially sad, given his charismatic influence in the dressing room.

The overall consequence was a season more like Rafa's first, where our League form was inconsistent but we excelled in Europe. The 2006–07 campaign highlighted the fact there's no magic formula in football, allowing you to plan years in advance and ensure you get better year upon year. My experiences at Liverpool prove it never works like that. Our best League seasons have arrived in isolation and been followed by changes that didn't work.

Like the supporters, I didn't disagree with the quality of the recruits at the time, although after being linked for so long with names of the calibre of Seville's Brazilian wide man Daniel Alves I could understand the sense of anti-climax. You ask yourself each summer on the first day of pre-season, are these the signings that will make us as good as we need to be? Would these lads get in the United, Chelsea or Arsenal side? Will our rivals be gutted we signed them? Too often, it seemed, the answer was no. We were pursuing four or five bargains; what we needed was one or two top-of-the-range players.

Bellamy was a particularly controversial purchase. He was seen as a 'bad egg', but he seemed misunderstood to me. I got on brilliantly with him and could see how driven he was and how much he loved his football. His problems seemed to stem from being too intense, as well as from a refusal to compromise when it came to speaking his mind. If he didn't understand or agree with a decision in training, he'd question it. Rafa's style of management was unsuited to him.

It did lead to some funny moments, though.

After his arrival, we were in the players' lounge when he spotted one of the lads' girlfriends. His eyes were virtually popping out as he asked who she was with.

'That's Xabi's bird,' he was told.

Xabi came into the dressing room the following morning and Bellamy couldn't stop himself.

'Tell you what, Xabi,' he said in his cheeky Welsh accent, 'you're punching well above your weight there, mate.'

The lads were laughing, although I'm not entirely sure Xabi knew what he meant.

Bellamy's high and low at Anfield arrived in the same week, when after putting us on the front pages for using a golf club in a fight with John Arne Riise, he scored the equalizer and created the winner in the game we'd been away 'bonding' for, in Barcelona. I was lucky enough to be back on Merseyside when the 'incident' at our Spanish getaway occurred. 'You won't believe what the fuck's gone on here,' was the alert I was given by Steven Gerrard. What can you say? A drunken night out went too far. The fact Bellamy and Riise scored the goals in the Nou Camp, and Craig celebrated it by practising his golf swing on the pitch, demonstrated how mischievous and funny I thought he was. 'Whatever anyone says about me, I played for the club I support, scored and made the winning goal against Barcelona in the Nou Camp, and scored in front of The Kop. No one will ever be able to take that away from me,' Bellamy said prior to his sale to West Ham. Can't argue with that.

Not everyone was upset he left though, especially the poor youth team player who isn't blessed in the good looks department, who was nicknamed 'Gorgeous' for the duration of Bellamy's stay.

With Bellamy sold after a year and players such as Gonzalez moved on after minimal impact, the only conclusion was the 2006 signings didn't work. The Premiership table confirmed this as we finished twenty-one points behind Manchester United. I'm not blaming the new players for our disappointing League performance, though. The circumstances at the start of that season undoubtedly played a part in our failure to take the step forward we expected.

Post World Cup, the effects of our twelve-month season caught up with us. It was no coincidence all our internationals started the season slowly and our worst results and performances came at the same time. I was as guilty as any of underperforming during this period, to the point where I began genuinely to fear if I'd gone past my peak. I'd heard so many stories after previous World Cups and European Championships about the fatigue players suffered the following season. If I'm brutally honest, I'd often brushed such comments off as a tame excuse. Only after I suffered the same syndrome did I fully appreciate how debilitating it felt. It was a strange sensation. I'd jump for a header and literally find it difficult to pull my legs off the ground. I'd run for a tackle and feel a yard slower. There was no sharpness in my game, and it was becoming a struggle to get through ninety minutes without feeling tired.

As I'm such a worrier, there were plenty of sleepless nights to endure at the start of that season, especially after my nightmare performance in the Goodison derby in September, when we were hammered 3–0. I genuinely feared I was finished. 'Is this what happens when your body can't handle the top level any more?' I asked myself. I was questioning if, in football terms, I was 'gone'. It happens to every player eventually, and although I wasn't expecting to fall victim at the age of twenty-eight, maybe this was it.

Rafa could justifiably have dropped me, but I owe him a lot for sticking by me during this dip. There were a lot of us in the same situation, so the manager assured us it was only a temporary problem. That didn't help us in our instantly aborted title bid, though. Any prospect of a challenge was gone after ten games following defeats to Everton, Bolton, Chelsea and Manchester United.

At times like that, the burden of responsibility Stevie and I felt to carry the team through difficult periods was too much. We've benefited from this reputation for much of our careers, and it's a duty we relish most of the time. I like being seen as dependable in that way. It's meant, if things have gone well, we've often been the ones to get most of the credit as the local lads always giving their all. The flip side is if results go wrong fans and team-mates have tended to look to us to get everyone going again. When I was struggling I needed others to step in and help me out, but that hasn't always happened. The best sides will have no passengers; equally they'll be able to accommodate a loss in form of one or two key players. Too often during my time at Liverpool it's seemed if Stevie and I hit a bad patch there's no one else to step up to the mark to cover for us.

As usual, and much to my relief, all our performances vastly improved and we rallied in the second half of the season. By then we were well off the pace in pursuit of Chelsea and United. The echoes with how Houllier's time had gone were unavoidable, but whereas the supporters lost faith quickly in Gérard, Rafa's ongoing European success meant he was still regarded as a messiah on The Kop.

Rafa won the hearts and minds of the fans much quicker than Gérard thanks to Istanbul. The speed of progress in his first two seasons meant the disappointments in the League in year three were not seen in such negative terms. Our progress through the Champions League, overcoming Barcelona and Chelsea once more, would always prove an impressive distraction to those critical of our domestic form. You don't get so much stick for losing away at Newcastle if you win in Barcelona a week later. These were pivotal, defining moments in our season, and Rafa always got it right. The portfolio of epic European victories was growing year upon year. It was an obvious conclusion we'd become a club more suited to the Champions League than the Premiership.

I'm not saying that's intentional, and it's not just the players or manager who have caused this. Go to Anfield on a Saturday at three p.m. when we're playing Wigan or Aston Villa, then go back three days later to watch us play Barcelona or Chelsea. It's like a different venue. The fans are up for it much more, the noise level is astounding, and the intensity generates a vibe that rarely fails to inspire us to play to our fullest potential. As a side we've been accused of failing to reproduce our European form in the League, but the allegation is fairer applied to the whole club. If most English sides had to endure the Anfield European atmosphere, we'd probably blow them away. All of us must take responsibility for that. It's up to us as players to get the crowd going as much as it's up to The Kop to perform every week. There seems to be a different mindset on and off the pitch. The Kop has had twenty years heading to League games with a feeling of trepidation having seen us struggle so often, yet the same supporters possess this supreme confidence and self-belief whenever they watch us in Europe, based largely on Rafa's recent success.

We also benefit from our knowledge of the European game. Never has a 1–0 home defeat been celebrated like that against Barcelona in the 2007 knockout stage. Because we had those two away goals in the Nou Camp, we could afford to lose. Perhaps fans at other clubs would have demanded we attack and finish Barca off, but The Kop has always been more understanding of the tactical side of the game. At that time, Barcelona had one of the most exciting attacking line-ups in the world. As a trio, Lionel Messi, Ronaldinho and Samuel Eto'o could destroy you, but we kept them largely at bay. Frank Rijkaard's side were European champions when we knocked them out. On its own this would have been a victory to rank alongside the Anfield greats, but during this particular era it had almost become expected as we claimed another historic scalp.

The same was true of Chelsea in the repeat of our 2005 semi-final. We knew Jose Mourinho and his players would be determined to get revenge, but playing the second leg at Anfield was crucial again. Mourinho hadn't seemed to learn his lesson with his pre-match comments, diminishing our achievements and ensuring a hostile reaction. 'He's the funniest thing to come out of London since Del Boy and Rodney,' I told the press on the eve of the match, and the line was plastered over the front of the *Echo* as Chelsea arrived.

We were at home. Nothing they could do or say could worry us. We knew after their previous experience here we could get to them.

The emotion of the 2005 success was repeated, but our performance was much more impressive. Chelsea's 1–0 lead was cancelled out by Danish centre-half Daniel Agger, one of our successful signings, from Brondby, and even though the tie went to penalties our standard of football had improved in the two years since the Luis Garcia semi. Whereas that win was based on solid defence, this time we created more opportunities in general play and could have finished them off before the shoot-out. Pepe's saves and Dirk Kuyt's winning penalty secured our second European final in three seasons, and as we headed to Liverpool's Sir Thomas Hotel again for what was fast becoming a traditional semi-final night celebration, our list of famous triumphs was rapidly expanding.

After my earlier dip, my personal performances were retaining their consistent quality too and I was sleeping soundly again. I'd never felt so strong and confident in what I was doing. You come into football not only to prove yourself at the top level, but to establish yourself as a player who can be trusted to deliver when it matters, which in my case means marking any striker in the world out of the game. My performances against Barca, and especially against Chelsea in the second leg, confirmed that when I was at my best I was a centre-half capable of taking on any forward in the world.

For the second time in Rafa's three years, and despite my difficult start to the season, I was named the club's player of the year, which was another proud accolade reflecting those European efforts. I was at the top of my game. I knew I was one of those who could be relied upon no matter who our opponents were. Whether it was a trip to the Nou Camp or a tricky League Cup tie against Reading, Rafa could rely on me. It was enough for him to invite me into his office and offer another new contract – and I was ready for him this time!

What was becoming clearer during every season of Rafa's management, however, was the split personality within Liverpool. We had our League side, which was inconsistent and continued to struggle to challenge Manchester United and Chelsea, and our European team, which could overcome anyone. The story of Jekyll and Hyde could have been written for us.

And it became increasingly apparent this wasn't the only division at the club. There was also the ongoing situation at The Academy, which came to a head in the summer of 2007 when Steve Heighway departed after three years of bickering with

Benitez's Melwood staff. I was hearing and reading rumours of tensions between Rafa and Rick Parry too, which was worrying. After embarrassingly heavy home defeats to Arsenal in the FA Cup and Carling Cup in January 2007, Rafa broke his silence with critical comments about the state of The Academy and our spending powers. Briefly, it created an hysterical story until Rick and Rafa met and brought some calm.

Despite the resolution, it was a hint of what was to follow, especially as the 2006–07 season continued amid the backdrop of Liverpool's takeover. David Moores was stepping down as chairman and the American revolution was underway. New owners Tom Hicks and George Gillett made their first appearance at Anfield on 6 March when we lost to Barcelona on the night but won the tie, seemingly intoxicated by the atmosphere and making grand announcements of their intentions to help Rafa make those final steps to the top of the English game.

We headed to Athens in May for the Champions League Final in positive mood, hoping to unify the club with our sixth European Cup, confident the American dollars would soon be flowing in no matter what the result. What followed were the opening exchanges of the most turbulent twelve months in Liverpool's history. Golden skies? We were about to walk through the most torrential wind and rain, at the end of which few at Anfield would be able to keep their heads held high.

12

The Liverpool Way

Before I became an established Liverpool footballer, my cousin Jamie Keggin was the only Kopite in the Carragher clan. He walked alone in our family for eighteen years, until my switch of loyalties meant those closest to me followed us across Stanley Park. After being a rival for so long, Jamie became a vital source of Anfield wisdom, providing a welcome insight into what he believed to be the essential requirement for a true Liverpudlian. Should anything go wrong off the field at the club, or someone speak out of turn in the press, Jamie will always remind us of a quote he has engraved in his mind which sums up the philosophy of Liverpool. It's attributed to former Liverpool chairman Sir John Smith, who led the club through its most triumphant period during the 1970s and 1980s. He said, 'We're a very, very modest club at Liverpool. We don't talk. We don't boast. But we're very professional.'

The ex-chairman must have spent the 2007–08 season banging his head on his coffin. My cousin Jamie has repeated his quote more in the last twelve months than the previous twenty-five years.

We'd experienced several seasons where simmering tensions had threatened to boil over behind the scenes at Anfield, but somehow we'd managed to avoid pressing the self-destruct button by ensuring events on the field rather than off it grabbed the headlines. Istanbul was played amid worries over Steven Gerrard's future which were ultimately resolved. The FA Cup was won despite growing uncertainty over the ownership of Liverpool FC. Even if you go as far back as the treble season, the future of the club was being debated during feisty shareholders' meetings. For the most part, such disturbances were kept in-house. There were rumours in the press every so often, but nothing to undermine the tradition of Liverpool as the club envied for the professional manner in which it conducted its affairs.

We'd always handled a crisis with dignity. Even managers who left the club would host a press conference to say goodbye, as Roy Evans did in 1998, and also Gérard Houllier following his dismissal in 2004. You wouldn't get that at any other football club, and I loved that uniqueness about Liverpool. Great servants reached the end of their time and were escorted through the Shankly Gates with dignity to receive the applause of the crowd, not shoved out of the back door shouting and screaming with their tail between their legs.

Athens was a turning point that signalled, temporarily I pray, the demise of those values which come under the definition 'The Liverpool Way'.

Rafa himself influenced a change of approach with his extraordinary press conference on the morning of 24 May following our 2–1 defeat in Greece. He took the opportunity publicly to demand instant action from Tom Hicks and George Gillett. 'The new owners say they will support us, but now is not the time to talk but to take decisions,' he said. 'It's not just about new faces, it's about the structure of the club.' These words sparked a chain reaction that brought problems into the open, almost cost him his job a couple of months later, riled Liverpool's owners into an ill-fated meeting with Jurgen Klinsmann, and ended Hicks's and Gillett's honeymoon relationship with The Kop, making them the targets of disapproval rather than appreciation.

I was heading for breakfast in our base at the Pentelikon Hotel when a journalist broke the news to me. 'Rafa has gone for the Americans over their failure to back him in the transfer market,' I was informed. I was taken aback. 'Give them a chance,' I thought. 'We only lost the Champions League final twelve hours ago.'

Obviously his concerns had been growing far more than any of the players were aware and he'd decided the time was right to express them, but I'd never guessed from his demeanour ahead of the game the problems had reached such a critical point, and I didn't feel airing them to the world's media would serve any purpose. I put it down to the disappointment of losing the final, although as the players' coach headed to Athens airport and the critical comments of the manager followed them across the Atlantic, I guessed the owners wouldn't be so sympathetic.

In most walks of life there's a basic rule we're all aware of: you don't go into work and slag off your boss. Such was Rafa's popularity, he must have thought the risk worth taking for what he believed would benefit the club. If Gillett and Hicks had fired him in the summer of 2007 after our second European Cup Final in three years, they'd have faced a serious fans' revolt. Rafa felt he was arguing from a position of strength.

Instead of reacting angrily, it must be presumed Gillett and Hicks decided to restrain themselves, bide their time and wait for what they perceived to be a more opportune moment to punish the manager for his public challenge to their ownership. In fact, instead of publicly responding to Rafa's remarks, the Americans seemed to react exactly how he wanted. Their actions spoke louder than words, and that impressed me. That was my definition of The Liverpool Way. Don't say it, do it.

Fernando Torres, Ryan Babel, Yossi Benayoun and Brazilian Lucas Leiva signed in the weeks that followed for fees in the region of £45 million and deals for Javier Mascherano and Martin Skrtel were completed in January 2008 costing around £25 million. It's hard for me to imagine this money wouldn't have been available had Rafa kept quiet. He may argue he provoked the decisive movement he wanted in the transfer market. Either way, the drama of his press conference appeared to have calmed down once the season was underway. Or so we thought. I could never have guessed the implications of Rafa's outburst would become so serious. The Athens press conference didn't register as big news on the plane home as much as in the newspapers and among the fans in the days that followed. We were too busy getting over our disappointment at losing the final to get wrapped up in club politics.

History is always written by winners. I could spend hours talking about Istanbul and reliving every second of that victory. I've forgotten much of what happened in Athens because I get no pleasure from recalling it. We played all right but didn't do enough to win the game. Unlike Istanbul, it wasn't an especially entertaining match and there were few chances for either side. AC Milan scored at crucial times, defended well and deserved their victory. Despite being stronger than in 2005 and heading into the game with more confidence, we never played to our full potential.

The mysteries of football will never cease to throw up contradictions. Tactically, we were more clever at the start of the game in 2007 than in 2005. Rafa learned from what happened in the first half in the Ataturk, played Steven Gerrard in a more advanced forward role and asked Javier Mascherano to perform Didi Hamann's role in the second half, denying Kaká the freedom he'd enjoyed two years earlier. An extra body in midfield also stopped Pirlo dictating play. If you analyse the game tactically, this strategy brought some success. We dominated possession and were never in danger of being ripped apart by Kaká in the way we were for forty-five minutes in Turkey.

But for all our improvement since our last meeting, the game exposed where work was still needed. There weren't enough goalscorers on the pitch for us in Athens. Our midfield consisted of Bolo Zenden, Javier Mascherano, Xabi Alonso and Jermaine Pennant, none of whom had short odds on the first goalscorer betting slips. Dirk Kuyt played as a lone striker instead of Peter Crouch, with Gerrard tucked behind, so the onus was entirely on those two to break the deadlock. Dirk scored late on, but there was never a point where we threatened to take control of the game.

AC Milan could argue they played much better in defeat in 2005 than in victory in 2007, but they'll always look at Athens as the completion of their revenge mission. I didn't feel they'd been avenged. It's easy for me to say, but the pain of defeat in 2007 was nothing compared to how it would have been two years earlier.

I was devastated to lose, of course. To win the Champions League once was enough to create history, especially in the manner we did it. To have done it twice within three years would have taken this to another level. There's always a hollow, sickening feeling after losing a final, but it's certainly eased when you can console yourself with the knowledge you've already won it before and you believe further opportunities to win it will come again. I'm greedy for more winners medals and as hungry for European success now as I was before my first Champions League win, but experience allows you to cope better with such setbacks.

One thing I've learned throughout my career is this: no defeat passes without attempts to over-analyse where it went wrong and find contributing factors. The explanation was simple in Athens: we didn't play well enough to win. Such an obvious statement isn't always enough in the modern game. On my return to Liverpool I read several articles about the preparation for the game not being up to scratch because our team hotel wasn't what it should have been and our families had to stay in some appalling conditions. This was true, but it had nothing to do with our performance. We didn't lose the European Cup because our rooms were a bit small. It's a ridiculous argument.

Fans told me they knew as soon as they arrived in Athens it wasn't going to be the same as Istanbul, and they had more valid reasons for feeling disillusioned with the trip. I can't ignore the fact a small but not insubstantial group of Liverpool supporters let the club down on the night of the final by forcing their way into the ground without tickets, or with fakes. Friends I'd arranged genuine tickets for couldn't get in and were left stranded, and stories filtered back to me about shambolic scenes outside the Olympic Stadium prior to kick-off. I saw frightening images of fans pushing in.

Those responsible have no excuse, but a catalogue of errors contributed to this, starting with UEFA. They were warned for weeks about potential problems. They picked a venue unsuitable for such a major match, the attendance was too small, and not enough seats were available to the clubs. It was an athletics stadium rather than a football arena, and by all accounts it was far too easy to bunk in. Liverpool's own ticketing policy came under criticism by some of our supporters as they tried to distribute a meagre number to the many thousands travelling to Greece.

Like the players, fans' views either get rose-tinted or tainted depending on the result. You won't hear a single horror story about Istanbul, but no one has a positive tale to tell about Athens. My mates told me they felt uneasy as soon as they got there because the atmosphere wasn't the same as Taksim Square. During the course of a season, Liverpool's European trips tend to attract the same group of die-hard Reds, but once you reach the final the bandwagon gets top heavy with those who are more interested in the 'event' rather than the football. There are some unruly elements – and this applies to every club, city and probably every country – who latch on to the biggest occasions and want to invade what the most loyal fans perceive as their 'territory'. I know that for many, travelling to Greece was less about seeing Liverpool win the European Cup and more about just 'being in Athens'. Thousands who missed out on Istanbul weren't going to make the same mistake twice. This is an unavoidable consequence of reaching a major final, and if the supervision isn't up to scratch, it gets magnified.

There's nothing like parading the Champions League trophy to hide any blemishes on and off the park, and had we beaten AC Milan in Athens I doubt there'd have been much post-match talk about poor organization; in the same way Rafa's morning-after-the-night-before briefing would have carried a much different tone. Instead, without the manager, the fans or the players knowing it, we returned for pre-season training a few weeks later with the Anfield time-bomb having already been set.

Far from planning for the 2007–08 campaign sensing added pressure, it seemed there was much to be positive about. New billionaire owners, a record signing, a fresh stadium announcement and the promise of our most realistic title bid for fifteen years. What could possibly go wrong?

Such was the relief when the Anfield takeover saga ended in March 2007, Liverpool supporters were willing to accept whatever Hicks and Gillett said at face value. They made the right noises, promising to build the arena on Stanley Park which had been planned for seven years, and vowing to invest in the team without plunging the club into debt. On the surface it was a good deal. I was one of those who'd welcomed the new owners to Anfield, believing they would provide the finances to build a new ground that, over the long term, would allow us to compete with Manchester United and Chelsea. I wasn't expecting a Roman Abramovich-style revolution, but I presumed the manager would still have his annual kitty of about £30 million a year, which would give him enough options in the transfer market. The arrival of a player of Torres's calibre from Atlético Madrid for £21 million seemed to confirm our confidence in what former chairman David Moores hoped were the 'ideal custodians' for the club. The only reservation was that Liverpool had to pass into foreign ownership. That was a sad consequence of modern football realities. I'd have preferred Mr Moores to stay as owner, but once he said he couldn't afford to keep us competitive without getting massive but risky bank loans there was no choice but to sell to the right bidder.

For a while, it seemed that would be Dubai International Capital. The chairman and Rick Parry introduced me and Steven Gerrard to the DIC chief executive Sameer Al-Ansari when they were on the verge of concluding their deal. I liked his enthusiasm for the club and handed him a couple of signed shirts, believing this was my future boss. Within a few weeks I was having another meeting at the Lowry Hotel in Manchester, ahead of England's international with Spain. This time Hicks and Gillett were shaking mine and Stevie's hands, telling us how good they'd be for Liverpool.

Neither of us had reason to doubt that DIC or Hicks and Gillett would be good for the club. We trusted the chairman and Rick to make the right decision; they knew far more than Stevie or me about why they'd changed their minds on DIC. Like the fans, if the club hierarchy was sure the Americans offered more chance of success and stability, we had to back them. We had no choice.

As is often the case in such circumstances, Liverpool's website rushed out quotes from us saying how enthusiastic we were about the future under the Americans, no doubt hoping we'd put the supporters' minds at ease. But what else would we say? We'd met them once, they said what we wanted to hear about buying players and building the stadium, and that was that. Privately, as I listened to their guarantees, that definition of 'The Liverpool Way' which I cling to was at the forefront of my mind: 'Actions speak louder than words.' You can put as much faith in the inspiring pledges of chairmen, chief executives, managers and players as you want, but there has to be something to show for these assurances. We were compelled to be as positive about the takeover as possible. There was no reason for me to be negative, but there was bound to be a certain amount of caution about whether promises would be delivered. I'd delay my real judgement until a later date.

Of the two new owners, I knew more about George Gillett. I had been aware of his interest in Liverpool longer than most courtesy of a conversation he'd had with Michael Owen the previous summer. Mo travelled to America for cruciate knee surgery following the World Cup in 2006; he was treated by renowned surgeon Dr Richard Steadman, a friend of Gillett's. Mo told me how keen Gillett was to buy Liverpool. His first bid was rejected because he didn't have deep enough pockets to assure the Anfield board he was the right option. This changed once he'd made a second offer backed by the Texan Tom Hicks, whom the club knew less about.

We have to acknowledge the supporters were guilty of a certain amount of naivety in their initial reaction to the takeover. The Americans' first press conference when they spoke in glowing terms about understanding the traditional values of the club played well to the fans, but from day one I was more realistic. For richer or poorer, we'd sold Liverpool to two ruthless businessmen who saw us as a money-making opportunity. They didn't buy Liverpool as an act of charity; they weren't intent on throwing away all the millions they'd earned over fifty years. If I had £500 million and decided to buy an American baseball team, do you think I'd just give away £100 million for players? The fact Gillett didn't have enough to complete the deal on his own was revealing in itself. It showed there wasn't the bottomless pit of funds the more optimistic of our fans believed. Anyone with a financial brain recognized they'd want a return on their investment. They were never going to pump money into the club they didn't expect to get back with interest.

Liverpool wasn't an attractive purchase because of the fans, the players, the manager or even our illustrious history. They wanted to buy us because the planned stadium offered a chance to generate tons of cash and increase the value of the club. DIC were criticized and had their bid seriously undermined when this information was revealed as part of a seven-year exit strategy. They'd buy Liverpool for £200 million, build the stadium and keep the team strong, and seven years on sell it for a handsome profit. Some fans didn't like the crudeness of such a scheme to exploit Liverpool's economic potential, but in reality everyone would have been a winner. The only way to treble Liverpool's value within seven years was to enjoy success on the pitch and build a new ground with a bigger attendance.

I doubt Gillett's and Hicks's plans differed, other than the fact they were less blatant about saying it and cleverly appealed to the fans' romantic idea of Liverpool remaining a 'family club' by announcing their sons, Foster Gillett and Tom Hicks Jr, would be on the board. Supporters wanted to believe the owners would embrace the club's mottos and traditions. Hicks and Gillett insisted they would.

This is why the months that followed left The Kop feeling so let down. It's hard enough for people outside Liverpool to understand our fans' mentality, let alone those from another country, and Hicks and Gillett badly misread it. You won't find a more loyal set of supporters, but try to kid them and you're in trouble. When serious mistakes were made in the running of Liverpool, the fans felt they'd been misled in order to win their support.

Some mistakes are worse than others, but in the history of Anfield none will be recalled more than the claim by Hicks and Gillett that 'we won't put any debt on the club'. Breaking this vow set the first alarm bells ringing; the embarrassing continual changing of the stadium plans was irritating too. It felt Stevie and I were being asked to endorse a new arena every month, looking at drawings and saying, 'Yes, it looks great.' I'm not an architect so I haven't got a clue which stadium should be built, only that it needs to happen, preferably before I retire.

The former chairman told us the reason he sold the club was to prevent it falling into too much debt when he paid for the Stanley Park project. It begged the obvious question: what had the new owners done that the old board couldn't?

It was an issue the fans rightly wanted to explore further. We'd spent heavily on Torres and Babel, but was this the club's money or the bank's? I'd read we'd won as much as £25 million from the Champions League in 2007, and the new TV deal was worth a fortune too, so why did we have to borrow so much? I couldn't understand it. Was it possible we were taking financial risks in the hope of immediate success on the pitch? If that was the case, the pressure for the manager to achieve annual progress in the Champions League and keep collecting the UEFA winnings was much greater than we'd imagined.

Not that Rafa or the players needed to be bothered by this. If I was a manager in Spain and I was told I could bid £21 million for a striker and £11 million for a winger, I'd take the cash and spend it without questioning where it came from. I don't believe many managers care where they're getting the financial backing as long as they're getting it. It's more understandable if fans, board members or journalists question the wisdom of such a spending policy because they're looking longer-term. As a local player who cares deeply about the future of Liverpool, I was interested in this information too. But managers have so little time to make an impact at a top club I'm amazed any would take a moral stance about their funds. Can you imagine it if I was a boss at a La Liga club?

'You can have as much as you like to buy what you believe to be the best striker in Europe, Carra.'

'Er, is it the club's money or have you got it from the bank?'

'We've taken a loan because we believe in your judgement.'

'No thanks, mate, I'd rather be skint.'

If breaking the promise about taking the club into debt and growing rumours of disagreements between Hicks and Gillett on the subject of the stadium and its funding caused only mild ripples of concern, what happened next led to chaos.

Another strange press conference on 22 November ended the uncomfortable ceasefire between Rafa and the board since Athens. Rafa sat for forty-five minutes answering questions with the same response: 'As always, I'm focusing only on training and coaching.' He broke off from this routine to declare himself interested in the vacant England job. He must have been really desperate to do that (although it still wouldn't have brought me out of international retirement). As usual, I was watching this on Sky television, shaking my head at the screen and texting friends to gather as much info as I could because I had no idea what was going on.

The reasons for this performance were explained later. Having sought assurances about his transfer plans in January, when he wanted to sign the centre-half Kakha Kaladze from AC Milan, he'd received a message from the board telling him to focus on coaching the side until a planned meeting in December. I believe Rafa suspected a plan was already in place to sack him and the owners were playing for time, holding back funds for his replacement. This prompted his bizarre but undoubtedly brave reaction. He must have felt if he didn't make his concerns public he'd lose his job anyway, so what did he have to lose?

As if to underline the point, he wore his tracksuit at St James's Park in Newcastle two days later for the only time I can recall in a Premier League fixture, and repeated criticisms of the hierarchy. He was effectively daring the Americans to arrange his funeral, especially when Hicks ended the dignified boardroom silence by telling Rafa to 'shut up' on the front page of the *Liverpool Echo*.

Within twenty-four hours, the *News of the World* back page was announcing Hicks's and Gillett's intention to sack Rafa because of his continual outbursts against their reign. Usually such a story would immediately be denied, but it wasn't. Instead, the club made a statement saying 'nothing had changed' despite the 'speculation'. This was more than rumour now, and Rafa must have known how close he was to the sack. There was an immediate change of tone from him after it was made public he was getting the bullet, no doubt sparked by the lack of support he was receiving from the owners.

I couldn't believe what I was reading from one day to the next. I picked up the *Echo* on Monday expecting to discover the club was dismissing the story about his imminent sacking, but there was nothing of the sort. Instead I saw quotes attributed to a 'source close to the manager' saying how grateful he was for the backing he'd had from the owners and wanted to talk to them. That made me more angry. I've grown up reading the *Echo* and it's always been the most reliable source of information regarding Liverpool FC. It's like the bible for the fans in the city. You read stories in other papers and you take them or leave them. If it's in the *Echo*, the first presumption is it's 100 per cent right. I expect to see 'sources close to' someone being quoted in the Sunday papers, not the *Echo*. It showed me how out of control the situation had become when people at Anfield weren't prepared to attach their name to such important words. Now, even the *Echo* – the closest paper to the club – was being used in the same way as one of the Sunday papers. What was going on here? Everyone was trying to be too clever, playing politics with little regard for how much damage it was doing. They were making it worse. The saying goes, 'Don't wash your dirty linen in public.' Anfield was starting to look like a launderette.

It must also be acknowledged that, although he'd been at the club for over three years, Rafa's education in the business of running a football club was exclusively Spanish. What seemed to many of us to be an unusual approach to getting what he wanted wasn't as much a departure for him. In La Liga, political battles have always been played out in public. It's the nature of their system because club presidents need the ongoing support of their fans when summer elections are held. This makes them as vulnerable to being shoved out as managers, so the coaches in Spain are cuter about exploiting situations to their advantage.

Rafa, like all Spanish managers, had experience of boardroom battles at his previous clubs so he was well equipped to handle himself at Anfield. His fall-out with a director at Valencia enabled

Liverpool to recruit him in the first place. 'I wanted a sofa and they bought me a lampshade,' he was famously quoted as saying during a disagreement with the Valencia board about a signing he didn't want. We knew what a clever operator we were getting.

You have to admire his mental strength and courage, especially as he continued to focus on preparing the team for tough fixtures while coping with the prospect of dismissal. He also knew no matter what the owners were planning he had a powerful ally in the form of The Kop. The fans instantly rallied behind Rafa, demanding the owners publicly support him.

As the story developed, it became clearer why they'd refused to do so. In the same week as Rafa's 'training and coaching' press conference the board had met Jurgen Klinsmann in America to discuss him becoming our next manager. The daily morning papers claimed an offer was made to Klinsmann prior to the German taking the Bayern Munich job. Incredibly, Hicks then backed up the stories with an admission to the *Echo*'s Liverpool FC correspondent Tony Barrett a couple of days later. With one sentence to the local paper, Hicks turned what most fans were happy to dismiss as an outrageous rumour into an astonishing fact. They went ballistic.

My Evertonian mate Seddo took great delight in the ongoing shambles.

'Go and buy the *Echo*, ha, ha, ha,' he texted me.

'Typical Blue,' I thought. If you want to know what's going on at Liverpool, ask an Evertonian. They're more interested in our club than their own.

Hicks said he was being honest in his answer, replying truthfully in the hope it might earn him some credit. But, like many of the decisions around this time, it showed a lack of understanding of English football. There are times when such admissions are counter-productive, especially as the story appeared to be dying a death.

Supporters expected me to come out and immediately condemn what was happening at the top of the club, but I found myself in an incredibly awkward position. You have to remember, like Rafa, the players are employees of the football club. I've never shied away from saying what I believe, but I'm not stupid. If Rafa Benitez can be sacked for speaking out of turn, so can Jamie Carragher.

At this stage, I had more sympathy for both sides than people imagined. I should clarify that I completely disagreed with their decision to consider Rafa's position when they did. It made no sense to me at all, particularly given the timing. We were near the top of the table, and although we'd endured a difficult start to our Champions League group after defeats to Marseille and Besiktas, we knew we could still progress with a few wins. I didn't agree with Klinsmann as a replacement, either. He was too inexperienced at club level and his CV is no match for Rafa's, at least at this stage of his career. In fairness to Klinsmann, he's one of the few to emerge from the sorry episode with any credit. He's not said a word about the controversy, and I respect him for this. He must have been livid that details of his private meetings were leaked.

Where I disagreed with many supporters was in their outrage that a manager had been approached while another was still in charge. It was wrong to think about replacing Rafa a few weeks into a new season, but once a decision had been taken it was inevitable a plan had to be put into operation and other candidates explored. Let's not plead innocence about this. Anyone who thinks representatives on behalf of Liverpool FC never spoke to Rafa Benitez while Gérard Houllier was still the boss must be very naive about how the football world operates. It's a nice idea to think Liverpool sacked Gérard and then asked themselves, 'I wonder if Benitez will be interested in the job?' but somehow I doubt it was like that. I'd be greatly concerned if it was. If Rafa had left and Liverpool had had no one else lined up, the board would have been accused of incompetence for leaving us in the lurch at a key point of our season.

There were also claims Klinsmann had been approached in case Rafa decided to leave Liverpool in the near future. This might have washed the previous summer, but not in November 2007, although it did explain why Hicks and Gillett were eyeing other candidates. Rafa had been linked with Real Madrid on at least two occasions during his three and a half years at the club, and had never distanced himself from those stories.

The sense I got was of a series of factors colliding to create a mess of everyone's making. There should have been guilty consciences all over the club as the situation spiralled out of control.

I avoided answering questions on the subject because it's not in my nature to compromise. I was 100 per cent behind the manager, but I understood why the owners were unhappy with him too. They'd been undermined by Rafa and now they were undermining him. It was a political rather than football battle, and although the fans wanted to see it in black and white terms, with the owners the bad guys and Rafa their hero, I saw far more shades of grey.

Steven Gerrard and I were constantly asked questions about the situation, and when we swerved the issue fans began to approach me and say they'd heard 'Rafa has lost the dressing room'. This is a phrase you often hear when a manager is under pressure, and it's one of the biggest myths in football. I've never known a manager to 'have the dressing room', never mind lose it. Whether it was Steve Heighway, Roy Evans, Gérard Houllier or Rafa Benitez, I've always played foremost for Liverpool Football Club and my own sense of pride, and never given less than 100 per cent in all circumstances. We're one of the biggest clubs in the world and the manager is under pressure from day one. Any player who doesn't give his all, whether we're going through a good or bad spell, shouldn't be here. My relationships with all those managers have been professional. It's the badge that comes first. Rafa has defined that professional relationship more than any boss I've known, and he knows as much as anyone where loyalties lie in a dressing room.

Look at the results we achieved in the biggest games after it became public Rafa's job was under threat. They speak out much more than any hard-hitting interview. On 24 November, when it was believed he was forty-eight hours from losing his job, we beat Newcastle away, 3–0. Just four days later we trounced Porto at Anfield in the Champions League. Our 4–0 away win in Marseille in mid-December to reach the knockout stage of the Champions League also arrived amid speculation a defeat would have brought the axe. Victory over Inter Milan in the last sixteen was achieved in similar circumstances. If you want to know how the dressing room felt, look at those results. The damaging headlines had no effect on how we played. Stevie and I talked about it every day. It was increasingly annoying seeing Liverpool's image being dragged through the mud, but it didn't stop us performing when it mattered. No circumstances exist where I wouldn't give my all for Liverpool.

We got sick of everyone around us fighting and wanted an immediate resolution rather than to get dragged into it. Some hope. No sooner had one issue died down as the results improved and Rafa remained in his job than the attention shifted elsewhere. Now Gillett and Hicks were arguing with each other. Foster Gillett, who'd been based at Melwood for a couple of months, returned home. It was a sign of how serious the situation had become. Until then, Foster was the one we had most dealings with. He made every effort to understand the club, joining the players in the canteen to discuss tactics or games he'd watched. I could see he wanted to be well informed about English football. When statements were made in the papers which inflamed the situation, it wasn't his father who was quoted, but Tom Hicks. As the only new member of the board actually based in the city, though, he must have felt more vulnerable to the fans' anger.

Liverpool should have known better after the joint-manager debacle at the end of the 1990s. You can only have one boss at a football club.

With DIC talking to Gillett about buying his share in the club just a year after he'd bought it, it became obvious he recognized the damage that had been done and was ready to sell. Hicks saw things differently. Once Hicks and Gillett began to air their grievances with each other publicly, the situation worsened.

Every idea I had of what 'The Liverpool Way' meant was contradicted by one particular interview conducted by Hicks on Sky Sports News on 17 April, 2008. If this phrase wasn't in danger of receiving the last rites, it was certainly in need of urgent medical attention afterwards. I thought of my cousin Jamie's John Smith quote again as I watched. 'We're a very, very modest club . . . we don't boast . . . we're very professional.' The interview began with a boast: 'Everton won't like that,' he commented after we beat Blackburn to secure an unspectacular fourth place in the League. The owners had arrived pledging funds to take on Manchester United and Chelsea; now we were rubbing Everton's nose in it simply because we'd finished fourth.

Then, after earlier telling Rafa to shut up and admitting a plan to sack him, Hicks announced the manager would get a one-year contract extension. It was clearly intended to be a vote of confidence, but any seasoned football observer will tell you a one-year deal isn't seen in such positive terms.

Hicks continued with a series of contentious statements, deflecting blame for our problems elsewhere, and accusing Gillett of the approach to Klinsmann. Hicks said he hadn't heard of Klinsmann. How could he have considered a man he didn't know becoming Liverpool's manager?

After the takeover was complete, I'd argued to friends there needed to be a greater Anfield connection on the board to balance out what Hicks and Gillett openly accepted was their limited understanding of our game and Liverpool in general. I'd have loved them to appoint a figurehead such as Kenny Dalglish to offer advice on key issues. The fans would have trusted Kenny to make the right judgements on such matters. He'd certainly have urged Hicks and Gillett to think twice about replacing Rafa mid-season, and would have been able to fill them in on the credentials of future managerial candidates. Looking to the future, I firmly believe a man of Kenny's stature should be on our board – and I'm not just saying this because he agreed to write the foreword to this book! It makes perfect sense. Manchester United have successfully operated with Bobby Charlton as a director throughout the Ferguson era.

What worries me about Hicks saying he'd never heard of Klinsmann is this: what happens when we *do* need to appoint another manager? Liverpool fans will shudder at the idea of names being checked on the internet. If Kenny was on the board, the owners would be able to ask his advice in the knowledge he has a grasp of what the supporters here expect. There's been a lot of talk about placing a fans' representative on the board too, but for me, appointing someone such as Kenny – a fan with experience of the ins and outs of football on and off the pitch – would be more appropriate.

The Klinsmann admission was just one of many concerns raised by the Sky interview. Attacking Rick Parry – he called his period as chief executive a 'disaster' – was not the Liverpool way, and to use such a word just two days after the anniversary of the Hillsborough tragedy was insensitive.

Hicks raised broader issues about how Liverpool had been run over the previous decade, particularly in the area of commercial development. Whenever I've heard criticism of this aspect of the club I've felt there's been a large dose of hypocrisy from the fans. If you compare us to Manchester United, there's a massive gulf in what they earn from merchandise or tickets that has developed over twenty-five years. That's why we're talking about a new stadium. The only reason supporters make an issue out of this now is because they've belatedly realized how far behind we are and accept that if you haven't got mega-money, you can't compete.

If you go back to 1990 when we won our last League title and United were often linked with unpopular takeovers such as those by Robert Maxwell or Michael Knighton, our fans were laughing at theirs. We were the family club that didn't have to sell its soul to win the title, whereas they were always focused on exploiting their brand name across the world. There's an inevitable inconsistency here. On the one hand we're a proud working-class club, but on the other we want our board to behave like ruthless capitalists and think it's great if American and Arab billionaires want to give us lots of money.

I've heard our supporters complain, rightly, about increased season ticket prices and regular kit changes, but then they say the club should be doing more to fleece supporters living in Malaysia or Thailand. We have supporters' groups who admirably wish to protect the Scouse roots of Liverpool FC and ensure there's always an affiliation between the club and the community. Some are resentful of what's often referred to as the 'out of town' influence at Anfield, where coaches from the rest of the country and flights from Ireland and Norway invade the city on a match day. At the same time, some of the same people will accuse Liverpool of being too slow to follow United to areas of Europe and the Far East to attract a wider fan base and raise money.

We can't have it both ways. If Liverpool really wants to be like Manchester United off the pitch as much as on it, sacrifices will have to be made to our identity – and we do want it, as proved by the fact we were so accepting of the American takeover and held SOS DIC banners on The Kop. Finding the right balance between how the traditional fans want us to be seen and becoming a 'brand name' across the world is tricky, but there's no point rewriting history to attack the old board for having difficulty coming to terms with these contradictions. It's only in recent times the fans have accepted we have to change and think in a more global sense about the club's future. If you'd have said we needed to pursue this path while Kenny was lifting the League title in 1990, there would have been a supporters' backlash. For Hicks to use the argument about our lack of commercial development as another stick with which to beat Parry was too simplistic and demonstrated a limited view of our recent history.

All the Sky interview achieved was to expose how deep the divisions at the club had become. As players, there was no possibility of publicly backing one side over the other, you simply had to make your mind up on the basis of what you read, saw and heard. I fail to see how the interview served any positive purpose, especially as at the time we were concentrating on the vital Champions League semi-final against Chelsea.

The owners told us they wanted the best for the club. Couldn't they see that what was happening was the opposite of what we needed? DIC were said to be ready to pay £400 million to buy the club off the Americans. That's what the fans wanted, but these figures disgusted me too. Liverpool had been bought for around £200 million a year earlier, but was now double its value. Think how many world-class players that £200 million could have brought to the club. Instead, if Gillett and Hicks did sell, they or their banks would make a huge profit. I felt ill thinking about it.

As far as I was concerned, there was no other conclusion: everyone at Liverpool had to get together urgently to sort out the situation, and that included Rick and the former chairman, who inevitably took criticism for selling to Hicks and Gillett instead of DIC. They said they had concerns when DIC didn't complete their first takeover attempt as quickly as expected, and after Gillett and Hicks made a bigger offer many shareholders said the board was obliged to rethink their options. Few opposed the deal at the time, largely because Rick and the chairman said they were convinced of the Americans' credentials. But if they could turn back time, maybe they'd act differently. In the meantime, all everyone involved can do is try to heal the wounds, if it's possible.

As I write this, the ownership of Liverpool remains uncertain.

Hicks claimed he wouldn't sell to DIC and Gillett retaliated by insisting he wouldn't sell to Hicks. If Hicks took full control he'd replace Rick Parry and David Moores, but they were working to ensure Hicks left first. In the biggest twist of all, the only man at the club who felt safe in the knowledge he would still be at Liverpool at the start of 2008–09 was Rafa Benitez. When he thinks back to his press conference in Athens and how it's played out since, maybe he's the one who wouldn't act any differently. He took major risks, but he's still the manager, which as far as Liverpool fans are concerned is the main thing. If you're reading this and there's been no progress in the boardroom battle, it must still be a difficult time to be a Liverpool fan.

My hope is that for all their differences, everyone in a position of power at Anfield will put aside their own agendas and think not only about 2008–09, but the next twenty-five, even fifty years of Liverpool Football Club. We can't have arguments played out in public every week, and we can't ever hope to catch Manchester United and Chelsea if we're too busy scrapping with one another to take the fight to them. Whatever our situation we have to get on with it and try to restore the dignity that has always been associated with Liverpool.

Inevitably, my discussing this issue may create new headlines at the start of the current season. There are those who may say there is a contradiction between my calling for a return to what I call The Liverpool Way and making comments that remind everyone of the problems at boardroom level. I sat down to write this book in the summer of 2007 with no idea of the crisis on the horizon. There were no plans to include such a difficult chapter twelve months ago. Having committed myself to as honest and forthright a view of my club as possible, it was impossible for me to ignore this situation or refuse to give my opinion on it. My thoughts have been expressed in this book as a consequence of events that were thrust into the public eye by others, not by me.

To onlookers, it must have seemed like everyone was falling out with each other at Anfield in 2007–08. The campaign began with Rafa's assistant Pako Ayesteran leaving the club. It took me by surprise. I headed in to Melwood one Friday at the end of August to be informed Pako had gone. Rafa said he was upset Pako had spoken to other clubs and accused him of disloyalty. I've never spoken to Pako since so didn't get to hear his side of the story. It was sad to see him go, but such circumstances regularly occur in football. Without wishing to sound uncaring, you have to move on quickly. He was replaced by another fitness coach and that was that so far as I was concerned. Some players were more affected by his departure than others. He had a particularly close relationship with the Spanish lads, and also got on with Steven Gerrard.

Although he didn't show much emotion, I also felt for the manager. He'd arrived from Valencia in 2004 with his own back-room team but, for different reasons, each had now gone. Paco Herrera, our highly rated chief scout and reserve team manager who identified many of Rafa's signings, left in 2006 to return to his family in Spain. The goalkeeping coach Jose Ochoterana fol-lowed him in 2007, and now Pako was gone too.

The day after Pako's departure we beat Derby County 6–0 at Anfield to stay top of the table and consolidate our best ever start to a Premier League season. It was far too early for predic-tions, but with Fernando Torres immediately settling in and Ryan Babel showing signs of promise, the mood was upbeat. But that afternoon was probably as optimistic as it got. A series of draws lost us momentum, and as the season progressed familiar failings were revived.

Our Champions League form ensured we had plenty to play for until the final weeks of the season. Beating Inter Milan and Arsenal added to our impressive list of scalps, but defeat to Chelsea in the semi-final meant, ultimately, those victories won't stand up to comparison with those in 2005. As in Athens, our loss to Chelsea prompted headlines about revenge for those earlier encounters, but it was nothing of the sort. Since 2005 we've played Chelsea in four semi-finals in four seasons, winning three. The law of averages was bound to catch up with us eventually.

The most encouraging aspect of an otherwise disappointing year was the impact of Torres. To score thirty-three goals in his debut season was beyond any expectations, and if he repeats that form in the years to come he'll be well on the way to securing legendary status.

I've mentioned already how the first day of pre-season training is spent assessing if our new faces are going to make us any better, and the instant excitement was hard to contain with Fernando. He's built for Premier League football, strong, fast and skilful – as he proved in the Euro 2008 final by outpacing and outmuscling Germany's Philipp Lahm to score Spain's winner. I'm glad I only have to mark him in five-a-sides. His presence alongside Steven Gerrard offers hope of more silverware in years to come. With Javier Mascherano added to the ranks permanently during the course of last season, the fans can see a strong spine to our line-up. The hope must be that unlike those other summers of transition, we'll add those missing elements to sustain a title challenge.

Secure in his position, Rafa was able to continue his rebuilding in the summer of 2008, purchasing a couple of full-backs in

Philipp Degen and Andrea Dossena, while moving on an established player in John Arne Riise and bringing Peter Crouch's Anfield career to an end. I was particularly delighted to see us chasing Tottenham's Robbie Keane to partner Fernando Torres. Keane's a player I've long admired who seemed to play well against Liverpool, especially at Anfield. On a personal level, I was also pleased to welcome Sammy Lee back to the coaching staff. He missed out on the assistant manager's job in 2004, but now ensures the local heartbeat of the club remains intact.

Naturally, we returned to Melwood for pre-season in the summer of 2008 confronted with the same subject that has plagued Liverpool since 1990, accentuated by Manchester United's latest Premier League and Champions League double. Should anyone at Liverpool be asked about our chances of catching United, I'll happily accept the supporters demanding only one satisfactory response from the players, manager and board: 'Actions speak louder than words.' We're all on the same side, after all.

13

Walk On

I stare at my medal collection and there's a gaping, lingering hole. It's a void I fear will never be filled before that dreaded moment when I wear the red shirt for the last time.

Since I turned thirty, the pain of having no League title medal seems to have intensified. I can't even really argue we've come close to ending our Premier League drought. We've started every summer with fresh hope, but by February it feels we're already asking ourselves where it's gone wrong and thinking ahead to the following season. It hurts more as you begin to appreciate time is as much a rival as those other top clubs you're trying to overtake. I may only have the three years left on my current Liverpool contract to win the League, and it will sicken me not to achieve it.

I'm fixated by this goal, consumed by my determination to bring the title back to Anfield. I don't just think about winning the League once a day, but sometimes as many as half a dozen times in an afternoon. Every conversation I have with fans and friends covers the same territory. Winning the title has become Liverpool's obsession, but whereas the supporters have their

lifetimes to realize the ambition of seeing us reclaim the League, as a player I'm rapidly running out of opportunities.

I'm at one of the few clubs capable of winning it, providing we do everything possible on and off the park. With Chelsea such a powerful financial force, and Manchester United able to build on strong foundations year to year, we're under no illusions about the size of our task. We're at a point in our history where only by doing everything 100 per cent right, especially making the right calls with transfers and selections, can we have any hope of finishing first.

It's not impossible I'll do it, and there's no way I'm ever going to accept defeat, but without wishing to sound negative, I have no choice but to prepare myself for the possibility it might not happen. Years ago the League was played over forty-two games and the saying went you couldn't afford to lose five matches in a season. We only lost four League games during the 2007–08 season but still fell well short of a title challenge. It's getting harder and harder.

I often ask myself how I'll look back on my career if I never win a title, and knowing the personal standards I've set I suspect I'll consider it a partial failure. That sounds incredibly harsh given the honours I have won at Anfield. Many is the time I've shared this view with my dad, only for him to put me straight. 'Behave yourself,' he'll tell me. 'Think of all you've won – the treble, Istanbul, all those Liverpool appearances and England caps. What a career.' Had I been offered all these medals at eighteen, I'd have snatched them, but there's something about thinking that way that makes me realize it's still not enough. It's as though I'm compromising my determination to keep winning trophies by accepting what I've already got. It's my nature to persistently demand more from myself and those around me. Arsène

Wenger echoed my thoughts when asked if he'd feel he'd under-achieved in management should he never win a European trophy. 'Even if I won one, I wouldn't feel it was enough,' he replied. I feel the same. I've spent thirteen years pursuing one League title. If I ever win it, I'll say it wasn't sufficient, I want to win it again. I'd compare my medal haul to others' and feel dissatisfied if they'd won more than me.

The trouble for those of us craving the League title is the two major obstacles in our way: Manchester United and Chelsea. How I'd love to do to United what Sir Alex Ferguson claims to have done to Liverpool – knock them off their 'fucking perch'. Ferguson announced this was his prime objective when he took over at Old Trafford in 1986 and it seemed an improbable hope at the time. Liverpool had eighteen League titles to United's seven. We also had our four European Cups to remind them how far behind they trailed. Kenny Dalglish had just won the double and was in the process of building what many argue is the great-est Liverpool side ever. Four years after Ferguson's appointment Liverpool were champions and still sitting very comfortably on their perch. In that year, 1990, it's widely assumed that had Mark Robins not kept United in the FA Cup with a winner at Nottingham Forest, the Ferguson era would have been brought to a premature end.

In the eighteen years since then, Ferguson has transformed United and they've left us behind on and off the pitch. As he celebrated winning his tenth title last May, agonizingly reducing the titles gap between United and Liverpool to one, he must have felt he was edging closer to realizing that boast of twenty-two years ago. After winning the Champions League in 2008, giving United three wins to our five, he even suggested he'd long seen off Liverpool.

Much as I respect Ferguson as a manager, I must disagree with him. He didn't knock Liverpool off their perch. Liverpool fell off it. He didn't have to lift a finger against us, let alone give us a shove. Every wound Liverpool has suffered has been self-inflicted. Ferguson's been in the privileged position since 1991 of having to do no more than walk past us once a season and kick us while we were down.

We've spent millions trying to punch back recently, but whatever we do they can retaliate by spending more. There are times I've come off the pitch at Old Trafford in the last few years and feared they didn't even have to break sweat to beat us. It's hurt going there because it's like an annual reality check. Every time we feel we've assembled a side that can compete, we're reminded what we're up against. Their size, stature, reputation and consistent success mean they can attract more expensive players than us.

When Liverpool were strong, had the best manager in the country and made the right signings, the roles were reversed and United were helpless. I vividly recall Ferguson trying to sign Peter Beardsley and John Barnes in the summer of 1987, but he had no chance once Liverpool made them their top targets. Today, players of the same ilk would choose Old Trafford ahead of Anfield. It's an uncomfortable truth we have to accept. Footballers go where they're sure they'll be competing for League titles, or where their £20 million valuations can be afforded. That's a promise we haven't been able to make for ten years. Our record transfer is £21 million, but United and Chelsea can buy two players of that value each summer.

One significant event in Anfield history changed the fortunes of both clubs, opening the door for United and sending us into an era where cup success was our main salvation every season.

That was the day Kenny Dalglish stepped down as Liverpool manager. Our slump began shortly after we failed to replace Kenny, allowing Ferguson to take advantage of our problems and prove himself the best manager in Britain. Had Dalglish stayed at Liverpool, I've no doubt the last eighteen years would have a different complexion. Ferguson has never had to beat the strongest Liverpool teams to win the title. We've made it easier for him and harder for ourselves. United may still have been the force they are, but they'd have had a far greater challenge from Anfield than we've ever given them. Kenny's brief reign at Blackburn showed what was possible. If he could go to Ewood Park and beat United to the title it's a fair assumption he'd have won a few more with Liverpool.

The years that followed Dalglish's departure sowed the seeds of our conceding title dominance to United. Kenny's replacement, Graeme Souness, bought badly. Roy Evans couldn't repair the damage quickly enough, and by the time Gérard Houllier was in charge United were already comfortably in the distance. Rafa Benitez took over at a time when the gap between us and United was greater than at any point since the 1950s. The pressure is on Rafa to win the title, and the longer he goes without doing so the more his position will be questioned.

Whenever I look at the conditions and circumstances he's worked under, I find myself asking, could anyone really have done better since 2004? We've won major trophies and enjoyed mostly adequate rather than fantastic League campaigns, but what more could we have done? If a world-class manager such as Benitez leaves Anfield considered a 'failure' for having not won the League, who will win it for us? Given the competition he's faced, I don't believe Rafa can be criticized for not winning the League. He's spent a lot of money, but United and Chelsea will always spend more. He's in exactly the same position Ferguson was around 1990 when he'd spent heavily on signings but was still struggling to compete because Liverpool were better. Let's not forget that United broke transfer records with Gary Pallister, Jim Leighton, Paul Ince and Roy Keane, and to bring Mark Hughes back from Bayern Munich. It was a massive investment at the time, but it took years for the benefits to show. United got it right eventually, but it was no overnight success.

Many of our fans hated United while we were successful and despise them even more now. Those deep-rooted feelings have never been there for me. I don't relate to the bitter rivalry between Liverpool and United in the same way I do Merseyside derby games. At the age of thirteen there was even an outside chance I could have joined them. My Sunday League team was invited to play a side from United's School of Excellence, and I impressed their scouts enough for them to ask my dad if I'd consider a trial. I was happy enough at Liverpool, obviously, but it was nice to be noticed.

Other than the fact United are our competitors, so inevitably each wants the other to lose, I see no justification for both sets of fans disliking each other so much, and certainly no more than those other sides we're hoping to beat in a title race. The intense competition between Liverpool and United is more geographical and historical than logical, to me. We're the two most successful clubs in English football, and if one succeeds it's usually at the cost of the other. We're also near neighbours, which always adds a derby feel to our fixtures. But I've never found a proper explanation for why the bad blood has spilled over between the fans. As clubs, we seem to have far more similarities than differences.

Perhaps Liverpool and United are a bit too alike and that's the cause of the problems. We both grew thanks to the influence of legendary Scottish managers, we both have a combination of passionate northern working-class support and followers from all over the world, and we're both used to winning the biggest honours. The saying about 'familiarity breeding contempt' probably has a lot to answer for at Liverpool versus United games.

I have tremendous respect for United's achievements. I see players such as Ryan Giggs and Paul Scholes as Manchester equivalents of me – good professionals who've always tried to handle themselves in the right way and put football first. And Ferguson is simply a brilliant manager. If he appears on the TV, I'll stop what I'm doing and hang on his every word. He has so much football wisdom, whether you're a United fan or not it's impossible not to be impressed. The fact he's a working-class Glaswegian, and a socialist too, means he's got a lot more in common with Scousers – apart from his football loyalties – than many would care to admit.

I hope we give him a better challenge in future than we've been able to for the last fifteen or so years, otherwise we may have to wait until he retires. Perhaps that will trigger their slump in the same way Kenny's departure led to ours. They'll certainly struggle to replace him. We may simply have to wait for the circle to turn.

Alternatively, I might have to carry my title-winning ambitions from the pitch to the dug-out.

A few years ago I'd have said I was 100 per cent certain to become a manager when I finish playing. Today, I'm likely to change my mind from one week to the next. Doubts have surfaced as I consider the consequences of managing a club. If you pushed me for an answer, I'd say it's highly likely I will make the step into management. I'd regret it too much if I neglected the chance, even if I harbour serious concerns about how I'd cope with the additional pressures of being a number one. It hurts me badly enough to lose as a player; this would increase ten-fold if I carried the extra burden of responsibility for the entire club.

I've seen from close quarters how management affects people. Good men have dedicated their lives 24/7 to the sole pursuit of winning three points every Saturday. When they've failed, the criticism has been intense and hurtful. Management is a profession that breeds feelings of anger, paranoia and insecurity in some of the most powerful personalities in the game. I'm not entirely sure I want to open myself up to the emotional turmoil. It's not just about my own state of mind either: there will be an impact on the rest of my family too. If I became a manager and it went wrong I'd hate my wife and children to see me go through a traumatic period or suffer because of the strains of my job. I could make a perfectly reasonable living doing other things and still stay involved in the game in a less hands-on capacity. So I do ask myself, 'Is it worth it?'

The other factor that may work against me is the strict condition I'd impose on any job offer. Basically, if I couldn't still live in Liverpool, forget it. I'm fussy that way. I won't uproot my children at this stage of their lives for the selfish reason of pursuing my career. That instantly puts me at a disadvantage compared to other players of my generation who fancy becoming a coach. The top managers have been prepared to make those kinds of sacrifices, but I won't, which effectively means unless I can get a management position in the north-west, it won't happen.

I've also noticed the recent trend (give or take one or two exceptions) that fewer top players become successful managers. All the best modern bosses ended their playing careers reasonably early, or in some cases hardly played at a high standard at all. Rafa Benitez, Gérard Houllier, Arsène Wenger, Jose

Mourinho and Alex Ferguson all come into this category. They had longer to study the game and work their way up from small clubs. There's a sense they're living out the dreams as coaches they weren't able to as players. A hunger is there which was never satisfied during their playing careers. And all these great managers have moved their families to another country, in some cases enrolling their children into new schools, in order to fulfil their managerial ambitions. They've gone those extra miles to manage the best clubs in Europe. Chairmen won't be able to look at me and expect the same attitude since they'd struggle to get me out of Merseyside.

If there is one club I will never turn down, naturally it's Liverpool. I wouldn't limit my ambition to managing Liverpool, of course – I'm more realistic than that – but to manage Liverpool would be the ultimate accolade if I follow that route. I've already made a tentative start to my coaching career at Anfield, earning my UEFA 'B' coaching licence at The Academy, working alongside those who first brought me through the ranks, Dave Shannon and Hugh McAuley. I'm not sure how far it will lead, but at least when I've finished playing the option will be there should any offers come my way. I didn't want to be in a position where if a call came I wouldn't be qualified to consider it. Although I'm committed to Academy football, I wouldn't consider coaching youngsters as an alternative option. I'm driven by the pursuit of honours in the professional game too much. Winning major trophies is what football is all about, and I couldn't stay in the game if that wasn't my prime objective at the end of every season.

The idea of being a future Liverpool manager excites and worries me. On the one hand, what better promotion can there be? Kenny Dalglish proved it was possible to make a successful transition from player to manager, but the fact the pressures took their toll on him serve as a warning. Then you look at the experience of Graeme Souness. Until 1991 he was seen as nothing other than a hero by the Liverpool fans. My dad still claims he's Liverpool's greatest player. Sadly, his reputation was tainted by his period as manager. I'd hate that to happen to me. To have achieved so much for the club, to have contributed to so many medals, and to have that tarnished, even forgotten, because of a series of mistakes during a three-year reign as manager? It doesn't make the job seem so attractive. Would I fall out with my mates on The Kop? They'd be in my ear asking me to sign or sell players, or questioning my decisions or tactics. You can't win every game, so there would inevitably be disagreements.

The fact I'm even thinking so negatively suggests I might talk myself out of the running if I'm ever considered. But, despite all this, there's an exciting reason for me to believe the Liverpool manager's job would be right for me. I happen to think I'd be good at it.

There's been a misconception over many years that I've reached the level I'm at by being a courageous lad who gives 100 per cent, making the most of the good management of others. While it may have been meant well, there's always been more to me than that. Grab most of the lads on The Kop and they'll give you bravery and commitment. That's not enough to play for Liverpool and England. My greatest asset has been the football brain I was lucky enough to be born with.

As a player, I've always thought like a manager. From as far back as I can remember I've understood the language of football – not just what's said, but in my reading of the game. I see where moves are developing a second earlier than some players. The reason I've been able to throw my body in the way of a goalbound shot so often is I've sensed the danger before it arrived. I've never been someone who merely absorbed information on the training pitch like a zombie and just did everything I was told without questioning it. I've taken on board all the positive coaching ideas I've been given by Evans, Moran, Houllier and Benitez and applied them to my own view of how the game should be played. I'm as likely to give instructions to my team-mates as receive them from the boss. I don't need to be told what to do all the time because I've reached a point in my career where I instinctively know what the game is about. I've taken responsibility with my own decision-making on the field. I've had this talent since I was a youngster.

Like any manager, I analyse opponents and consistently assess my own side's strengths and weaknesses. Throughout the season I'm thinking about the players I've decided aren't good enough and should be shipped out, and I'm looking closely for those I feel would add quality to our line-up. I'm forever dropping hints to the manager about players I think should be targets. There have been plenty of times I wish I could have stopped a transfer from happening, or influenced the boss to make a move for a particular player. As manager, I'd have the power to make those decisions, standing and falling by my own judgement. I like that idea.

My press conferences would be entertaining too, although whether this would sit comfortably with those who'd prefer a quiet manager I'm not so sure. Of all the managers I've worked with, I suspect I'd have more in common with Houllier, in that he lost his temper much more than Benitez and Evans. I wouldn't be able to stop myself having a go at someone if they provoked me. I suspect I'd be a cross between a traditional English manager, saying it as it is, and the kind of foreign boss who's had so much influence on my career.

'You never stop learning in football,' Ronnie Moran taught me, and he was sixty-five at the time. I'd take on board modern ideas and ensure I was well informed of any advancements in the game, but I'd go out of my way to be honest and blunt in my assessments of a performance, as I have been as a player. I'm not a fan of the 'coach speak' that has infiltrated our game in recent years. You know what I'm talking about. Sometimes I hear a manager talk and it's like they've swallowed a UEFA 'what to say in press conferences' manual, using big words and phrases they think sound impressive but which are more designed to make them sound intelligent. I'd stand by 'The Liverpool Way' principles of Bill Shankly. He once said, 'Some people try to confuse you with their language. I wouldn't say someone was avaricious, I'd say they were bloody greedy.'

People might ask what kind of football a Jamie Carragher team would play, but I don't believe managers can be categorized in such a way. The players at your disposal must dictate your philosophy. The manager of Manchester United can afford to choose to play any style he wants, recruiting the players to suit his system. Go to the bottom of the League and you'll find managers who'd love to get their side performing like Real Madrid but they don't have players capable of doing so. A good manager is one who can adapt to the resources at his disposal rather than expect his players to do what they can't.

I've already said football teams tend to reflect the personality of the boss, so I'd look to assemble a physically and mentally strong squad that understood the value of keeping possession of the ball. I'd always want two or three flair players in attacking roles, and if there's one commodity every manager agrees is proving as important as any in the modern game, it's pace. Find a player with speed and skill nowadays and you could have a world-beater on your hands.

If you ask me where I'll be in ten years' time, I'd settle for being Liverpool's assistant manager. That seems like a less pressurized role, but influential enough to give advice on where the team needs to improve. I suppose the only problem with that is whether any manager would put up with me telling him what he should do, and whether I'd get frustrated if my boss ignored my ideas. I'm bursting with so many of my own views on the game I'm sure I'd find the temptation to have a go too much to resist.

Fortunately, I've plenty of football left in my legs before I need to make my next series of momentous career choices. I'm not feeling the impact of turning thirty yet, and there are plenty of centre-halves who've gone on to thirty-four or thirty-five at the highest level. But, such are the demands at Liverpool, I can't escape a sense of trepidation when younger defenders arrive, and what that might mean for my role over the next few years. There's another phrase in English football which I can't stand and I'm determined will never be applied to me: 'squad player'. Just saying it sends a shiver down my spine. The day I'm seen as a squad player at Anfield I'll know my time is up. I might feel differently in a few years, but I'm as resolute as ever to play every second of every fixture.

I hate missing games, no matter what the occasion. There have been times I've been rested for Carling Cup matches and even that annoyed me. It hurts me to know there's a game in which I can play but I've not been selected, no matter how reasonable the explanation for my absence. That comes from a lifetime of being accustomed to preparing for each training session with a clear objective in mind. Match day. When it arrives, I expect to be involved. If I'm not, I'm not happy. I can't understand why any professional footballer wouldn't want to be doing his job when the whistle blows.

If I'm rotated more as I get older, no one will be more interested than me in my reaction to featuring in fewer games. I'm not a good substitute and I have no respect for those who've built a reputation at a big club by settling for being bit-part players, filling in when the first choices are given a rest. There are players who've averaged ten League games a season and described themselves as title winners. You'll see them when you turn on the television on the last day of a season. They're the ones popping the champagne and shoving their way into the centre of the photographs as the trophies are being presented. They talk about their honours lists as if they were central to the success, but their major contribution was usually a last ten minutes here and there and a six-out-of-ten display in a comfortable midweek home victory against Bolton or Wigan. I see such players as winners by association; they've taken a ride on the coat-tails of the great players around them because deep down they know they're not at the same level. If you're only playing around ten games a season, it's a clear hint you're at a club that is beyond your capability and you shouldn't be there.

I have more regard for someone such as Nicky Butt, who was a regular at Manchester United for years before Ferguson brought in more central midfielders. Butt could have stayed to line his pockets with medals, playing a few games here and there. Instead he opted for a fresh challenge at Newcastle where he knew he wasn't going to get the same success. It shows he had pride and would play every week for a club that wasn't competing for the title rather than make a false claim of 'winning' more at Manchester United by sitting on the bench for two thirds of the season.

If I was at Liverpool and didn't play a part in a trophy win, you wouldn't see me celebrating as much as I have on those momentous occasions in the past. That's not being selfish but being proud. I'd feel a cheat. I'd rather those who did the job grabbed all the glory. In 2001 I threw my Charity Shield winners medal into the crowd immediately after the game for precisely that reason. I'd started the match on the bench because Gérard Houllier told me he wanted to give John Arne Riise his debut against Manchester United, and he thought the experience would help him. I was only told I was on the bench when we arrived at the Millennium Stadium, and I was so furious to be left out, no contribution I made would have eased my disappointment. It was a mistake to chuck the medal away, and I got it back later, but they were my feelings then and they haven't changed seven years later. As a footballer, you only fully appreciate and understand success when you've contributed to it. I've played my part in all Liverpool's most recent victories, which is why each one is so precious.

If I'm not a regular in the side – and I hope that's many years away – I will move on. There are those who advise you to quit at the top, but I disagree. I'd love to finish my career at Anfield, but if the time comes to consider another Premier League club or a competitive Championship team (in the north, of course), I'll do so. I intend to play until my body can't take it any more. You're a long time retired in this profession and I know how much I'm going to miss the game when it comes to an end. I love playing football and won't stop until I have to.

I'll miss the routine of being a footballer because it's all I've known. It's comforting, reassuring, to know you're heading to Melwood to see the lads and train every day, and you plan your life around the calendar of the fixture list. Although I get too intense about the game sometimes and can think about it too much, I'm not sure what I'd do if it didn't matter to me professionally any more. I can't imagine having no concern about who Liverpool are trying to sign, or what day we're playing the Merseyside derby, or what match we've been scheduled on Boxing Day or over the New Year. I'll find it weird.

Once it all comes to an end, there'll be an enormous sense of emptiness. What will I do with myself? I've learned to switch off much more in recent years, taking the advice of those who've told me to enjoy the game rather than get too down when results go wrong. My wife and children have given me a focus away from the game, and there are other interests I have, although even these tend to reflect my personality. I'm a fan of the American TV comedy show *Curb Your Enthusiasm*, which is about a middle-aged guy who gets wound up by the most minor inconveniences in life. I think I see something of myself, and what I might become in the future, in the character. Maybe you'll see me walking the streets of Bootle looking like Larry David, complaining about everything and anything. I've always been a fan of *Only Fools and Horses* and *The Royle Family* too, mainly because I recognize so many of the personalities and situations from my own life.

I'm also an avid reader of books – usually sport-related, of course. I hand my family a list of new titles every Christmas so I've always something to poke my nose into on Liverpool's away trips. I've read most players' autobiographies, which was one of the reasons I was so keen to get my own thoughts off my chest. My two favourites are actually related to Manchester United: *Managing My Life* by Alex Ferguson and *Back from the Brink* by Paul McGrath.

When it comes to music I'm an Arctic Monkeys and Oasis fan, although the Scousers still outgun the Mancs on that score as my favourite song is 'In My Life' by The Beatles. Sky TV played it over a montage of our Istanbul victory in 2005, so the song, which I already loved, will always carry significance for me.

But as I said, I've no intention of winding down the football yet. I want to drip every last ounce of sweat I can before I play my final game. At the very least I hope still to be at Liverpool when the new stadium is built on Stanley Park in 2011. In fact, I've pencilled in a date for the diary for the first game in the arena. I'd love it to be opened with my testimonial, Liverpool v. Everton, although given how long it's taking to build the stadium it's more likely I'll play this in the current Anfield in a few years' time.

I've been due a testimonial since 2007, when the club offered me a year of events to mark my tenth anniversary, but I wasn't so keen on the timing. I wanted it delayed for a more appropriate moment later on. I preferred a one-off celebration, and the prospect of the two clubs that have defined my football career from boy to man being at the centre of it, with all the money going to local charities, should make it a fitting finale if my Liverpool playing days are nearing their end. I want to do my bit to help bring the clubs' fans closer together again, and try to heal the bad blood which has developed over the last twenty years.

I also like the idea of having an ex-players' match where our treble side takes on our Champions League winners. I suspect there will be blood shed in the fight for the services of Steven Gerrard if that comes off. Maybe he and I will have to play a half for both teams.

It seems strange for me to be thinking about a testimonial at thirty, especially as I've every intention of adding more dramatic chapters to this book in years to come, but you become more aware of what's on the horizon as each pre-season approaches.

Other than the eternal quest for the League title, there are lingering regrets I've reflected upon as I've pieced together my story to this point. Everyone has disappointments, even if some of the mistakes you made early on helped you become the player and person you are. I wish, for instance, I'd settled as a centre-half much sooner than I did. If I had, the reputation I have as a player now would have arrived seven or eight years ago. I'm sure it would also have helped my England career progress more impressively. Others may argue it was my period as a striker, midfielder and full-back which allowed me to see the game from so many different angles, making the switch to central defence a comfortable one. That's a matter for me to debate when I'm finished.

I see less stressful options than management available once I hang up my boots, such as a career in the media, possibly as a television pundit. There's already interest in me from some TV channels, and you can see why so many ex-professionals jump at the opportunity. It's a lot easier getting paid to tell the managers where they're going wrong than being on the wrong end of the criticism.

I haven't wanted to commit myself to punditry too often because if you're a young player who makes that move too early, that's pretty much it for you. You become associated with that field of work, you settle into it, and then it's harder to move back into football. But if I'm not managing it's most likely I'll pursue a career in the media, joining the illustrious names of ex-Anfield stars passing judgement on the next generation of Liverpool teams. There seems to be no shortage of demand for us, much to the aggravation, it seems, of Liverpool managers who feel extra pressure when they hear a legend slagging off the team. It's never bothered me. One or two went a bit far during the Houllier era, but overall I see them all as passionate fans who know the game, expressing an informed, balanced opinion. So many of us are thinking of following them on to TV in the future it strikes me as hypocritical to have a go at pundits.

In fact, I'm not sure as a club we've always shown enough respect to former heroes. I've my own idea about ensuring the great names of the past are never forgotten: handing them an ambassadorial role on the club's behalf. It would be fantastic if we invited a different former player as our special guest every time we travelled to a European game. The club would only have to pay the price of one extra air ticket on the plane to Europe. The Kop legend could watch us train, have lunch with us, sit in the directors' box and get a real sense of belonging to the club again. It would also help the modern players – many of whom may need a history lesson on the efforts of those who made the club what it is – understand what Liverpool FC really means. Perhaps one day I'll be the one to benefit from such a scheme.

I don't want to sound like I'm in retirement mode, but you do have to think carefully about what you'll do when that final whistle blows. I've been planning ahead for a while, investing in areas outside football but which inevitably mix business with my pleasures. Last year I opened the first of what I intend to be a chain of sports-themed family restaurants. My business partners, Paul and Julian Flanagan, approached me four years ago with the proposal and it's proved a great success. Paul and Julian are passionate Liverpudlians who've helped transform our city centre with their trendy bars and modern hotels. The Sir Thomas Hotel, which they also own, was effectively the official Liverpool FC party venue following our Champions League triumphs. We had the idea of creating a healthy-eating restaurant to address the growing problem of child obesity in this country, and with my backing it's hoped we'll get more children thinking about what they eat, as well as feeling inspired to be more active. 'Café

Sports: England' is planning to expand across the rest of the country. We're looking to open in Ireland, Wales and as far afield as Dubai, too.

It's important for me to give something back to the community. Liverpool and Bootle mean so much to me, and I'm determined to do what I can to help continue their regeneration, and encourage youngsters to fulfil whatever potential they might have. I've been able to do this in several ways. If there's a charity auction to be held, I'm happy to donate signed shirts and football boots. Since breaking into the Liverpool team I've handed my gear to youth clubs and football teams in Bootle who needed to raise money to buy kits or equipment. For obvious reasons, the Alder Hey Children's Unit has always been in my thoughts over the years too.

To me it's a tiny gesture to raise funds, but I was honoured to be awarded with the Freedom of the Borough of Sefton for my efforts two years ago. I was shocked to hear I was receiving the award, which among other things now means I'm legally allowed to walk sheep through the streets of Bootle. Seriously, I felt privileged to be recognized by my own community in such a way. Once more, I shared the accolade with my family. The people of Bootle may have been showing their gratitude towards me, but it pales into insignificance compared with my debt to them.

Bill Shankly famously said, 'Football is not a matter of life or death; it is much more important than that.' Now, we all know he was wrong. Tragically, too much has happened at Liverpool since Shankly coined this much-repeated sentence for it not to have been questioned, even if there is still a great deal of truth behind the sentiments he was trying to express. But in my city, in my town and in my family, the importance of football has been central to everything I am. It's defined me, given me the opportunity to provide for my own wife and children, and allowed me to fulfil the ambitions my dad had for me when he took his lad to those places I remember on the fields of Marsh Lane. Whatever I do with myself when I stop playing, football will always be there. I owe everything to the game, and everything to the place where I was born and the people who live there. I'll never lose that affection.

I also feel that Shankly quote has deeper meaning for me. My becoming a footballer was a matter of life and death. When I look over my career it all leads back to that distressing decision my mum took three decades ago. Everything begins for me the moment she looked a doctor in the eye and insisted she would give birth to her baby, regardless of the medical advice she was hearing. That was the day she proved no matter how tough the circumstances or how painful the outcome might be, if you showed the right character and stood firm behind what you believed was right, everything could turn out for the best.

My mum said she was sure someone was watching over me from the moment I was born. As I re-read the pages in my life, I think she was right.

Career Record

Liverpool appearances/goals (to end 2007–08)

	Appearances	Goals
League	360	3
FA Cup	29	0
League Cup	26	0
Champions League	74	1
UEFA Cup	28	0
European Super Cup	2	0
World Club Championship	2	0
Charity Shield	2	0
Total	523	4

Honours

FA Cup	2001, 2006
League Cup	2001, 2003
Champions League	2005
UEFA Cup	2001
European Super Cup	2001, 2005
Charity Shield	2001, 2006
FA Youth Cup	1996

International caps

England (full caps)	34
Under-21s	27

Debuts

Liverpool: 8 January 1997 v Middlesbrough (away), League Cup (sub)

England (full): 28 April 1999 v Hungary (away), friendly (sub)

First goal

Liverpool: 18 January 1997 v Aston Villa (home), Premier League

Index

Ablett, Gary 70

Abramovich, Roman 227, 247, 259, 260–1

AC Milan 237, 250
    beating in European Cup final (2005) 250–2, 268–81, 286–7
    wins European Cup final (2007) 348–9, 350–2

Academy, The (was School of Excellence) 23, 34, 67, 68, 70, 70–1, 77, 78, 346

Agger, Daniel 344

AK Graz 252

Al-Ansari, Sameer 354–5

Alaves 179–80

Alder Hey Children's Hospital 12, 394

Aldridge, John 70, 77, 172

Alonso, Xabi 92, 234, 241, 245, 257–8, 262–3, 276, 340, 351

Alves, Daniel 339

Ancelotti, Carlo 275

Anelka, Nicolas 149

Arsenal 35, 120, 148, 266
    beating in FA Cup Final (2001) 172–3

Aston Villa 107

Atkinson, Ron 103

Ayala, Roberto 239

Ayesteran, Pako 222, 372

Babbel, Markus 105, 123, 138, 140, 160, 162

Babel, Ryan 350, 372

Bailey, John 44

Baldini, Franco 219

Ball, Alan 50

Banks, Gordon 191